Paradoxical Resolutions

PARADOXICAL RESOLUTIONS

American Fiction since James Joyce

CRAIG HANSEN WERNER

UNIVERSITY OF ILLINOIS PRESS   Urbana   Chicago   London

8/1983
Am. Lit.

LIBRARY OF CONGRESS CATALOGING IN PUBLICATION DATA

Werner, Craig Hansen, 1952–
    Paradoxical resolutions.

    Bibliography: p.
    Includes index.
    1. American fiction—20th century—History and
criticism.   2. Joyce, James, 1882–1941—Influence.
I. Title.
PS379.W43   813'.54'09   81-11423
ISBN 0-252-00931-2   AACR2

To Mom and Dad

Acknowledgments

Inevitably, this book represents a collaboration with the many people who have touched my life, within or without the academic world. Among those whose contributions demand special recognition are Bernard Benstock and Keneth Kinnamon, who guided me through the writing of the early drafts; and Richard Barksdale, Nina Baym, Ed Davidson, Jim Hurt, and Emily Watts, who helped sharpen my critical abilities. James Justus and David Hayman provided many useful suggestions on improving later drafts of the manuscript. I wish also to acknowledge the support of the University of Mississippi Graduate College, in particular of Joseph Sam and Dale Abadie, in the publication of this book. Bill Ferris, Evans Harrington, and Gerald Walton have provided administrative assistance whenever needed. Ann Lowry Weir and Roger G. Clark of the University of Illinois Press have provided cheerful and valuable help.

My colleagues past and present—especially Steve Schultz, Dave Dorsey, Ben Fisher, Fred Dolezal, Barbara Ewell, and Mike Allen—have frequently suggested new ideas and forced me to clarify my own positions. My students—of whom I wish to recognize Sue Christel, Kevin Stewart, Jim Adkins, and Steve Yarbrough as both representative and outstanding—have in a very real sense made the five years I have spent working on this book worthwhile through their living reactions to the literature we love.

Bob Smith, Frank Krutzke, Dan Tynan, and Charles Sanders—all teachers in the truest sense of the word—first inspired and then validated my belief in education as a life-affirming vocation. Barbara Talmadge, Barbara Seidman, Steve Bernard, Brian Berry,

Acknowledgments

Mike DeLong, Patti Justis, Geoff King, and Missy Kubitschek have kept me going both personally and intellectually.

Finally, my deepest thanks go to my brothers Brian and Blake and to my Dad and Mom, who bore with me from the first cries of "Read, Mommy, read" through the final typing of the final draft.

Contents

CHAPTER ONE

Paradoxical Equanimity: James Joyce and the Tradition of the American Novel

If James Joyce taught us anything, it was that everything is inevitable and that nothing can be predicted. Inevitably recent American novelists reacting to Joyce's achievement manifest his influence in unpredictable ways. Unpredictably they have forged a compromise, which in retrospect seems inevitable, between the conflicting realistic and romantic traditions of the American novel.

The realistic-romantic dichotomy exists in the criticism of American fiction under many guises. "Realism" and "naturalism" often are used interchangeably, as are "romance" and "symbolism." Precise definitions of the terms descend quickly into the chimeric and often contribute more to particular theses than to actual clarification of the problem. Richard Chase, whose *American Novel and Its Tradition* is largely responsible for the dominant interpretation of the American novel as a romance form,[1] refuses to attempt any strict definition, arguing that "the main difference between the novel and the romance is in the way in which they view reality." The novel, he continues, "renders reality closely and in comprehensive detail. It takes a group of people and sets them going about the business of life. We see these people in their real complexity of temperament and motive. They are in explicable relation to nature, to each other, to their social class, to their own past." The romance, conversely, "feels free to render reality in less volume and detail. It tends to prefer action to character, and action will be freer in a romance than in a novel, encountering, as it were, less resistance from reality . . . the romance will more freely veer toward mythic, allegorical, and symbolistic forms."[2]

Almost all major American novelists mix elements of these two forms, and it is more difficult to assign particular aspects of their work to either tendency than Chase sometimes implies. Still, the feeling that symbolic significance is somehow incompatible with realistic settings has often contributed to the ambiguity of the resolutions of American novels. Richard Poirier identifies this uneasy mixture of elements as a direct reflection of a deeper limitation, contending that no "interesting" American writer can be clearly identified as "romantic" or "realistic" because "Nearly all of them have written in protest against the environment of the 'rest of life' which contradicts the dreams of their heroes and heroines."[3]

Some writers, usually those normally classified as "romantics," attempt to resolve this protest by separating their essentially powerless characters from the hostile social realities—Natty Bumppo pursues the receding frontier, Huck Finn lights out for the territories, Ike McCaslin repudiates his participation in a corrupt society. Some writers, usually the "realists," picture their characters, however sympathetic their struggle, as similarly powerless victims unable to escape crushing environments—Isabel Archer returns to her stultifying life with Osmond, Sister Carrie rocks futilely toward the future, Bigger Thomas hears the door to the execution chamber clang shut. Some (and it is quite possible that each of the previous writers belongs in this category) leave their characters suspended in the midst of unresolved ambiguities which are as paralyzing as either overt dissociation or victimization—Ishmael can never really escape the spectre, both real and symbolic, of Moby-Dick; Jean Toomer's Kabnis can never establish communication with the South, the North, or his own elusive racial identity.

All have great difficulty establishing a meaningful connection between social reality, the individual psyche, and the metaphysical structure of the universe. Some characters deny reality to attain an ambiguous freedom; the environment denies human potentiality by destroying others. Life transpires in fragments, disconnected chunks. Symbolic-romantic meanings and realistic-naturalistic details perpetually strain away from one another.

Joyce reestablished the connections in his own work, and provided a general model for American writers struggling with these difficulties, by redefining symbolism and realism to support his vision of the possibility of human equilibrium *within* a hostile environment. At times it seems that Joyce is merely rushing to mutually exclusive extremes. The street furniture littering the Dublin of Leopold Bloom and Stephen Dedalus extends realism to a logical (or perhaps nightmarish) conclusion. No detail appears too trivial for Joyce's attention. Characters and objects are sometimes charged with significance, but at other times they seem mere ciphers in an overwhelming urban environment. Conversely, the metaphysical, psychological, and historical allusions in *Finnegans Wake* often threaten to obliterate the realistic identities of HCE and ALP.[4]

Through it all, however deceptive a particular passage or work, Joyce abandons himself to neither extreme. As Harry Levin observes, Joyce "defined the double responsibility of the imaginative writer as a task of mediation between the world of reality and the world of dreams."[5] An actual mediator, rather than a covert agent in either "world," Joyce drew his power from his refusal to attempt to separate them. To Joyce, dreams derive from the impact of reality and in turn shape the individual's perception of that reality. Leopold Bloom's visions of degradation and triumph in "Circe" are rooted in his troubled marriage. Stephen Dedalus' perceptions of hostility and betrayal on every Dublin street corner reflect his Byronic image of the artist as an exile armed only with silence and cunning. (This image—as we wander deeper into the hall of mirrors—was engendered by such realistic details as the turmoil of the Simon Dedalus household and Stephen's own weak eyesight which brought on his earliest victimization by authority in *A Portrait of the Artist as a Young Man*.)

Joyce's practice emphatically rejects T. S. Eliot's assertion that art embodies a preexisting "universal" emotion, "by finding an objective correlative; in other words, a set of objects, a situation, a chain of events which shall be the formula of that *particular* emotion; such that when the external facts are given the emotion is immediately evoked."[6] Rather, Joyce examines the detailed experience of his *particular* characters in their *particular* situations and only then expresses their "universal" significance. He presents what George Kent calls a "legitimate universalism." Writing on Gwendolyn Brooks, Kent notes that "her poems tend not to represent a reach for some preexisting Western universal to be arrived at by reducing the tensions inherent in the black experience. Their universalism derives, instead, from complete projection of a situation or experience's *space* and *vibrations* (going down deep, not transcending). Even where a preexisting univeral may be paraphrasable, the true roots of the poet's universalism are in her power of enforcing the illusion that the vibrations from the space her imagination has encircled are captured and focused with all the power and significance which the raw materials afforded."[7] In just such a manner, Joyce captures the significance inherent in the Dublin of his youth and the Europe of his maturity.

Above all, Joyce battles to liberate *experience*, to admit the full range of human life into the work of art. Joyce's most important weapon in this battle is not silence, exile, or abstract cunning; it is his "scrupulous meanness" of observation, his refusal either to raise or lower his eyes from the concrete experience, in both its real and its dream aspects. This focus on the particular at times results in harsh attacks on the very people he wishes to liberate. But it also frees him from cultural preconceptions which arbitrarily dismiss his insights concerning the significance of human endeavor on the grounds that they fail to support "universal" truths.[8] When Joyce affirms, his affirmation stems from specific experiences.

To apply this in terms familiar to the criticism of the American novel: Leopold Bloom attains transcendence; he does so not by dissociating himself from his environment, but by experiencing a series of realistically rooted incremental movements toward equanimity. Bloom's moments of transcendence occur late in *Ulysses*—in "Circe" and "Ithaca." His adoption of Stephen and his acceptance of Molly's adultery are the clearest examples. At the end of "Circe" Bloom gazes upon the prostrate Stephen and sees his own lost son, Rudy. Bloom's decision to continue to watch over Stephen thereafter not only becomes a practical good deed, but also allows Bloom to express his frustrated paternal love toward a surrogate son. In "Ithaca" Bloom's equanimity in the face of Molly's sexual affair with Boylan is justified on both practical and metaphysical grounds, including "the futility of triumph or protest or vindication: the inanity of extolled virtue: the lethargy of nescient matter: the apathy of the stars."[9] Both situations are essentially symbolic; both involve Bloom's revaluation of his relationship with the concrete universe and can be read as symbolic statements on the nature of human relationships. But neither elevates the romantic self above its environment. Rather, both readjust Bloom's position *within* that environment. Bloom's symbolic assumption of fatherhood in the vision of Stephen and Rudy comes as the climax of a long series of realistic events which shape Bloom's thoughts: the funeral of the pauper child in "Hades," the birth of Purefoy's son and his repeated encounters with "lost" sons such as Patrick Dignam and Stephen Dedalus himself. Similarly, Bloom's equanimity in the face of domestic betrayal stems from a vast accumulation of marital history: his sexual estrangement from Molly, his constant encounters with Dubliners whose blustering open conflicts are at best comic, at worst repugnant (the Citizen, Dennis Breen, the British soldiers), and his extreme physical weariness at the end of a long day. Bloom's realistic surroundings, therefore, condition the nature of his transcendence. That transcendence does, of course, maintain its symbolic significance. Bloom will not succumb to despair because human warmth is possible; he will not be crushed by defeats since he can see himself in a cosmic (and comic) perspective. He apprehends the nature of the universe in a way which will help him resist the crushing environment. But there is no doubt that he will remain *within* that environment, and that his symbolic perceptions will be integrated into his outwardly unchanged life on the streets of Dublin.

Just this certainty has traditionally eluded American novelists. Strether's perceptions in themselves are convincing, but what effect will they have on his life in Woolett, Mass.? Could Huck Finn maintain his morally sound relationship with Jim in slaveholding St. Petersburg? Some novelists, most notably Melville in *Moby-Dick*, have been acutely aware of this problem. Ishmael cannot drop too deeply into his dreams in the crow's nest or he will be broken on the very solid deck. Still, while recognizing the dichotomy, Melville cannot resolve it. Whitman's lines "Do I contradict myself? Very well then, I contradict myself" could well serve as a motto for classic American novelists' treatment of the relationship between the hero and his community.

Since Joyce (or, perhaps more accurately, since the publication of *Ulysses*) American novelists have been less willing to accept this irresolution. Arming themselves with a variety of Joycean techniques and concepts, they attempt works which combine the metaphysical profundity of the great romantics, the social relevance of the naturalist reformers, and the depth of characterization of Jamesian realism. Joyce's young contemporaries, writers such as William Faulkner and Richard Wright, frequently adopted specific Joycean techniques in ways which increased the impact of their work. Still, their sensibilities had been basically formed by the time they read Joyce. Only the generation which began writing during and after World War II has fully assimilated Joyce's example.

This book explores the diverse ways in which the current generation has created a post-Joycean tradition in American fiction. Several critics, most notably David Hayman, Vivien Mercier, and Robert Martin Adams, have examined particular aspects of post-Joycean writing. All concentrate on European writing, however, and Hayman concerns himself primarily with writers who have "understood Joyce," positing a "correct" reading which I doubt exists. At any rate, my concern is not so much to contribute to our understanding of Joyce as to study both the understandings and the misunderstandings which have helped shape the contemporary American novel. In his introduction to *In the Wake of the Wake* Hayman asks, "Would the same thing not have occurred without Joyce?"[10] Hayman suggests no answer. The same question and the same prudent response seem appropriate for this study. I would note, however, that the contemporary novel, both in Europe and in America, in fact did happen and is happening *with* Joyce. I have attempted both to recognize this fact by employing Joyce as a touchstone for discussion of individual works and to admit the autonomy of the new generation of American writers by deemphasizing Joyce when the later works demand differing points of reference.

The writers of this generation only occasionally "copy" specific aspects of Joyce's work. Often they trace their literary lineage more directly to either Wright or Faulkner (or, in the case of Thomas Pynchon, to Samuel Beckett). But the aspects of Faulkner's and Wright's work which seem most appealing to them are those which parallel the romantic-realistic reconciliation pioneered by Joyce. My purpose here is not to argue, à la Harold Bloom, that Joyce represents the highest achievment in the novel and that his successors merely re-create his world on progressively smaller scales.[11] Even those writers such as William Melvin Kelley and Willam Gaddis, who are most directly and obviously conscious of Joyce, have shown that it is possible to take particular aspects of Joyce's work and extend them in ways which increase their effectiveness and significance. At any rate, considering "influence" in the narrow sense, implying that later writers have done little more than re-create earlier achievements adds little to our understanding of most novels. Rather than limiting my discussion to tracing specific connections, I propose to examine influence as part of a writer's context which involves three interlocking factors: 1) the author's individual experience and temperament; 2) the social reality in which he lives; and 3) his literary and aesthetic tradition, which is in part self-created and which includes his awareness of major predecessors. Often in this study I shall explore the ways in which the first two factors lead an individual author to differ from Joyce's positions on specific issues.

Diversity characterizes contemporary American fiction as it characterized Joyce's work. Some contemporary writers delight in Joyce's technical achievement. John Barth, Russell Banks, Ronald Sukenick, and Raymond Federman manipulate and extend Joyce's stylistic innovations, while Ernest Gaines, John Updike, and Ralph Ellison consolidate his advancement of traditional forms. Other writers reexamine Joyce's conception of the relationship between the artist and his work. Jack Kerouac and Norman Mailer participate directly in their works; James Baldwin and Saul Bellow emulate Joyce's control of biographical distance; Flannery O'Connor assumes the Joycean pose of "absent" controller of the epiphanies. Still other writers reexamine Joyce's thematic concerns. Toni Morrison, William Melvin Kelley, and William Burroughs perceive the political implications of Joyce's work, while Donald Barthelme and William Gaddis extend his aesthetic themes. Pynchon, like Joyce, encompasses a wide range of seemingly incompatible extremes. Only the arranger's ingenuity limits the permutations, possible arrangements of the writers. But whatever the categories imposed, all share the Joycean desire to escape the limitations imposed by too narrow a conception of either "symbol" or "reality." Seen in historical perspective, the American novelistic tradition remains contradictory; no simple thread unites the authors I shall consider. The contradictions in the tradition reflect the activity of a large number of individuals striving for their own resolutions. No longer a sign of acquiescence and confusion, the contradictions in the contemporary American novel testify to the the health of a tradition able, in conflict, to cohere.

CHAPTER TWO

The Dangers of Domination:
Joyce, Faulkner, Wright

JOYCE BEWITCHED, BEDEVILED, and bemused his contemporaries. Whether insulting older established writers (as he did Yeats), ignoring young "rivals" (as he did Eliot), or carefully controlling closer relationships (as he did with Pound and Beckett), Joyce's attitude was clear; he offered his contemporaries a great deal, while they offered him little save an amusing spectacle. As a result, most of the allusions to "modernist" literature in *Ulysses* and *Finnegans Wake* are parodic, while novels seriously imitating aspects of Joyce's works fill the literary history of the 1920s and 30s. In the United States, superficial imitations of Joyce abounded. Thomas Wolfe employed mythic parallels in *Of Time and the River*, John Dos Passos juxtaposed narrative voices throughout his *USA* trilogy, and Sherwood Anderson self-consciously imitated Joycean prose rhythms in *Dark Laughter*. But none of the direct imitators turned the Joycean influence to their artistic advantage as well as two writers less concerned with emulating particular Joycean accomplishments: William Faulkner and Richard Wright.

Both Faulkner and Wright adapted Joycean techniques to their own voices in a way which helped them, in their greatest works, rise at least momentarily above the conflict of romantic and realistic modes. Neither successfully adapted Joyce, however, until he had written an "apprentice" novel which failed, at least partially, because it alluded too frequently and directly to Joyce. Faulkner's *Mosquitoes* and Wright's *Lawd Today* carefully "re-create" *A Portrait of the Artist as a Young Man* and *Ulysses* respectively. More mature works such as Faulkner's *As I Lay Dying* and *The Sound and the Fury* and Wright's *Uncle Tom's Children* continue to employ easily recognizable Joycean techniques, but are more successful because the writers pursue their own lines of development rather than constantly shaping their novels to correspond to a Joycean model. While the Joycean influence is even less direct in works such as Faulkner's *Go Down, Moses* and Wright's *Native Son*, it is more profound. In these works, Faulkner and Wright bring romantic and realistic meanings into at least a temporary balance by using Joycean concepts of the connection between real and symbolic psychological experience.

The sharpest distinction between Faulkner's and Wright's mature applications of Joyce and their less successful attempts lies in their increased willingness to differ with Joyce when their individual perceptions so demanded. Faulkner, a much less self-absorbed artist than Joyce, derived his artistic sensibility largely from his historical situation as a member of the declining southern aristocracy. To a degree, the southern sense of history molded Faulkner into a romantic. The idealism of the Sartorises and the more articulate Compsons inspires frequent Faulknerian raptures, but the decline of his family's fortunes and the decay of southern institutions instilled a strong realistic element in his writing. For every Sartoris, he saw a Snopes; for every Quentin, a Jason. The best of Faulkner's novels express his awareness of both sides of this dichotomy, which has no close parallel in Joyce. Unlike Faulkner, Wright, also a native of Mississippi, felt no romantic attachment to the southern past. As the son of a black sharecropper, Wright confronted the harshest social deprivation, and his writing emphasizes the difficulty of resisting impersonal forces. Working from this naturalistic sense of the power of the environment, Wright expands his vision to include his characters' attempts to articulate the symbolic meaning of their own lives.

William Faulkner

William Faulkner's *Mosquitoes* portrays a peripheral character, whose name the other characters have a good deal of trouble remembering, as "a liar by profession."[1] The character's name is Faulkner. No one examining Faulkner's statements concerning himself should overlook this early self-portrait. In particular,

Faulkner's retrospective account of his lack of early knowledge of James Joyce's works "reworks" facts. In 1932 Faulkner told Henry Nash Smith he had not read *Ulysses* when he wrote *The Sound and the Fury*. But Faulkner also told the readers of *Mosquitoes* about an amazing bayou ranch specializing in corn-fed lamb-fish. Both stories should be accepted only with caution. In fact, Faulkner not only knew Joyce's works but also adapted Joycean techniques, beginning with his work of the 1920s and culminating in *Go Down, Moses*, helping him to rise at least momentarily above the conflict of romance and realism.

As critics have increasingly recognized, the evidence indicates that Faulkner had read *Ulysses*, probably in its entirety but certainly in excerpts, by 1925. Phil Stone gave Faulkner a copy of *Ulysses* which he dated 1924. Sherwood Anderson actively publicized the book in Faulkner's New Orleans circle, and Hamilton Basso remembered discussing the novel with Faulkner in 1925. Perhaps the clearest evidence of Faulkner's selective memory regarding Joyce lies in his 1931 admission to Paul Green and Milton Abernathy that he had been telling people he hadn't read Joyce. At the same time, he entertained his traveling companions by quoting *Ulysses* from memory.[2]

Despite this dissimulation, Faulkner never attempted to deny his high respect for Joyce's achievement. Joyce was the only writer whom Faulkner sought out when he visited Paris in 1925. He considered Joyce and Thomas Mann to be the greatest writers of his time, and he told Richard Ellmann in 1958 that he "considered himself the heir of Joyce in his methods in *The Sound and the Fury*."[3] Faulkner *was* to become a legitimate heir to Joyce, but not before composing two "Joycean" apprentice novels in which the influence contributed more to confusing Faulkner than to aiding him.

Even if no external evidence existed, the specific echoes of *Ulysses* in *Mosquitoes* (and the earlier *Soldiers' Pay*) would strongly suggest that Faulkner not only read Joyce, but made a conscious effort to adapt his techniques and themes. Faulkner's description of Mr. Talliaferro's thoughts as he bends over the sleeping Jenny echoes Joyce's description of both Bloom's and Molly's mental processes. Mr. Talliaferro kneels near Jenny, thinking, "Hard this floor his old knees yes yes Jenny her breath

Yes her red soft mouth where little teeth but showed parted blondness a golden pink swirl kaleidoscopic a single blue eye not come fully awake her breath yes yes."[4] This verbally parallels Molly's final thoughts in *Ulysses*: "Then he asked me would I yes to say yes my mountain flower and first I put my arms around him yes and drew him down to me so he could feel my breasts all perfume yes and his heart was going like mad and yes I said yes I will yes" (*U*, p. 783). But the rhythm and content of Mr. Talliafero's thoughts more closely resemble Bloom's as he watches a woman board a carriage: "Watch! Watch! Silk flash rich stockings white. Watch!" (*U*, p. 74). Similarly, David's thoughts as he trudges along in the swamp have analogues in "Proteus"; both David and Stephen walk along the sand, eyes closed, meditating on the sea, time, and man's relation to the paradoxical unchanging flux.[5]

Despite these parallels between *Mosquitoes* and *Ulysses*, Joyce Warren's suggestion that *Portrait* exerted a greater influence over Faulkner's novel seems just.[6] *Mosquitoes*, like *Portrait*, concerns itself almost obsessively with artists and aesthetic theories. Warren, however, miscalculates when she concludes that, like *Portrait*, *Mosquitoes* "presents the artistic theory which is to direct his [Faulkner's] greatest work."[7] Basing this conclusion on the parallel between Gordon and Stephen Dedalus, Warren assumes that both characters present their creators' views in more or less unadulterated forms.[8] This seems highly questionable; Joyce treats Stephen with a good deal of irony, even in *Portrait*.[9] Still, Warren is safe in identifying Joyce with Stephen. She risks much more in seeing Gordon as Faulkner, for, whereas Joyce concentrates the focus in *Portrait*, Faulkner has gone to great lengths to diffuse it in *Mosquitoes*.

Faulkner's self-portrait in *Mosquitoes* involves many characters. On the level of serious aesthetic discourse, Julius rather than Gordon serves as Faulkner's mouthpiece.[10] His statement of an essentially romantic creed closely resembles Faulkner's own public position on the nature of "universal truth":

> Life everywhere is the same, you know. Manners of living it may be different—are they not different between adjoining villages? family names, profits on a single field or orchard, work influences—but man's old compulsions, duty and inclination:

the axis and circumference of his squirrel cage, they do not change. Details don't matter, details only entertain us. And nothing that merely entertains us can matter, because the things that entertain us are purely speculative: prospective pleasures which we probably will not achieve. The other things can only surprise us. And he who has stood the surprise of birth can stand anything. [*M*, p. 243]

Gordon, Julius, and Fairchild (who is based on Anderson but shares Faulkner's love of "local color" and grotesque detail) all contribute to the thematic climax during their walk down the rat's alley (*M*, pp. 335–40). This scene, in which the three characters develop the "Passion Week of the Heart" theory (*M*, p. 339) as a defense against their hostile environment, clearly resembles the "Circe-Eumaeus-Ithaca" sequence in *Ulysses*, where Stephen and Bloom finally bring sensitivity and humanity into tenuous contact.

In addition to these "serious" reflections, Faulkner includes numerous satirical self-caricatures in *Mosquitoes*. Faulkner the liar heads a file which includes the overly serious aesthete Mark Frost,[11] Eva Wiseman, whose poetry is Faulkner's own,[12] and the nephew carving his pipes who reflects Faulkner's wry image of himself as a simple country craftsman. Despite his use of Joyce's work as a general model, Faulkner presents a gallery of sketches, serious and comic, rather than a single full-length portrait.

The most important difference between *Portrait* and *Mosquitoes* is that Joyce understands his own position, whereas Faulkner appears to be groping in the dark. As his later works demonstrate, Faulkner preferred leaving artistic theory to take care of itself while he concentrated on the concrete events of Yoknapatawpha County. In *Mosquitoes* Faulkner seems aware of a conflict between the romantic artistic ideals of his trio and the experiences he presents in the novel, but he seems unsure of how to resolve the contradiction. When Patricia and David travel through the swamp, Faulkner juxtaposes Pat's vision of escape with the problems of heat, insects, and exhaustion. This discrepancy between dream and reality epitomizes the dilemma of the classical American writer.[13] While Faulkner satirizes Pat's silly romanticism in the swamp scene, he apparently endorses Gordon's romantic conception of himself as the king Halim. The "Passion Week of the Heart," an extension of Gordon's self-image into artistic terms, appears to be an attempt at the classic American transcendence through dissocation. But Faulkner ends the novel on a note of social satire, and *Mosquitoes* collapses amid unresolved contradictions.

Faulkner's ascent to greatness following *Mosquitoes* is a well-worn literary story. *The Sound and the Fury* and *As I Lay Dying* so clearly surpass any reasonable expectations created by Faulkner's earlier work that they seem composed by a different writer. Chase sees the key to Faulkner's development in Joyce's influence.[14] Since the Joycean influence was present in the early works, however, it seems more accurate to emphasize Faulkner's new attitude toward Joyce. Joycean techniques which seemed intrusive in *Mosquitoes*, largely because Faulkner attempted to link them to Joycean aesthetic themes, contribute to the impact of specifically Faulknerian themes in the first novels of his maturity. Chief among these techniques are the stream-of-consciousness approach to narration and the use of mythic parallels in structuring the realistic action. Neither novel contains many direct allusions to Joyce, although it is possible to see parallels between Stephen Dedalus and Quentin Compson (the sensitive young men) and Molly Bloom and Addie Bundren (the women who motivate action while remaining motionless themselves). Chase, Robert Martin Adams, and Michael Groden have explored Faulkner's use of Joycean techniques in *The Sound and the Fury* at length, but relatively little attention has been granted Joyce's equally important influence on *As I Lay Dying*.[15]

Faulkner relies more heavily on stream of consciousness in *As I Lay Dying* than did Joyce in *Ulysses*. The entire novel consists of brief glimpses into a variety of streams of consciousness. As Peter Swiggart observes, Faulkner's use of stream of consciousness tied to a first-person narrator rules out third-person descriptions of the realistic object inspiring the thought, a technique which Joyce often employs. Rather, Faulkner creates "a symbolism that reflects a character's interpretation of experience and does not necessarily describe the world in which he lives."[16] Faulkner's treatment of stream of consciousness reflects what, in *As I Lay Dying*, remains an essentially romantic sensibility. The difference between Faulkner's and Joyce's sensibilities also affects their choice of unifying devices. Traditional naturalistic details keep the stream of consciousness from reducing *Ulysses* to a chaos of mental impressions. Bloom's lemon soap and his potato talisman, for instance, periodically draw his attention and redirect his thought processes, linking various sections of the book. Similarly naturalistic details—the H.E.L.Y.'S sandwich men, the Ascot Gold Cup race, the bookseller's cart at which both Bloom and Stephen stop, even so mundane a detail as a cloud momentarily covering the sun— verify that all the characters of *Ulysses* inhabit the same world.

To be sure, realistic details also help unify *As I Lay Dying*. The sound of Cash's adze draws comment from Darl, Jewel, Tull, and Peabody.[17] The buzzards circle ubiquitously throughout the final half of the novel.

Faulkner relies primarily, however, on symbolic associations to unify his work. Occasionally Joyce, too, indicates affinities between characters through symbolic details. Stephen and Bloom, for example, both wear black all day, emphasizing their similarity in attitude and their alienation from most Dubliners. But even this affinity has its origin in realistic experiences—Stephen's poverty and continued mourning, and Bloom's attendance at Dignam's funeral. In contrast, Faulkner uses symbolic detail, derived only indirectly from realistic experience, as his primary method for establishing connections between characters. Vardaman expresses his bewildered love for Addie symbolically: "My mother is a fish" (*AILD*, p. 79); Jewel's love for horses not only motivates his actions but also serves to differentiate him from the bovine Dewey Dell; Darl perceives the link between Addie and Jewel symbolically: "Your mother was a horse, but who was your father?" (*AILD*, p. 202). Similarly, the frequent descriptions of Anse as a "steer" (*AILD*, pp. 58, 59, 69) stress his alienation from his family, an alienation which stems from his spiritual emasculation. These symbolic identifications unifying *As I Lay Dying* suggest that Faulkner sees the central meaning of the novel on a romantic rather than on a realistic level.

Perhaps its mythic structure contributes even more to the success of *As I Lay Dying* than stream of consciousness. Richard P. Adams believes that Faulkner read and agreed with Eliot's essay on *Ulysses*[18] which sees the use of myth as "a way of controlling, of giving a shape and a significance to the immense panorama of futility and anarchy which is contemporary history."[19] While most critics agree that the Easter story provides the mythic base for *The Sound and the Fury*, no similar consensus exists on *As I Lay Dying*. The Demeter-Persephone-Kora myth, the William Morris translation of *The Odyssey*, the figures of Adam and the anti-Christ as presented by *The Golden Bough*, and the journey of King Edward I and his dead Queen Eleanor have all been suggested as legendary parallels for the Bundrens' journey.[20] Perhaps the presence of a general mythic parallel is more important than that of any particular myth. Faulkner's description of his "plan" for *As I Lay Dying* makes his desire for "universal" significance clear, but does not deal in particular models: "I simply imagined a group of people and subjected them to the simple universal natural catastrophes, which are flood and fire."[21]

Several questions arise concerning Faulkner's juxtaposition of the universal and the particular. Does the meaning of the Bundren journey lie in its similarity to other mythic journeys, or in its realistic indication of the family's sociological predicament? Is *As I Lay Dying* a celebration of the Bundrens' heroic qualities, or a parody of their grotesque struggle? Is it a romance or a realistic novel? The answers lie somewhere between the extremes. Seen in isolation, the journey appears grotesque. Seen purely as myth, it reduces the realistic characters to the status of hapless automatons. The human significance of the journey stems from the characters' ability to recognize the contradictions surrounding their own lives, in their struggle to perceive and perhaps articulate the meaning behind the ritual of Addie's burial.[22]

The dominant critical position, a position which relies heavily on Addie's only monolog, sees two central themes in *As I Lay Dying*: the superiority of deed over word, and the redemptive potential of physical love.[23] Faulkner develops these themes in a manner which admits a great deal of ambiguity. Addie indeed argues for a focus on the concrete: "So I took Anse. And when I knew that I had Cash, I knew that living was terrible and that this was the answer to it. That was when I learned that words are no good; that words don't even fit what they are trying to say at. When he was born I knew that motherhood was invented by someone who had to have a word for it because the ones that had children didn't care whether there was a word for it or not. I knew that fear was invented by someone that had never had the fear;

pride, who never had the pride" (*AILD*, pp. 163–64). But Addie is also the novel's primary metaphysician. Along with Darl, she evinces the fullest awareness of the romantic conflicts of abstract universal forces. While Addie provides the center of physical love in the novel and inspires whatever heroism the Bundrens achieve,[24] she also perceives her children as nothing more than symbolic counters in a romantic clash of love and duty. Her statement, "I gave Anse Dewey Dell to negative Jewel. Then I gave him Vardaman to replace the child I had robbed him of. And now he has three children that are his and not mine. And then I could get ready to die" (*AILD*, p. 168), dehumanizes her children as much as Anse's more obvious insensitivity. Addie's monolog may imply abstract thematic resolutions, but Faulkner's presentation of their realistic impact demonstrates her failure to resolve the conflict between the realistic and the symbolic significance of her own life.

At times Darl seems to effect such a resolution. At the moment of the ford disaster, he momentarily freezes time and perceives the redemptive potential inherent in the realistic catastrophe: "But I did not realize the reason for the rope until I saw the log. It surged up out of the water and stood for an instant upright upon that surging and heaving desolation like Christ. Get out and let the current take you down to the bend, Cash said. You can make it all right. No, I said, I'd get just as wet that way as this" (*AILD*, p. 141). But Darl can never respond on the realistic level to such opportunities for conscious heroism. Instead, the stoic sufferer Cash and the brave but impulsive Jewel perform the heroic actions[25] while Darl descends into madness and arson. The final glimpse of Darl filters through his own fractured consciousness: "Darl is our brother, our brother Darl. Our brother Darl in a cage in Jackson where, his grimed hands lying light in the quiet interstices, looking out he foams. 'Yes yes yes yes yes yes yes yes'" (*AILD*, p. 244). Unlike the final sympathetic "yes" of *Ulysses*, Faulkner's "yes" is accompanied by hysterical laughter. Where Joyce's characters resolve the contradictions of experience, Faulkner's are destroyed by them. The cacophonous ironic conclusion of *As I Lay Dying* stresses that Faulkner, while developing a mature ability to employ Joycean techniques and an increased control over his juxtapositions of the real and the romantic, remained a very American writer in his willingness to accept their unresolved destructive conflict.

According to the critical consensus, Joyce's influence on Faulkner fades gradually after *As I Lay Dying* and vanishes almost entirely after *Light in August*. This position overemphasizes specific details and overlooks the general nature of Faulkner's later novels. Only in the works of the late 1930s and early 1940s, culminating in *Go Down, Moses*, does Faulkner succeed, as Joyce had done twenty years earlier in *Ulysses*, in reconciling the realistic and romantic modes.

Even in specific detail, Faulkner does not abandon Joycean models as completely as critics such as Robert Martin Adams imply.[26] Faulkner's concern with the juxtaposition of mythic patterns and realistic experience continues unabated. In *Go Down, Moses* Faulkner moves from the literary myths of *As I Lay Dying* to two social myths: the myth of the wilderness, and the myth of the Negro. Neither myth is imposed upon the realistic action; each is embedded in the minds of characters living within the realistic setting.[27] This conception of myth sets the stage for Faulkner's resolution of *Go Down, Moses*'s symbolic and realistic meanings.

In addition, *Go Down, Moses* uses several varieties of the Joycean stream of consciousness. There are fairly standard stream-of-consciousness passages, such as Roth Edmonds's as he contemplates Lucas Beauchamp in "The Fire and the Hearth": "He's more like Old Carothers than all the rest of us put together, including Old Carothers. He is both heir and prototype simultaneously of all the geography and climate and biology which sired Old Carothers and all the rest of us and our kind, myriad, countless, faceless, even nameless now except himself who fathered himself, intact and complete, contemptuous, as Old Carothers must have been, of all blood black white yellow or red, including his own."[28] But this passage is not quite analogous to the internal monologs of either *Ulysses* or *As I Lay Dying* which attempt to capture the cadence of each character's thought patterns. Its prose rhythms bear no immediate relationship to Roth's mental constitution. In fact, the rhythms echo those associated with Isaac: "Fifty dollars a month. He knows that's all. That I reneged, cried calf-rope, sold my birthright, betrayed my blood, for what he too calls not peace but obliteration, and a little food" (*GDM*, pp. 108–9) or Gavin Stevens: "It doesn't matter to her now. Since it had to be and she couldn't stop it, and now that it's all over and done and finished, she doesn't care how he died. She just wanted him home, but she wanted him to come home right. She wanted that casket and those flowers and the hearse and she wanted to ride through town behind it in a car" (*GDM*, p. 383). Throughout *Go Down, Moses* the stream-of-consciousness passages share a tone and rhythm which Irving Howe has aptly referred to as Faulkner's "stream of eloquence."[29] This stream of eloquence, which reaches its culmination in Part IV of "The Bear," shares many characteristics with the stream of consciousness. It shifts between levels of consciousness with opaque subjective (rather than clear rational) connections between thoughts. Unlike Joyce's stream of consciousness, however, it allows Faulkner to speak in a collective historical voice that takes its cadences from famous speeches, ledgers, the Bible, slaveholders' rhetoric, Jeffersonian political theory—in short, all of the sources which mold the characters' sensibilities, their senses of myth, while remaining largely beyond their conscious knowledge.

This stream-of-eloquence technique allows Faulkner to balance the realistic and symbolic elements of his characters' struggles to come to terms with their experience. The structure of *Go Down, Moses* gradually deflates the romantic plantation mythology of "Was" and culminates in the harsh realism of the title story, which closes the novel.[30] The key to the novel's unity lies in Ike's recognition, in Part IV of "The Bear," of Carothers McCaslin's incestuous miscegenation, the very real sin underlying the romantic awe in which most characters, black and white, hold the legendary family founder. This sin unifies the themes of the decline of the wilderness and racial oppression, the central myths of the novel. Both derive from the arrogance which led Old Carothers to believe he could possess first part of God's creation and ultimately other human beings.

Within this structure Faulkner presents a number of characters who are unable or unwilling to reconcile the romantic and the realistic aspects of their experience. Carothers, although not a character in the novel's present, typifies the "romantic" pole of Faulkner's continuum. He lives in a myth of himself, acting out his fantasies of power, seemingly blind to the realistic implications of his actions which consistently dehumanize his black "family" and his own soul. Roth Edmonds plays a similarly unconscious role in acting out the myth of white superiority in "The Fire and the Hearth" and "Delta Autumn." At the other end of the continuum are characters, mostly black, who make no attempt to act out mythic fantasies because they have been victimized by circumstances beyond their understanding, very much in the tradition of American naturalism. Carothers's slave mistress, Eunice, unable to comprehend the horror of Carothers's subsequent sexual relations with their daughter Thomasina, drowns herself, providing the realistic legend balancing Carothers's romantic legend. Rider, destroyed by his own grief and by white insensitivity, similarly falls victim to forces he cannot understand. All of these characters, and most of the others in *Go Down, Moses*, share an inability to connect the symbolic and realistic demands of their situations.

Unlike *As I Lay Dying*, however, *Go Down, Moses* does not abandon the reader to a contemplation of the irreconcilable disjunction. Rather, through the juxtaposition of Isaac McCaslin and Lucas Beauchamp, Faulkner provides a meditation on the possibilities of reconciliation and heroism. Isaac attempts to confront the problem from an essentially romantic posture; Lucas, from a realistic one. Each shows enough awareness of the other's orientation to attain a convincing, though limited, heroism which recalls Joyce's similarly measured resolution of *Ulysses*.

The traditional view of Isaac as a saintly figure, best argued by R. W. B. Lewis,[31] has come under increasing attack with the growing recognition of "The Bear" as an intrinsic part of *Go Down, Moses* rather than a self-sufficient short story. The purely heroic interpretation of Isaac's attempt to dissociate himself from Carothers's complex sin by repudiating his inheritance either ignores or underemphasizes a central realistic fact: the repudiation accomplishes nothing, and in fact perpetuates oppression by placing control of the land in the hands of the increasingly mercenary Edmonds clan. Sam Fathers would certainly not have approved of Ike's decision,[32] and Faulkner's own statement on heroism demands a qualification of the canonization of Isaac:

. . . there are some people in any time and age that cannot face and cope with the problems. There seem to be three stages: The first says, This is rotten, I'll have no part of it, I will take death first. The second says, This is rotten, I don't like it, I can't do anything about it, but at least I will not participate in it myself, I will go off into a cave or climb a pillar to sit on. The third says, This stinks and I'm going to do something about it. McCaslin is the second. He says, This is bad, and I will withdraw from it. What we need are people who will say, This is bad and I'm going to do something about it, I'm going to change it.[33]

When Isaac confronts Roth's mistress in "Delta Autumn," Faulkner makes it clear that he has transformed nothing, not even his own moral being. But he has recognized the seriousness of the problem and has refused to repress his insight.[34] The girl's question, "Old man . . . have you lived so long and forgotten so much that you don't remember anything you ever knew or felt or even heard about love?" (*GDM*, p. 363), qualifies Isaac's triumph but does not destroy it. He *has* been willing to forego the material rewards which accompany acceptance of the myths he repudiates. He is limited, but not hypocritical; his realistic actions accord with his romantic beliefs. They simply—realistically—lack the power to effect wide change.

Although Lucas Beauchamp only rarely has been seen as the hero of *Go Down, Moses*, his position in the novel provides the necessary complement to Isaac's. Denied the opportunity for large romantic gestures by his racial identity (to repudiate his inheritance would be to condemn himself to a life of entrapment within the myth of the "nigger," against which his financial independence serves as his chief weapon), Lucas nonetheless understands both his symbolic and his realistic situations and acts accordingly. Lucas refuses to participate in the myth which states that he, as a black man, must accept whites as superiors. He infuriates Roth because he "never once said 'sir' to his white skin" (*GDM*, p. 131). Lucas refers directly to interracial kinship, an absolute taboo, when confronting Zack: "I'm a nigger . . . but I'm a man too. I'm more than just a man. The same thing made my pappy that made your grandmaw" (*GDM*, p. 47). By withholding his acceptance of the basic racial symbolism of his society, Lucas walks a dangerous line. He survives partly through luck when his gun misfires and partly through the very practical cunning which allows him to outwit both Roth and the salesman without overstepping identifiable social boundaries in "The Fire and the Hearth."

Like Isaac, Lucas has flaws. He shares something of Old Carothers' materialism but, unlike Carothers, maintains his sense of human values.[35] When the treasure hunt threatens to destroy his marriage, Lucas withdraws (though he never rejects it theoretically). Though he acts primarily on the basis of concrete facts while Isaac acts almost totally on the basis of abstract concepts, Lucas too lives with an awareness of both the real and the symbolic significance of his actions. He cannot destroy the myth of the nigger, but he can, to a limited degree, refuse to participate in it, providing a symbol of its emptiness and futility.

In the end, then, Isaac and Lucas, like Joyce's Bloom, demonstrate the possibility of successfully coping with their hostile environment by perceiving and accepting both the symbolic significance of their actions and their realistic results. Both will continue to live in Yoknapatawpha County; neither will light out for the territories or wind up in a padded cell in Jackson.[36] Faulkner accepts neither the romantic conception of transcendence through dissociation nor the naturalistic abandonment to victimization. He does not throw down his pen in despair. The successful resolution of the modes in *Go Down, Moses* marks the point of greatest similarity, though certainly not most obvious resemblance, between the works of Faulkner and Joyce.

Richard Wright

Richard Wright's reading of the great American realists is widely recognized as the key to his development as a writer. The key to understanding his mature work is recognizing the equal importance of his reading of the great modernists, particularly Joyce. The major phase of Wright's career culminates in *Native Son*, which combines his perceptions of man as both naturalistic and existential victim. The resolution rests on Bigger Thomas's unifying consciousness, which draws together realistic and symbolic levels of experience. But Wright created Bigger only after experimenting first with Bloom-style "everyman" figures and later with more sensitive, if still inarticulate, Dedalian minds.

Too often presuppositions concerning the lack of "universality" in black life have led critics to dismiss even *Native Son* as a mere "slice of life." Wright, indeed, identified a naturalistic base for his work: "All my life had shaped me for the realism, the naturalism of the modern novel."[37] His favorite American writer was Theodore Dreiser, and actual events inspired most of his novels: "How Bigger Was Born" recounts experiences behind *Native Son*; a newspaper clipping inspired "The Man Who Lived Underground," one of his most obviously symbolic stories. As a theorist, however, Wright was not solely or even primarily a realist. His "Blueprint for Negro Writing" stresses aesthetic craftsmanship and the *subjective* basis of literature.[38] To embody the naturalistic and symbolic aspects of his theory in his novels, Wright turned to Joycean techniques.

Unlike Faulkner, Wright made no attempt to deny Joyce's influence on his writing. In a 1939 Federal Writers' Project guide to New York, Wright identified Joyce as a major influence on black writers of the time. He later recommended Joyce to many of his acquaintances, including Ralph Ellison.[39] Reading and discussing *Portrait* and *Ulysses* in 1935 inspired Wright to rewrite early drafts of "Big Boy Leaves Home" and "Down by the Riverside," expanding them from realistic sketches to symbolic confrontations between man and fate.[40] The early Joycean influence most clearly affects *Lawd Today*, which Wright began writing in 1934. Like Faulkner's *Mosquitoes*, *Lawd Today* fails largely because it keeps the Joycean model too much in the foreground.

Lawd Today is Wright's *Ulysses*; its hero, Jake Jackson, is his Leopold Bloom. Like Bloom, Jake leaves his wife in the morning, lives through an "average" working day, and, following a nighttime excursion to a brothel, returns home. Both Edward Margolies and Katherine Fishburn identify the ironic function of the mythic background in *Lawd Today*, which takes place on an "important" day, Lincoln's birthday, rather than on the "insignificant" June 16. They insist too strongly on seeing this as a mark of Wright's independence from Joycean models.[41] During the 1930s, Eliot's interpretation of Bloom as an emblem of the emptiness of modern man in comparison with the mythic hero was dominant.

It seems likely that, given the numerous parallels between *Ulysses* and *Lawd Today*, Wright saw his bitterly ironic use of the mythic parallel as yet another echo of Joyce.

The variety of styles in *Lawd Today* also derives from *Ulysses*. But whereas Joyce chose his styles to reflect the increasingly weary physiological condition of his characters, Wright has no unifying rationale behind his technical progression. Several of Wright's styles allude directly to *Ulysses*. Often the allusions accentuate Wright's inability to integrate his perceptions. His use of newspaper clippings (*LT*, Iiii) seems artificial when compared with either Joyce's parodic commentary in the headlines of "Aeolus" or his realistic portrait of Bloom's reading in "Eumaeus." Jake's mock-epic battle with his hair (*LT*, Iiii) works better as an isolated passage but again suffers from comparison with Joyce's "Cyclops." The conclusion of Wright's battle openly mocks Jake: "He was breathing hard. He resorted to the comb again. A hot skirmish on the left and right flanks had each warweary strand clinging to his scalp like troops in shell holes under bombardment. The enemy was conquered! Jake peered into the mirror. His head was a solid mass of black slickness. He smiled, thinking with satisfaction *If a fly'd light on that he'd slip up and break his neck. . . .*"[42] Joyce's resolution balances parody and compassion: "And they beheld Him even Him, ben Bloom Elijah, amid clouds of angels ascend to the glory of the brightness at an angle of forty-five degrees over Donohoe's in Little Green Street like a shot off a shovel" (*U*, p. 345). Similarly, the experiments with no analog in *Ulysses*, such as the bridge game (*LT*, Iiii), succeed only erratically.

The descent into the racial unconsciousness (*LT*, Iiv), which has a source in "Circe," is Wright's most effective experiment. By omitting phrases identifying speakers whose voices merge in a lengthy conversation, Wright stresses the underlying similarity in the personalities of the black postal workers. This similarity stems from common historical experiences of oppression (*LT*, p. 156) and a common folk culture (*LT*, p. 159). The merging reflects Wright's naturalistic view of sex and violence as the motive forces for all human beings (*LT*, p. 162). Here style reinforces content.

Despite occasional successful experiments, however, Wright fails to balance the symbolic and realistic elements of *Lawd To-*

day. Joyce's stylistic experiments in *Ulysses* provide a sense of the interplay between external stimuli and the characters' subjective reactions. When Bloom listens to Simon Dedalus sing, the music blends with and redirects his thoughts: "It soared, a bird, it held its flight, a swift pure cry, soar silver orb it leaped serene, speeding, sustained, to come, don't spin it out too long long breath he breath long life, soaring high, high resplendent, aflame, crowned, high in the effulgence symbolistic, high, of the ethereal bosom, high, of the high vast irridiation everywhere all soaring all around about the all, the endlessnessnessness . . ." (*U*, pp. 275–76). In *Lawd Today*, conversely, music serves merely to fill in the realistic setting; Jake sings while dressing (*LT*, p. 24) but his song does nothing to direct his consciousness to the comic mood associated with the battle with the hair which immediately follows. This lack of subtlety in Wright's use of Joycean techniques mars *Lawd Today*. Frequently Wright's treatment of symbols recalls Frank Norris more than Joyce. The endless stairs in Jake's opening dream symbolize his plight, but they seem tacked onto the realistic setting of the novel, like the caged bird in *McTeague*. Unlike Stephen Dedalus' ashplant, which is at once a walking stick and the sword Nothung capable of destroying time and space in "Circe," they lack a realistic component. Wright also fails to integrate the mythic parallel into the realistic action; the day-long radio broadcast on Lincoln's life, which appears to be tuned in even at the raucous Calumet Club (*LT*, p. 172), is unconvincing.

Many of the specific failures of *Lawd Today* stem from Wright's conception of his everyman figure as a debased victim who lacks the ability to understand either his symbolic or his realistic situation. Wright aggravates the problem with his uncertain use of stream of consciousness. Frequently Wright's stream-of-consciousness passages do nothing more than echo the narration: "He wondered if his pal, Bob, were up. *Dammit, that's the big trouble with Bob; he always sleeps so late*" (*LT*, p. 61). At best they comment directly on narrative: "He remembered still another scene when Howard had hurt his feelings. He had been before the Board and Howard had used the word 'Negro' in front of Swanson. *He could've called me colored at least.* It was all right for one Negro to call another Negro 'nigger'; but when in front of white folks one ought to be careful. *And that word ain't the same when a white man uses it. There's something he puts in it that ain't right"* (*LT*, p. 120). The shifts of narrative stance seem pointless. Jake's inability to see anything beyond the naturalistic level of experience renders Wright's reports of his mental processes generally uninteresting. Jake is a true victim; his mind has been destroyed. Wright's sporadic symbolism fails to merge with the realistic action. This disjunction emphasizes the overwhelming power of the naturalistic forces which render *Lawd Today*, more than any of Wright's later works, a limited slice of life.

If *Lawd Today* is Wright's *Ulysses*, then *Uncle Tom's Children* is his *Dubliners*: a series of short stories unified through thematic and symbolic patterns filtered through gradually widening perspectives. Both *Dubliners* and *Uncle Tom's Children* served as proving grounds for techniques which were refined in later novels. The overall structure of the two books is remarkably similar. Joyce divided *Dubliners* into sequences of stories concerning childhood, adolescence (which Joyce defined as young adulthood), maturity, and public life. He concluded the volume with a story written after the others, which revalues the preceding sequence by considering a greater complexity of experience. *Uncle Tom's Children* progresses similarly. After an initial story concerning the youthful Big Boy, the next stories progress from Mann, whose lack of awareness identifies him with Joyce's adolescents, to Silas, whose resistance, while impotent, reflects his more mature understanding of his own victimization. The volume's original concluding story, "Fire and Cloud," focuses on the public responsibility of Reverend Taylor.

Wright added "Bright and Morning Star," a story which revalues the conclusion of "Fire and Cloud" much as "The Dead" revalues "Grace." If *Dubliners* had ended with "Grace," the volume would have seemed bitterly ironic, concluding with a picture of God as the great accountant in the sky. "The Dead" adds humanity to *Dubliners* by examining both Gabriel Conroy's lack of sensitivity and his final attempts to sympathize with other human beings. Similarly, the addition of a story greatly alters the emotional impact of *Uncle Tom's Children*. The cry of *"Freedom belongs to the strong"*[43] from "Fire and Cloud" concludes *Uncle Tom's Children* on a naively optimistic note of interracial cooperation. Aunt Sue's bewildered confrontation with betrayal in "Bright and Morning Star" reflects Wright's awareness that the formulaic solutions of the communists in "Fire and Cloud" underestimate the persistent complications of American racism. Aunt Sue's death in defense of her half-understood ideals combines the victimization which dominated the first three stories and the political insight, revalued on a more complex level, of "Fire and Cloud." This death, convincing on a realistic level, results from her dreams of a better future and transforms her, like Gabriel, into a symbol of silently struggling humanity. Keneth Kinnamon considers the story a failure impinging on the thematic unity of *Uncle Tom's Children*. He observes that the concluding paragraph of "Bright and Morning Star" echoes "The Dead" in rhythm and imagery:[44] "Focused and pointed she was, buried in the depths of her star, swallowed in its peace and strength; and not feeling her flesh growing cold, cold as the rain that fell from the invisible sky upon the doomed living and the dead that never dies" (*UTC*, p. 384). Aunt Sue, like Gabriel Conroy, combines the realistic situation of a social class, an individual personality, and a symbolic vision of mortality in a universe of hope and despair.

Along with this increasingly complex balance of realistic and symbolic meanings, *Uncle Tom's Children* includes stream-of-consciousness passages far more effective and less intrusive than those in *Lawd Today*. Aunt Sue's thoughts as she seeks Johnny's gun do more than simply echo the narrator:

She thought of Johnny-Boy's gun in the dresser drawer. Ahll hide the gun in the sheet'n go aftah Johnny-Boys body. . . . She tiptoed to her room, eased out the dresser drawer, and got a sheet. Reva was sleeping; the darkness was filled with her quiet breathing. She groped in the drawer and found the gun. She wound the gun in the sheet and held them both under her apron. Then she stole to the bedside and watched Reva. Lawd, hep her! But mabbe shes bettah off. This had t happen sometime . . . She n Johnny-Boy couldna been together in this here South . . . N Ah couldn't tell her about Booker. Itll come out awright n she wont nevah know. Reva's trust would never be shaken. She caught her breath as the shucks in the mattress rustled dryly; then all was quiet and she breathed easily again. She tiptoed to the door, down the hall, and stood on the porch. Above the yellow beacon whirled through the rain. She went over muddy ground, mounted a slope, stopped and looked back at her house. The lamp glowed in her window, and the yellow beacon that swung every few seconds to feed it with light. She turned and started across the fields, holding the gun and sheet tightly, thinking, Po Reva . . . Po critter . . . Shes fas ersleep . . . [*UTC*, pp. 369–70]

As Sue watches Reva, her thoughts reveal the protective impulse behind her actions. The rustling mattress cuts off the stream of consciousness as Sue attempts to silence herself entirely to avoid waking Reva. Finally, Sue's image of the sleeping girl suggests Reva's limited perception of, and involvement in, the complexities around her. The symbolically resonant images in Sue's stream of consciousness indicate levels of awareness which remain inarticulate. Like Jake Jackson, Aunt Sue is an "everyman" figure. Like Jake, she fails to consciously understand the nature of her victimization. Unlike Jake, she acts on the basis of an unconscious apprehension. Her martyrdom is both real and symbolic, like that of Bigger Thomas in *Native Son*.

In Bigger, Wright created a character who combines aspects of Bloom and Stephen Dedalus. As Wright's essay "How Bigger Was Born" recounts, Bigger was in some sense an everyman figure: "there was not just one Bigger, but many of them, more than I could count and more than you suspect."[45] But he is also, at least potentially, an incarnation of his creator. Wright's close emotional identification with Bigger motivated his explanation of *Native Son*'s realistic roots. Wright perceived his own "imagination as a kind of self-generating cement which glued his facts together, and his emotions as a kind of dark and obscure designer of those facts" (*NS*, p. vii). This conception of the shaping power of the imagination links Wright, as he recognized, with the great American romantics. He saw Bigger's feeling of alienation as a socially grounded extension of the metaphysical conflicts at the center of his predecessors' work:

> Early American writers, Henry James and Nathaniel Hawthorne, complained bitterly about the bleakness and flatness of the American scene. But I think that if they were alive, they'd feel at home in modern America. True, we have no great church in America; our national traditions are still of such a sort that we are not wont to brag of them; and we have no army that's above the level of mercenary fighters; we have no group acceptable to the whole of our country upholding certain humane values; we have no rich symbols, no colorful rituals. We have only

a money-grubbing, industrial civilization. But we do have in the Negro embodiment of a past tragic enough to appease the spiritual hunger of even a James; and we have in the oppression of the Negro a shadow athwart our national life dense and heavy enough to satisfy even the gloomy broodings of a Hawthorne. And if Poe were alive, he would not have to invent horror; horror would invent him. [*NS*, p. xxxiv]

This apprehension places the "naturalist" Wright, who looked to Dreiser for much of *Native Son*'s plot, squarely in the tradition of American romanticism.

The horror of *Native Son* filters through Bigger's consciousness, which only gradually attains an awareness of the symbolic universe it unconsciously reflects in apprehending realistic events. Bigger certainly does not equate his own situation with that of the rat he kills; he does not interpret the blanket of white snow which plagues his attempted escape as a symbol of white oppression. Nonetheless, as numerous critics have recognized, the dense symbolic texture sets the book apart from numerous other proletarian novels and from Wright's own early works.[46] By the end of the novel, Bigger is capable of consciously choosing to reject the chaplain's proffered cross and to accept Jan's friendship because of their symbolic significance.

Although *Native Son* is probably the least Joycean of Wright's major works, the development of Bigger's awareness resembles that of Stephen Dedalus, whose increasing awareness of the symbolic meaning of his environment allows him to assume responsibility for his own life. Wright's analogous treatment of Bigger's consciousness extends the techniques of perspective employed in *Uncle Tom's Children*. Where the earlier work shifted characters in order to broaden perspective on thematic issues, *Native Son* intensifies the technique by showing the progression within a single mind. Bigger, trapped at the outset in his realistic environment, gradually comes to terms with that environment through his increasing awareness of the symbolic significance of his own actions.

This progression centers on Bigger's understanding of the murders of Mary Dalton and Bessie. He kills Mary almost unconsciously, because of his fear of being found in a white girl's bedroom. During the early stages of his flight, Bigger reacts to the killing on a literal level, although the surrounding imagery clearly intimates the larger social context of his act: "The reality of the room fell from him; the vast city of white people that sprawled outside took its place. She was dead and he had killed her. He was a murderer, a Negro murderer, a black murderer. He had killed a white woman. He had to get away from here. Mrs. Dalton had been in the room while he was there, but she had not known it" (*NS*, p. 86). Bigger reacts to the specific crime, but the basic reality indicated in the imagery points to the fact that the crime in fact represents a general condition. No black man can act without having his actions in some measure determined by the presence of a "vast city" of whites, represented immediately by the uncomprehending Mrs. Dalton.

Only after he kills Bessie, with far less motivation, does Bigger begin to recognize the meaning of the first murder. He now recognizes the rage engendered by the encompassing forces of whiteness:

> In all of his life these two murders were the most meaningful things that had ever happened to him. He was living, truly and deeply, no matter what others might think, looking at him with their blind eyes. Never had he had the chance to live out the consequences of his actions; never had his will been so free as in this night and day of fear and murder and flight. He had killed twice, but in a true sense it was not the first time he had ever killed. He had killed many times before, but only during the last two days had this impulse assumed the form of actual killing. Blind anger had come often and he had either gone behind his curtain or wall, or had quarreled and fought. And yet, whether in running away or in fighting, he had felt the need of the clean satisfaction of facing this thing in all its fullness, of fighting it out in the wind and sunlight, in front of those whose hate for him was so unfathomably deep . . . [*NS*, p. 225]

This helps explain Mary's murder but applies less well to Bessie's. Bigger now understands the social symbolism behind his behavior, but again the imagery points to symbolism which he cannot yet comprehend. The fear directed at the whites' "blind eyes" inspires Mary's murder. But Bigger fails to comprehend the existential roots of his own "blind anger" which leads him to kill a black woman who can by no definition be counted among those with an "unfathomable" hatred for Bigger.

Not until he prepares for his execution does Bigger understand his actions fully. He rejects the purely social interpretation of the murder's symbolic significance. Max expresses this interpretation in his "guilt of the nation" speech: "This man is different, even though his crime differs from similar crimes only in degree. The complex forces of society have isolated here for us a symbol, a test symbol. The prejudices of men have stained this symbol, like a germ stained for examination under the microscope. The unremitting hate of men has given us a psychological distance that will enable us to see this tiny social symbol in relation to our whole sick social organism" (*NS*, p. 354). But this passage, like much of Max's speech, self-destructs and cautions against overemphasizing the symbolic dimensions of *Native Son*. Bigger is not *merely* a symbol: he remains a human being, whatever his symbolic significance. Max's interpretation of Bigger as a symbol of "millions of others, Negro and white" (*NS*, p. 368), as an organism under the microscope of Marxist "science," fails to account for the racially motivated aspects of the murder, pursuit, and trial. No white man would have murdered out of fear of aiding a drunken girl; no white murderer would have been subjected to the press vendetta aimed at Bigger.

The key to understanding Bigger's actions lies in a full acceptance of his humanity.[47] Whatever symbolic value accrues to Bigger stems from an acceptance of his experience on its own terms. Facing death, Bigger himself expresses this acceptance: " 'What I killed for must've been good!' Bigger's voice was full of frenzied anguish. 'It must have been good! When a man kills, it's for something. . . . I didn't know I was really alive in this world until I felt things hard enough to kill for 'em. . . . It's the truth, Mr. Max, I can say it now, 'cause I'm going to die. I know what I'm saying real good and I know how it sounds. But I'm all right. I feel all right when I look at it that way . . .' " (*NS*, p. 392). With this speech, Bigger passes from the social to the existential understanding of his own life. He sees that his own realistic experiences are of more importance than any system, such as Max's, designed to explain them.

In this brief passage, he draws his real and symbolic experiences together by accepting simultaneously his literal, social, and existential blackness.[48] Bigger's triumph lies not in the murders themselves. He no longer believes, as he did following Bessie's murder, that he has freed himself through violence. Whatever freedom Bigger attains occurs in the act of accepting the murders, not in the actual murders. He accepts both his actions *and* their consequences. He accepts his guilt and impending death. Though still a victim, he is no longer an unconscious victim. Bigger Thomas ultimately understands the balance of symbolic and realistic elements in his life as profoundly, if not as articulately, as do Stephen Dedalus and Leopold Bloom. Wright does not resolve the realistic and romantic modes as thoroughly as Joyce or Faulkner. Bigger's symbolic freedom cannot be realized within his environment. Still, within Wright's fictional world, Bigger's awareness of the symbolic significance of his naturalistic fate represents the highest achievement. Dreiser's Clyde Griffiths shares Bigger's fate, but Hawthorne's Hester Prynne, as Wright perceived, shares more of his sensibility.

The Many Mirrors:
Joyce's Techniques

IF STYLE MAKES THE MAN, Joyce was a crowd. Different writers read different Joyces—Dublin(er)'s Joyce, Stephen Joyce, Homer's Joyce, Humphrey Chimpden Joyce—and react accordingly. Joyce had no one style, yet he has influenced nearly every stylistic development in contemporary fiction.

General theories of Joyce's stylistic development abound. Critics who read the works of the heroic Stephen Joyce often embrace the aesthetic theory of *A Portrait of the Artist as a Young Man*. Accepting Stephen Dedalus as Joyce's spokesman (and assuming that the Joyce of 1910 foresaw the Joyce of the 1930s), they trace a lyric-epic-dramatic development in Joyce's work. This development can be seen as moving toward either symbolism or realism. When Stephen posits an ideal "dramatic" art in which "the esthetic image . . . is purified in and reprojected from the human imagination," he provides the foundation for symbolist readings. When he speaks of the artist who "remains within or behind or beyond or above his handiwork, invisible, refined out of existence, indifferent, paring his fingernails," he provides the base for realistic readings.[1] The realists argue that, as Joyce gradually distances himself from his material, his insight into experience increases. Freed from personal limitation, he polishes his mirror to better reflect life in all its breadth and depth. *Dubliners* and *Portrait* prepare for the realistic triumph of *Ulysses*, a masterpiece of both external and internal mimesis. Conversely, the symbolists contend that Joyce increasingly distances himself from the narrow naturalism of *Dubliners*. Concentrating increasingly on the

33

artistic (un)consciousness, he departs totally from the mimetic mode in *Finnegans Wake*. While the symbolist theory considers Joyce's final work more fully, the realistic theory avoids an inordinate emphasis on "Circe" in its consideration of *Ulysses*. Neither approach seems adequate in itself.

Perhaps it is more accurate to image Joyce's stylistic development as a tuning fork seeking to isolate a single frequency. While the prongs vibrate between two extremes, a single note emerges for the listener's ears. *Dubliners* and *Portrait* sound the realistic-social and symbolic-psychological extremes. *Ulysses*, while shifting back toward *Dubliners* with its emphasis on physical detail, maintains the psychological overtones of *Portrait*. *Finnegans Wake*, while oscillating back toward the self-absorbed style of *Portrait*, echoes the sounding of a realistic historical bass-line in *Ulysses* which conditions the artist's lyrical freedom. The harmony, the realistic-symbolic stylistic equilibrium, emerges only from the entire canon.

Grand theories aside, Joyce's works suggest specific techniques for use by contemporary writers attempting to reconcile the modes. The epiphanies of *Dubliners* and *Portrait*, the mythic substructures of *Ulysses* and *Finnegans Wake*, and Joyce's continual linguistic experiments have all been adapted by relatively traditional as well as openly experimental novelists. Their success in harmonizing the diverse chords of their works varies substantially, but very few are willing to accept the limitations of writing in a single key.

Dublin(er)'s Joyce: Ernest Gaines, Flannery O'Connor, Russell Banks

Although Joyce did not invent the epiphany, he effectively "patented" it. Stephen Dedalus' theory of the epiphany as "a sudden spiritual manifestation whether in the vulgarity of speech or of gesture or in a memorable phase of the mind itself"[2] capitalizes upon the developmental work of several predecessors. Anton Chekov's short stories often rely on seemingly innocuous details which, when viewed from the right perspective, yield unexpected spiritual insights. Though University College Dublin professor Gerard Manley Hopkins remained largely unknown until the publication of his poetry in 1918, his inscapes anticipate Joyce's epiphanies. Nonetheless, *Dubliners* remains the first book of short fiction to rely primarily on the technique which has since revolutionized the short story, whether as published by the *New Yorker* or by the Fiction Collective.

Joyce's terminology, rather than Hopkins's, has been accepted largely because Joyce helped transform the modern idea of the "short story collection." Prior to *Dubliners*, short story volumes were, with few exceptions, collections of random pieces.[3] Since *Dubliners*, many have instead sought the unity long associated with the best volumes of poetry, the unity of Hopkins's canon. *Dubliners* provides three basic techniques for unifying story cycles: 1) focusing on one well-defined setting, the central unifying technique of Ernest Gaines's *Bloodline*; 2) developing a group of central thematic issues from different perspectives, an approach shared by *Bloodline* and by Flannery O'Connor's *Everything That Rises Must Converge*; and 3) manipulating narrative stance to reflect shifting authorial attitude toward the subject matter, the style which unifies Russell Banks's *Searching for Survivors*.[4] As Faulkner's *Go Down, Moses*, Wright's *Uncle Tom's Children*, and Sherwood Anderson's *Winesburg, Ohio* intimate, each of these techniques filters down to the present through American writers as well as through Joyce. At some times the Joycean influence is indistinguishable from that of his successors; at other times the difference is crucial.

For Ernest Gaines, Joyce provided an escape from Faulkner. Gaines acknowledges that Faulkner strongly influenced his own early novels, *Catharine Carmier* and *Of Love and Dust*, both of which share the classic inability to resolve contradictions. Unable to endorse Faulkner's commitment to the old aristocratic South, Gaines shares Faulkner's distrust of the new order.[5] Only in *Bloodline* does he resolve this tension—not by abandoning the Faulknerian influence, but by revaluing it using Joycean techniques. Commenting on Jerry Bryant's discussion of the influences on his early novels, Gaines observes: "I don't think it's possible for me to break away from the influence of jazz or blues or Negro spirituals or Greek tragedy or James Joyce or Tolstoy."[6] In another interview, Gaines includes both *Dubliners* and *Ulysses*, the two Joyce works most often claimed by the realists, on a list of the books which have most influenced his writing.[7]

Joyce's obsession with the Dublin of his youth attracts Gaines, who himself returns time after time to Bayonne, the Louisiana setting which provides the most obvious unifying device for *Bloodline*. Most immediately, however, Faulkner's Yoknapatawpha County rather than Joyce's Dublin appears to have inspired Gaines's conception of Bayonne.[8] A more distinctive Joycean contribution to *Bloodline* lies in Gaines's juxtaposition of the perspectives of the five stories to clarify his attitude toward Faulkner's historical nostalgia. Gaines begins *Bloodline* with a naive limited narrator in "A Long Day in November" and gradually expands to the seemingly omniscient manipulative narrator of "Just Like a Tree."[9]

"Just Like a Tree," taken out of the context of *Bloodline*, seems typically Faulknerian. Its rapidly shifting perspectives clearly derive from *As I Lay Dying*, as do many of the grotesquely comic incidents (such as the accident at the gate). Out of context, the story, which ends with the death of the black matriarch Aunt Fe, expresses the Faulknerian theme of the destruction of the old southern code, fatally flawed but potentially noble, by an inhumane present. Gaines approves of the emotional attachment of the young white girl, Anne-Marie Duvall, to Aunt Fe; her simple gesture of coming through the gathering storm to deliver the gift of the scarf, though it will not alter the situation which led to the bombing deaths of the black woman and two children, is admirable. Gaines sympathizes with Anne-Marie's comment that the blacks "must think we white people don't have their kind of feelings,"[10] and the sympathy invites a reading of "Just Like a Tree" as a eulogy for the vanishing South. Out of context, it seems to express Gaines's helplessness before the contradictions which force him to admire the system which enslaved his ancestors. When considered with an awareness of the developing thematic and technical perspectives of *Bloodline*, however, "Just Like a Tree" expresses a different idea. In context, it marks a resolution of Gaines's realistic and symbolic perceptions; it rejects the southern system, despite its noble elements.[11] The first four stories in *Bloodline* present Gaines's attitude toward the code represented by Anne-Marie Duvall and demonstrate his increasing ability to confront the complexities of life. They mark his resolve to leave the old securities behind and to commit himself to the future.

. The narrators of the first two stories, "A Long Day in November" and "The Sky Is Gray," are young children incapable of understanding the sources of their painful experiences. Sonny in "A Long Day in November" retreats from his parents' emotional confrontation, a confrontation which cannot be resolved because of the limitations of his father's perspective. Sonny's father, Eddie Howard, destroys his car because it symbolizes his obsession with the new ways which threatens to destroy the family unit, traditionally the only refuge from the harsh outer world. Given his alternative, Eddie makes the right choice—but he fails to perceive the limits of his perspective. Seeing only creeping Snopesism and retreat to the past as alternatives, Eddie cannot commit himself to a future which will improve his son's prospects. His solution parallels Sonny's final retreat: "I hear the spring on Mama and Daddy's bed. I get 'way under the cover. I go to sleep a little bit, but I wake up. I go to sleep some more. I hear the spring on Mama and Daddy's bed. I hear it plenty now. It's some dark under here. It's warm. I feel good 'way under here" (*B*, p. 79). Neither father nor son has made it out of bed.

In "The Sky Is Gray" the young narrator, James, heroically accepts his mother's rejection of white sympathy and charity, marking a break with the perspective of even the "well-disposed" whites committed to the Faulknerian South. Placed in an untenable position where the price of food is dignity, he chooses to keep his dignity. Although he does not comprehend the reasons, James will not act out the role of helpless victim that has been assigned him under the old code. At the end of the story, his mother refuses to allow him even Sonny's symbolic retreat into comfort: "The sleet's coming down heavy, heavy now, and I turn up my coat collar to keep my neck warm. My mama tells me to turn it right back down. 'You not a bum,' she says, 'You a man'" (*B*, p. 117). James confronts the cold world but cannot understand the significance of his own actions, much less convert them into realistic benefits. He has bought his manhood at the cost of his youth.

Proctor, the central consciousness of "Three Men," lacks a

mother to fall back on. As has often been observed, his dramatic situation resembles that of Johnny in *Of Love and Dust*. Proctor begins the story with an unquestioning reliance on the old code: "I told Grinning Boy to let my uncle know I was in trouble. My uncle would go to Roger Medlow—and I was hoping Roger Medlow would get me off like he had done once before. He owned the plantation where I lived" (*B*, p. 132). He is willing to call on "Ole Massa" to gain physical freedom. But Munford demands that Proctor reject the code and accept prison in order to maintain dignity: "you don't go to the pen for killing the nigger, you go for yourself. You go to sweat out all the crud you got in your system. You go, saying, 'Go fuck yourself, Roger Medlow, I want to be a man, and by God, I will be a man. For once in my life I will be a man'" (*B*, p. 141). Proctor, symbolically akin to James at the end of "The Sky Is Gray," tentatively accepts Munford's position: "I lit a cigarette and looked up at the window. I had talked big, but what was I going to do when Medlow came? Was I going to change my mind and go with him? And if I didn't go with Medlow, I surely had to go with T. J. and his boys. Was I going to be able to take the beatings night after night?" (*B*, p. 155). At least Proctor, unlike Eddie Howard, asks the right questions. But even if he does reject the old system, he will remain its physical victim. *Of Love and Dust*, like the first stories in *Bloodline*, presents no alternative to the old code. "Three Men," while leaving the realistic solution in doubt, intimates the possibility of symbolic refusal of cooperation.

While "Bloodline" does not resolve its realistic and symbolic dimensions, it explicitly challenges the nostalgic vision of southern mores. Mr. Frank clearly stands in the position of an admirable Faulknerian aristocrat opposing the onslaught of the Cajun Snopeses. But General Christian Laurent—or Copper, as Mr. Frank insists on calling him (the split name emphasizes the disjunction between realistic and symbolic meanings in the story)—refuses to recognize the old aristocracy. The mature narrator, Felix, feels sympathy for both figures, but his final image of Laurent "walking fast the way soldiers walk" (*B*, p. 217) points to his commitment to the future. Still, he shares Laurent's dilemma. Laurent answers Frank's question concerning the existence of an army prepared to attack the Southern system with an image of contradiction: "'There aren't any men, are there, Christian?' 'Yes and no,' Copper said. 'Spiritually, yes, and they're waiting for me. Physically, in the sense of an organized Army, no'" (*B*, p. 207). Symbolically, "Bloodline" resolves the volume: a revolution must take place. Realistically, it leaves the important questions open, since Laurent cannot implement his plan.

"Just Like a Tree," if read with an awareness of the unambiguous rejection of Anne-Marie Duvall's code in the preceding stories, resolves *Bloodline*. The shifts in point of view within the story indicate that no one character can resolve the issues. In fact, Gaines's resolution hinges on the juxtaposition of Emmanuel and Aunt Fe, the only two major characters whose thoughts he does not portray directly. William Burke argues that this silence underlines the opposition of the old black matriarchy and the new "masculine" black revolution.[12] It seems more logical, however, to invert this assumption and see Fe's and Emmanuel's actions as aspects of a coherent movement which both understand.

Fe's declaration that "I ain't leaving here tomorrow" (*B*, p. 248) implies that she wills her own death. Her final blessing on Emmanuel (*B*, p. 247) indicates her understanding of his determination to act despite white retaliation. Symbolically representing the old order willing itself out of existence, her death grants the future to the "soldier" who, unlike General Christian Laurent, can act with practical goals in view. In addition, her death withholds a negative symbol from those who desire to retreat from the confrontation and accept the Faulknerian code. Abandoning her roots would appear to provide further proof of black weakness, perpetuating the code which lies not only behind the gift of the scarf but also behind the bombings. Her death, then, serves both as a symbolic statement of support for Emmanuel and as a realistic action pledging that "Just like a tree that's/planted 'side the water./Oh, I shall not be moved" (*B*, p. 221).

Gaines, then, manipulates his perspective to transform a Faulknerian statement on the passing of the Old South into a call for commitment to the new order. The silence of two major characters stresses the insufficiency of individual perspectives (such as Anne-Marie Duvall's) either within the story or within the book as a whole. Aunt Fe's death is an epiphany which completes the *Dubliners*-style development of *Bloodline*.

Flannery O'Connor's attitude toward Joyce involved both admiration for his craft and contempt for his philosophy. In "The Enduring Chill," Asbury, an aspiring artist, attempts to draw a Jesuit priest into a conversation on Joyce:

> "It's so nice to have you come," Asbury said. "This place is incredibly dreary. There's no one here an intelligent person can talk to. I wonder what you think of Joyce, Father?"
> The priest lifted his chair and pushed closer. "You'll have to shout," he said. "Blind in one eye and deaf in one ear."
> "What do you think of Joyce?" Asbury said louder.
> "Joyce? Joyce who?" asked the priest.
> "James Joyce," Asbury said and laughed.
> The priest brushed his huge hand in the air as if he were bothered by gnats. "I haven't met him," he said. "Now. Do you say your morning and night prayers?"
> Asbury appeared confused. "Joyce was a great writer," he murmured, forgetting to shout.
> "You don't, eh?" said the priest. "Well you will never learn to be good unless you pray regularly. You cannot love Jesus unless you speak to Him."[13]

As David Aiken demonstrates, O'Connor undercuts Asbury's smug self-approval, using the satirized priest as a satiric norm. Aiken further contends that, despite an "elaborate series of correspondences" between Asbury and Stephen Dedalus extending into "details of diction and syntax," Asbury "is not part of the intellectual and artistic vanguard of society; and he is not Stephen Dedalus."[14] In fact, O'Connor would not have approved of Asbury even if he had been Stephen Dedalus. Stephen's identification of the artist with either a priest or the God of his own creation implies that man can rival God as a creative force—a position which O'Connor viewed as a misguided show of arrogance.[15]

This extreme temperamental difference, coupled with O'Connor's offhand dismissal of Joyce as a writer who "could not rid himself of his Catholic inheritance no matter how he might try,"[16] leads Melvin Friedman to the mistaken corollary that O'Connor's "novels and stories are in every sense traditionally constructed and make no use of the experimental suggestions of a Joyce."[17] This seriously underestimates both Joyce's influence and O'Connor's craftsmanship. *Everything That Rises Must Converge* stands as one of the major post-*Dubliners* short story cycles. O'Connor clearly heeded Joyce the technician while rejecting Joyce the philosopher.

Forrest L. Ingram reads the first seven of the volume's nine stories as a cycle but argues that "Parker's Back" and "Judgement Day" "disturb the aesthetic unity" of the volume.[18] In noting that the first seven stories in *Everything That Rises Must Converge* do not appear in print in the order in which they were written, Ingram fails to observe that *only* the title story, written fifth but placed first, violates that chronology. This strongly suggests that "Parker's Back" and "Judgement Day" were written as continuations of the seven-story cycle which O'Connor approved before her death. Indeed, "Parker's Back" represents a culmination of the volume's two thematic positions: the grotesque triviality of contemporary life, and the need to escape the self through a terrifying apprehension of God. "Judgement Day" serves as an ironic coda which reemphasizes O'Connor's didacticism and extends the satire to include the North.

O'Connor's moral vision emerges through her sophisticated use of nondidactic techniques pioneered by Henry James and James Joyce. Writing on the development of fictional technique, O'Connor, who advised correspondents to study *Dubliners* as a model for short fiction, observes that

> along about the time of Henry James the author began to tell his story in a different way. He began to let it come through the minds and eyes of the characters themselves, and he sat behind the scenes, apparently disinterested. By the time we get to James Joyce, the author is nowhere to be found in the book. The reader is on his own, floundering around in the thoughts of various unsavory characters. He finds himself in the middle of a world apparently without comment. But it is from the kind of world the writer creates, from the kind of character and detail he invests it with, that a reader can find the intellectual meaning of a book.[19]

O'Connor, like Joyce in *Dubliners*, immerses the reader in the "thoughts of various unsavory characters," leaving the progression of stories and her own stylistic modulation to express and criticize the characters' moral situations. Occasionally O'Connor presents her didactic judgments by employing norm characters, such as the priest in "The Enduring Chill." But more frequently she makes her points by juxtaposing either separate stories or images within individual stories.

"Everything That Rises Must Converge," like "The Enduring Chill," typifies the early movement of the volume. Julian, like Asbury, deceives himself almost entirely. The narrative voice seemingly accepts Julian's vision of his relationship with his mother: "The further irony of all this was that in spite of her, he had turned out so well. In spite of going to only a third-rate college, he had, on his own initiative, come out with a first-rate education; in spite of growing up dominated by a small mind, he had ended up with a large one; in spite of all her foolish views, he was free of prejudice and unafraid to face facts" (*ETR*, p. 412). By the end of the story, however, it is clear that an absolute failure of charity and love accompanies Julian's inability to confront the facts of his own empty life. The story's final lines, "The tide of darkness seemed to sweep him back to her, postponing from moment to moment his entry into the world of guilt and sorrow" (*ETR*, p. 420), echo the conclusion of Joyce's "Araby:" "Gazing up into the darkness I saw myself as a creature driven and derided by vanity; and my eyes burned with anguish and anger" (*D*, p. 35). Like Joyce's child narrator, Julian is unable to place his experience in perspective. O'Connor, while maintaining Julian's point of view, stresses his continuing inability to advance beyond himself toward a spiritual recognition of the debased world he represents.

While the early stories of *Everything That Rises Must Converge* satirize grotesque spiritual dwarfs, an insistently didactic voice begins to assert "positive" values in "The Comforts of Home" and "The Lame Shall Enter First." While Thomas in the former merely mouths platitudes which his actions belie, Sheppard in the latter must confront the implications of his moral failure. Again O'Connor's narrative voice reflects the social worker Sheppard's shallow apprehension of spiritual reality: "He had never been inside a confessional but he thought it must be the same kind of operation he had here, except that he explained, he did not absolve. His credentials were less dubious than a priest's; he had been trained for what he was doing" (*ETR*, p. 449). O'Connor does not simply leave the reader to this deluded voice; rather, she structures the story to emphasize its inadequacies. Norton's arguments for going to Hell, grotesque echoes of Huck Finn's decision not to betray Jim, carry more spiritual weight when juxtaposed with Sheppard's complacency:

Something in the depths of Johnson's eyes stirred. All day his humor had been glum. "I ain't going to the moon and get there alive," he said, "and when I die I'm going to hell."

"It's at least possible to get to the moon," Sheppard said dryly. The best way to handle this kind of thing was with gentle ridicule. "We can see it. We know it's there. Nobody has given any reliable evidence there's a hell."

"The Bible has give the evidence," Johnson said darkly, "and if you die and go there you burn forever."

The child leaned forward.

"Whoever says it ain't a hell," Johnson said, "is contradicting Jesus. The dead are judged and the wicked are damned. They weep and gnash their teeth while they burn," he continued, "and it's everlasting darkness." [*ETR*, p. 461]

Johnson, unlike Sheppard, acts in accord with his beliefs. His "communion" presents the first image of true faith in *Everything That Rises Must Converge*:

The boy raised the Bible and tore out a page with his teeth and began grinding it in his mouth, his eyes burning.

Sheppard reached across the table and knocked the book out of his hand. "Leave the table," he said coldly.

Johnson swallowed what was in his mouth. His eyes widened as if a vision of splendor was opening up before him. "I've eaten it!" he breathed. "I've eaten it like Ezekiel and it was honey to my mouth!" [*ETR*, p. 477]

Although he can never accept Johnson's example, Sheppard, unlike the previous central characters, ultimately recognizes the depth of his own failure. After the police take Norton, he realizes that "I did more for him than I did for my own child" (*ETR*, p. 481). Although Sheppard attempts to resist this "revelation" (*ETR*, p. 481), Norton's suicide (which, unlike the death of Julian's mother, comes *after* the guilty character has recognized his failure) forces Sheppard to confront the implications of his moral shortcomings. The didactic note introduced by Johnson echoes throughout the cycle's climactic stories, which extend the theme of "The Lame Shall Enter First" and stress the necessity of accepting the pure confrontation with God, no matter how devastating to the individual's self-approval.

The layered epiphanies of "Parker's Back" provide O'Connor with her most effective didactic vehicle. Parker, whose name and actions identify him with the biblical figures of Moses, Jonah, and Obadiah, is the first character to confront the divine terror of his universe (the tattoo) and to accept his own identity (his given name). Where the narrative voice and O'Connor's moral position were separate in the earlier stories, in "Parker's Back" O'Connor's didactic note, introduced by external characters such as Johnson, finally sounds through the central narrative consciousness.

Parker's sullenness dominates the narrative voice from the beginning: "Parker understood why he had married her—he couldn't have got her any other way—but he couldn't understand why he stayed with her now. She was pregnant and pregnant women were not his favorite kind" (*ETR*, p. 510). But as the story's final line implies, he himself passes through a period of gestation leading to his emergence into a new world with a new name: "There he was—who called himself Obadiah Elihus—leaning against the tree, crying like a baby" (*ETR*, p. 530). The narrative voice shares in Parker's rebirth; like the protagonist, it ultimately abandons self-absorbed cynicism and accepts the vulnerability expressed in the final "cliché."

Parker's very limitation prepares him for his revelation. His sullen refusal to obey orders leads to his apocalyptic epiphany, with its echoes of Moses and the burning bush:

> As he circled the field his mind was on a suitable design for his back. The sun, the size of a golf ball, began to switch regularly from in front to behind him, but he appeared to see it both places as if he had eyes in the back of his head. All at once he saw the tree reaching out to grasp him. A ferocious thud propelled him into the air, and he heard himself yelling in an unbelievably loud voice, "GOD ABOVE!"
>
> He landed on his back while the tractor crashed upside down into the tree and burst into flame. The first thing Parker saw were his shoes, quickly being eaten by the fire; one was caught under the tractor, the other was some distance away, burning by itself. He was not in them. He could feel the hot breath of the burning tree on his face. He scrambled backwards, still sitting,

his eyes cavernous, and if he had known how to cross himself he would have done it. [*ETR*, p. 520]

Unwillingly, Parker confronts the reality of divine power in his immediate surroundings. This leads directly to Parker's uncompromising decision not only to accept, but actually to obey the eyes of God which he has tattooed on his back: "Parker sat for a long time on the ground in the alley behind the pool hall, examining his soul. He saw it as a spider web of facts and lies that was not at all important to him but which appeared to be necessary in spite of his opinion. He was as certain of it as he had ever been of anything" (*ETR*, p. 527). Sarah Ruth's refusal to acknowledge Parker's conversion heightens the religious tension of the ending. Although she serves as the external didactic voice throughout the story and, as a mother figure, generates Parker's rebirth, she cannot share his total apprehension of God. Ironically, her insistence that religious experience transpires outside institutions leads her to a simplistic, literal-minded rejection of Parker's tattoo as mere idolatry.

"Parker's Back" resolves the tension between the realistic satirical elements and the didactic metaphysical elements of O'Connor's vision. The story is very nearly an epiphany in the religious sense; God's nature manifests itself suddenly in the secular world.[20] O'Connor never sacrifices Parker's humanity in the interest of her didactic point. He is not transformed beyond recognition. He remains a naturalistic victim; he will never convince Sarah Ruth of his salvation. But he is, in the only sense important to O'Connor, saved. "Judgement Day" intimates that O'Connor doubts that an individual salvation will transform the world; Coleman's southern insights do not even transfer to New York City. O'Connor's final judgment returns to the harsh satire of "Everything That Rises Must Converge" and completes a pessimistic frame surrounding the progress towards salvation seen in the central seven stories. O'Connor's Catholicism kept her from approving of Joyce, but Joycean techniques did not keep her from expressing her Catholicism.

Both Gaines and O'Connor follow the Joyce of *Dubliners* in building their short story cycles on solid realistic bases. Russell

Banks's *Searching for Survivors* rejects most realistic conventions, seeking what Jerome Klinkowitz calls a "playful disruption of content, to make the reader astonished by a world otherwise taken for granted."[21] Whether Banks's mode is romantic or realistic may be a meaningless question; Klinkowitz claims that the "Superfictionists," including Banks, have moved as far beyond Beckett as Beckett moved beyond Joyce, and that no adequate critical vocabulary exists for discussing their works. While the Superfictionists do indeed exercise a dazzling stylistic freedom, they are not original in their willingness to manipulate and mock literary conventions, which have been under attack from the times of *The Tale of Sir Thopas, As You Like It, Don Quixote,* and *Tristram Shandy* down to the era of the master parody *Ulysses.* Klinkowitz's work, of course, is part of a long tradition of critical rebellions (typified by *Preface to Lyrical Ballads*) which proclaim important breaks from past models. Nonetheless, as in many past rebellions, the best work emerging from the new movements (typified by "Tintern Abbey") builds on the very models against which it ostensibly rebels. In *Searching for Survivors* Banks follows Joyce both in his approach to the short story volume and in his attempt to escape the contradiction of realistic and symbolic modes.

Banks, in fact, evinces little of Klinkowitz's concern with distancing himself from his predecessors. Invoking the Joycean artistic creed, Banks describes his own creative vocation as based on "Silence, exile, and cunning, then. The first inevitably brings with it the second, while the third is merely the survival tactic traditionally regarded as characteristic of rodents and other small, fanged mammals."[22] Banks's concern with survival provides the key to, as well as the title for, *Searching for Survivors.* An example of Banks's desire "to reveal in his work the conditions that permit continued existence,"[23] *Searching for Survivors* consists of fourteen stories unified not by setting or theme, but by a movement toward a style recognizing the concrete roots of emotional disruptions. Rather than establishing a clear overall progression, the way Gaines and O'Connor do, Banks intertwines three identifiable groups of stories with seven "single" pieces. The sequences are "Searching for Survivors—I" and "Searching for Survivors—II," the volume's first and last stories; the two "royalty" pieces,

"The Investiture" and "The Masquerade"; and the three "With Che" stories. "The Neighbor" and "The Lie," the two stories at the center of the volume, also form a coherent thematic unit emphasizing cruelty, deceit, and human isolation.

Banks's apparent freedom from the logic of reality suggests that he is an essentially romantic writer. He has in fact characterized the new fiction as avoiding psychological and social realism.[24] Indeed, the opening lines of "Searching for Survivors—I" appear symbolic in intent. The story is "set" in present-day Massachusetts, but begins: "Poor Henry Hudson, I miss him. It's almost as if I had been aboard the leaking *Discovery* myself, a cabin boy or maybe an ordinary seaman, and had been forced to decide, Which will it be, slip into line behind the callow mutineers and get the hell out of this closing, ice-booming bay and home again to dear, wet England? Or say nay and climb over the side behind the good Commodore, the gentle, overthrown master of the *Discovery*."[25] Even the symbolic associations which Banks develops rest not on the narrator's "real" experience but on his memories of a Hudson automobile which was his friend "Daryl's father's obsession" (*SFS*, p. 2). The first story ends with the image of "Hudson and his three loyal sailors . . . dragging the shallop filled with their dwindling supplies all the way across the endless, silent ice pack" (*SFS*, p. 5). Banks meditates on loyalty and/or human commitment as the only defense against an emotionally frigid world. Clearly, symbolic details provide most of Banks's "meaning" in this traditional sense.

But the deeper significance of the story stems from the narrative voice which transfers its horror at the prospect of isolation from the concrete automobile to the abstract explorer. The narrator feels the emotional isolation associated with the Hudson automobile, but, rather than tracing the feeling back to its concrete human source, Daryl's father, he transfers it to another symbol, Henry Hudson. This attempt to reconstruct reality in abstract terms fails. The horror remains, and the narrator's refusal to recognize its concrete origin leads him to aggravate his own sense of isolation by creating an "allegorical" fantasy of Daryl: "for a second I thought I felt lonelier than I'd ever felt before. I knew that nowadays loneliness was probably the last thing old Daryl was troubled by" (*SFS*, p. 4). This could point to two separate misapprehensions of Daryl. The narrative voice could be condemning Daryl as materialistic and shallow, or overestimating him as a well-adjusted citizen free from existential ennui. Whichever reading one prefers, Banks's story is not simply a "fiction" independent of reality. Its effectiveness stems from the tension between the abstract and concrete in the narrator's imagination.

Banks's attitude toward the fictional modes reflects a similar tension. Stating that "Almost all novelists today are allegorists," Banks simultaneously praises and rejects the romantic tradition of American fiction: "A truly noble lineage, but one that in our time seems to have become increasingly irrelevant to the needs and abilities of a democratized consciousness so heightened or 'expanded' by information (input) as to be unable any longer to suspend disbelief. It's a blood-line gone watery thin."[26] Declaring his independence from this lineage, Banks embraces a distinct line of fictional development which "allows men to communicate with other men in such a way as *both* will be astonished by what is said about the world they live in."[27] Citing the examples of the early Hemingway, Henry Miller, and Jack Kerouac, Banks argues for a kind of personal realism: "Nothing is separate from existence, least of all art, and therefore the artist must allow himself to run the same risks in his work that he and all other men are forced to run in their lives."[28] Though rhetorically resembling a realistic manifesto, Banks's statement clearly defines the "risks of life" in a way which admits a full range of psychological and symbolic perils similar to those confronted by Leopold Bloom amidst the Cyclopses and Circes of Dublin.

Explaining his own "Cardinal" stories, "The Investiture" and "The Masquerade," Banks identifies social pressures which have made most Americans, not only novelists, into allegorists. Banks comments: "What's my 'thing on royalty'? Maybe proletarian American fascination with an image that defines Family in an archetypal way. One of the difficulties of being American is that we are stuck in a kind of historical and cultural cul-de-sac and end up describing our secular, democratic, materialist lives with religious, monarchic, idealistic images. Thus Che Guevara becomes an image we use to describe Oedipal conflicts. We seem to get our psychological realities in the most inappropriate ways—if we

have a historical continuity, that's probably it."[29] Both the "Cardinal" and the "With Che" groups, despite their apparent lack of
continuity, describe similar psychological realities. The motif of
fluid identity, reflecting an underlying insecurity with an Oedipal
role, pervades both sequences. The narrator in "With Che in New
Hampshire" imaginatively confronts the residents of his home-
town, Crawford, N.H., after a lengthy absence. He creates an image of himself as a hardened revolutionary, but Banks's style draws
attention to the contrivance: "Everything I own is in the duffle
bag I carry, and I own nothing that cannot be left out in the rain. I
want it that way" (*SFS*, p. 7). Continually altering details of his
own idealized physical appearance, the narrator ends the story by
imagining a ritual shaving on his return to Crawford. Being shaved
presents him with his own features, now unfamiliar and discon-
certing, a result of his allegorizing propensity: "I was swung back
down into a seated position and was allowed to peer at my face for
the first time in several years. I was stunned by the familiarity of
my own face, and also by the remarkable strangeness of it" (*SFS*,
p. 15). In creating his persona, he has departed so far from his own
character that he no longer recognizes himself.

After constructing a pastoral interlude for himself in "With Che
at Kitty Hawk," the narrator, obsessed with the "religious, monarchic, idealistic" image of Guevara, collapses into silence (and, by
extension, death) in "With Che at the Plaza." The image of the
revolutionary monarch Che mingles with the image of the estab-
lishment monarchs Kennedy, Johnson, and Sinatra. The narrator
grows confused; he fails to establish imaginative rapport with the
Che figure, who dissolves into an Oedipal nightmare of "the ma-
chismo laughter of Latin American sadism" (*SFS*, p. 72). The narrator feels victimized by the very image which he has established
as his ideal. Realizing that this symbolic destruction indicates a
severe collapse of his emotional equilibrium, the narrator admits
that "This Guevara thing was getting out of hand. I was beginning
to wish I had never met the man" (*SFS*, p. 73). The absence of any
human contact in the final scene of the story emphasizes the destructiveness of the narrator's commitment to abstract images
which have left him in the position of a Hudson (or of Daryl or
Daryl's father) without companions.

The pressure to recognize the concrete roots of symbolic conflicts culminates in "Searching for Survivors—II," at once a love story (for the narrator Reed's brother, killed in a train wreck) and a "realistic" restatement of the emotional isolation of "Searching for Survivors—I." "Searching for Survivors—II" stands apart from the rest of the volume in its relatively traditional present-tense-with-flashbacks narrative technique. The narrator casts little doubt on whether the events "really happened." He has slight inclination, though Banks has made it clear that he has the power, to disrupt the reader's perception of a sequence of "real" events dominating Reed's consciousness. The death of his brother Allen crystallizes Reed's feelings of isolation, his sense that he is stranded "in a place where a war had been lost" (*SFS*, p. 153). Reed's loving attention to the details of his relationship with his brother, even to a piece of material which might have come from Allen's sock, provides the only real sense of "the conditions that permit continued existence." The narrator's act is, finally, imaginative. He can no longer embrace his brother physically, but he can commit his imagination to the people who have shaped his life, rather than committing it to collapsing fantasy images of Che Guevara and Frank Sinatra. Banks writes that "What is in a man's life, tho, will be in his work."[30] *Searching for Survivors* pleads that the man not attempt to deceive himself—through uncontrolled and unrecognized allegories—about the actual contents of that life. Fiction becomes a tool for confrontation. To Banks, as to Joyce, the only hope (admittedly a desperate one) lies in reconciling the world of reality with the world of the dream.

Joyce Hero: Sylvia Plath, Jack Kerouac, James Baldwin

Like the Shakespeare of Stephen Dedalus' *Hamlet*, James Joyce broods behind and within his own creation. In *Portrait*, Joyce recapitulates the story of the events leading ultimately to the creation of the book itself. The resulting combination of *Bildungsroman*, *Künstlerroman*, and self-advertisement often inspires and intimidates young novelists setting out to establish the image of their own artistic development.

Despite its manipulation of point of view and its dense symbolic patterns, *Portrait* was not particularly revolutionary in its technique, even in 1916. During the previous century Jane Austen's *Emma* introduced the basic devices for controlling perspective which Joyce exploited in *Portrait*, and Henry James had developed their theory and practice. Joseph Conrad's dense symbolic textures predate Joyce's by more than a decade. So young novelists reacting to *Portrait* most frequently respond not to its style but to its content, the extraliterary Joycean mystique.

Joyce, of course, holds an insurmountable advantage over potential imitators. His mystique, based on accomplishments still many years in the future at the time of *Portrait*'s publication, guarantees his *Bildungsroman* a sympathetic (or at least a respectful) reading. Few readers familiar, directly or through hearsay, with *Ulysses* and *Finnegans Wake* dismiss Joyce's self-esteem as simple posturing. No beginning novelist shares this advantage, yet several American novelists of the past two decades, among them Sylvia Plath, Jack Kerouac, and James Baldwin, have risked being dismissed as egoists incapable of transcending their own experience and have succeeded in establishing compelling public images.

Interestingly, *The Bell Jar*, *On the Road*, and *Go Tell It on the Mountain* all criticize some aspect of the Joycean mystique. All three novelists seem to agree with Breon Mitchell's claim that *A Portrait of the Artist as a Young Man* "frees its hero from the traditional goal of integration into society."[31] Sharing this "romantic" reading of *Portrait* as Joyce's statement that the artist must transcend mundane reality, all three dismiss the transcendence as unrealistic. Plath emphasizes the psychological destructiveness of a self-absorbed rejection of reality, Kerouac sees the inevitable collapse of the energy needed to sustain transcendence, and Baldwin demonstrates that the very terms of the transcendence derive from the environment ostensibly left behind. In fact, Joyce criticizes in Stephen Dedalus the same tendencies which Plath, Kerouac, and Baldwin criticize in Joyce. Stephen Dedalus withdraws into the paranoid pages of his diary at the end of *Portrait*; he cannot sustain his flight, and at the start of *Ulysses* he is back in Dublin. Whatever his pretensions, he remains very much the son of the storytelling father and the Dublin streets which he consciously rejects. Joyce anticipates his followers even in their attacks. Just as Joyce follows in most essentials the pattern established by *Hamlet*, Plath, Kerouac, and Baldwin adapt that established by *Portrait*. In effect, they become Joyceans while fleeing Joyce.

The Bell Jar follows *Portrait* in its concern with the interaction of the artist and her image within the work. While explicitly criticizing what she sees as Joycean self-absorption—the attempt to escape from the community—Plath implicitly accepts a large part of Joyce's aesthetic emphasis on the importance of the re-creation (as opposed to simple reporting) of personal experience. Esther Greenwood explicitly rejects *Finnegans Wake*. Joyce is one aspect of the oppressive environment which leads to her mental breakdown. But Esther remains Plath's Stephen Dedalus, an autobiographical figure who in turn creates her own Stephen Dedalus figures, Elly Higginbottom and Elaine, in an attempt to come to terms with her own life. In addition, Plath draws heavily on Joyce's work for the thematic and structural principles which unify *The Bell Jar*.[32]

Early in the novel Esther contemplates spending her next semester "writing on some obscure theme in the works of James Joyce. I hadn't picked out my theme yet, because I hadn't gotten around to reading *Finnegans Wake*, but my professor was very excited about my thesis and had promised to give me some leads on images of twins."[33] She evinces little enthusiasm for the project, which has been forced upon her to gratify the professor's image of her as a prize student. When Esther begins reading the *Wake*, she remains uninspired. Its opening paragraphs reinforce her perception that the world has collapsed into incomprehensibility:

> Lifting the pages of the book, I let them fan slowly by my eyes. Words, dimly familiar but twisted all awry, like faces in a funhouse mirror, fled past, leaving no impression on the glassy surface of my brain.
> I squinted at the page.
> The letters grew barbs and rams' horns. I watched them separate, each from the other, and jiggle up and down in a silly way. Then they associated themselves in fantastic untranslatable shapes, like Arabic or Chinese.
> I decided to junk my thesis. [*TBJ*, p. 139]

This retreat from social involvement culminates in Esther's desire to abandon her real identity entirely. Early in the novel she adopts the pseudonym Elly Higginbottom as a social tactic (*TBJ*, pp. 13–23). Following her decision to abandon the thesis, however, Esther determines to "become" Elly, in part to escape from Joyce: "I would be simple Elly Higginbottom, the orphan. People would love me for my sweet, quiet nature. They wouldn't be after me to read books and write long papers on the twins in James Joyce" (*TBJ*, pp. 148–49). Previously Esther has attempted to create a purely fictional double by writing her own *Bildungsroman*: "My heroine would be myself, only in disguise. She would be called Elaine. Elaine. I counted the letters on my fingers. There were six letters in Esther, too. It seemed a lucky thing" (*TBJ*, p. 134). But only a total merging (confusion?) of art and life can satisfy her. Despite her attempt to re-create herself through alternate identities, Esther cannot write a novel about "Elaine" because, as Stan Smith observes, she "lacks the critical distance from her character that both the imputed [Esther as retrospective narrator] and the actual [Plath] author of *The Bell Jar* possess."[34]

Indeed, *The Bell Jar* raises questions concerning Plath's own aesthetic distance from her material. Unlike Joyce, who wrote *Portrait* before he had enjoyed any substantial literary success, Plath wrote *The Bell Jar* with an established poetic reputation. Although she was to commit suicide within a month of the novel's publication, Plath's life had seemingly developed into something very like that which Esther Greenwood wishes for herself. Is it therefore accurate to join Marjorie Perloff and Gordon Lameyer in reading the ending of *The Bell Jar* as the protagonist's successful "rebirth"?[35] Of course, there is a danger of reading too much irony into the conclusion, in light of Plath's ultimate failure to escape the suicidal urges recounted in *The Bell Jar*. But Plath's treatment of the double motif and her treatment of the birth-death patterns, both of which owe much to Joyce, suggest that she intends Esther's reemergence to be seen ironically.

Lameyer provides the strongest argument for an optimistic interpretation of *The Bell Jar* in his article on Plath's use of the double motif. Plath wrote her honors thesis on the double in Dostoevsky's *Double* and *The Brothers Karamazov*, and Lameyer argues persuasively that the manifold doublings in *The Bell Jar* reflect a Dostoevskyan vision of the divided self. But Lameyer's argument that the death of Joan Gilling, one of Esther's doubles in the mental hospital, allows Esther to "be free of her bell jar of stifling distortions and become psychically reborn"[36] is questionable. In his search for a Dostoevskyan source for the resolution of the double motif, Lameyer looks beyond the two novels on which Plath concentrated in the thesis. But Plath suggests another source entirely in her references to the twin motif in *Finnegans Wake*. Lameyer suggests that, by killing off her "dark" double, Esther frees herself from the double's power. But the Joycean twins Shem and Shaun never escape one another. Destroying each other, they spring up again in new incarnations; they are forced to surmount the same obstacles throughout eternity. If Plath intended to follow Joyce rather than Dostoevsky, the ending of *The Bell Jar* appears significantly darker.

No conclusive proof exists for either reading of the double motif, but *The Bell Jar*'s structure, assuming that the various elements of the book's conclusion reinforce rather than contradict one another, supports the cyclic Joycean reading of the resolution. Throughout *The Bell Jar* patterns involving the movement from birth to death, and from death to rebirth, abound. Each movement builds to an epiphany revealing a truth to Esther. The sequence of epiphanies can be seen as a progression aimed at the final affirmative epiphany of Esther's triumphant return to the social world.

Portrait, Plath's probable source for the technique, can be read in the same way. Stephen Dedalus certainly intends his final prayer, "Old father, old artificer, stand me now and ever in good stead" (*P*, p. 253), as a final cry of independence in the name of art. Nonetheless, Joyce undercuts Stephen's pretense. Stephen invokes a father figure, but he has been entirely unable to establish either spiritual or realistic contact with "fathers," familial or religious, throughout the novel. If he is invoking the mythic father Daedalus, Stephen is Icarus, doomed to fall. Joyce deflates even Stephen's minor epiphanies. The first chapter, for example, ends with Stephen's vindication by Father Conmee (*P*, p. 59), but the second chapter opens with Uncle Charles smoking his foul tobacco in the outhouse—hardly a fitting sequel to Stephen's triumph. By the end of the second sequence of chapter two, the first major epiphany has itself become the source of Simon Dedalus' comic epiphany: "Father Dolan and I, when I told them all at dinner about it, Father Dolan and I had a great laugh over it. You better mind yourself, Father Dolan, said I, or young Dedalus will send you up for twice nine. We had a famous laugh over it. Ha! Ha! Ha!" (*P*, p. 72). The juxtaposition of the epiphanies reduces Stephen's stature by placing him in a wider, less egotistical perspective.

Plath employs a similar deflating structure in *The Bell Jar*. Each epiphany leads only to a contradiction. The first movement toward rebirth climaxes with the image of Esther in her womblike bath: "The longer I lay there in the clear hot water the purer I felt, and when I stepped out at last and wrapped myself in one of the big, soft white hotel bath towels I felt pure and sweet as a new baby" (*TBJ*, p. 181). The purifying bath, however, transforms Esther only for a few hours, until the drunken, vomiting Doreen is brought to her door. Similarly, Plath undercuts death-oriented epiphanies. Esther attempts to drown herself but experiences an unwanted epiphanic recognition of the world's beauty: "I fanned myself down, but before I knew where I was, the water had spat me up into the sun, the world was sparkling all about me like blue and green and yellow semi-precious stones" (*TBJ*, p. 181). Her attempts at suicide and at forging new beginnings for herself are equally unsuccessful. She remains paralyzed by the conflict between life and death, the classic American opposition.

Esther cannot effectively destroy her dark twin even though she feels momentarily responsible for Joan's suicide. Even if Esther does bear responsibility for Joan's death, the implications are ambiguous. Has she, as Lameyer believes, destroyed her insanity? Or has she destroyed her psychic wholeness, and therefore herself? Plath substantially qualifies Esther's success. Her rebirth may *appear* conclusive; she has completed the "ritual for being born twice" (*TBJ*, p. 275). She is in the throes of an epiphany at the end, when, "guiding myself by them, as by a magical thread, I stepped into the room" (*TBJ*, p. 275). But, like the previous epiphanies, this too will pass. Even if Plath had lived, *The Bell Jar* would represent a constant reminder that the only certainty short of death is the physical epiphany of the beating heart. Its refrain, "I am, I am, I am" occurs twice in the novel: once preceding Esther's unsuccessful attempt to drown herself (*TBJ*, p. 178)—in association with an epiphany of death—and once immediately preceding the ritual rebirth (*TBJ*, p. 274)—in association with an epiphany of life. The only uncontradicted epiphany affirms nothing, save life's involvement with the unreconciled doubles.

Joyce escaped these debilitating contradictions by attaching them firmly to fictional characters from which he distanced himself. Though he links his perspective closely to Stephen's, Joyce never surrenders the narration of *Portrait*. The ironic structural treatment of Stephen's epiphanies establishes Joyce's "superior" understanding. But Esther tells her own story. At no point can we be sure that Plath does not identify herself directly with her protagonist. While *The Bell Jar* contradicts Esther's epiphanies, it remains attached to her emotions throughout. Stan Smith identifies the essential problem in his discussion of the relationship between Esther the character and Esther the narrator: "The book itself supposedly fulfills that ambition to write a novel whose frustration contributed to the breakdown it records. If the younger Esther stands in schizoid relation to her own experiences, retrospectively analyzing them . . . Esther the narrator assumes the same kind of stance to her past, seen as an initiation rite to be scrupulously and objectively tabulated."[37] Although Smith does not add the observation, Plath assumes nearly the same stance to Esther the narrator. Neither the narrator nor the artist has escaped the debilitating analytical perspective which contributed to Esther the character's original breakdown. The process of becoming an artist, at least an artist with an autobiographical orientation, condemns the artist to a paralyzing solipsistic relationship to her own past. Plath's protagonist desperately seeks some kind of traditional reintegration into society, though she maintains a longing for the kind of artistic integrity associated with the Joycean hero identified by Mitchell. *The Bell Jar*, then, even while using many of Joyce's approaches to the *Bildungsroman*, critiques the solipsism which made the "romantic" *Portrait* possible.

Jack Kerouac would have horrified James Joyce, who almost never acted without purpose. In *On the Road* Kerouac dedicated himself to expending energy in the hope of generating holy visions somewhere in the nights of Denver, San Francisco, Nebraska or Mexico, New Orleans or New York. It may seem incongruous, therefore, that in certain visions Kerouac saw himself as a new incarnation of Joyce.[38] Part of this claim was no doubt tongue in cheek. But, insofar as Kerouac saw himself as a stylistic innovator breaking from literary conventions, as had Joyce and Henry Miller, it appears to have been made with total seriousness.

Kerouac's stylistic "breakthrough" was "spontaneous prose," a kind of automatic writing which derived from jazz as well as from Joyce. The essay "Essentials of Spontaneous Prose" defines the technique as "blowing (as per jazz musician) on subject of image."[39] Calling for abandonment of "periods separating sentence structures" and for writing with "No pause to think of the proper word," Kerouac recommends "swimming in sea of English with no discipline other than rhythms of rhetorical exhalation."[40] As the briefest glance at his endless manuscript revisions proves, Joyce wrote in nothing even vaguely resembling this style. Nonetheless, a legitimate connection exists between *Portrait* and spontaneous prose. The very awkwardness of Kerouac's style reflects his belief that the style and the story are inseparable, that one's writing should embody the total rhythm of one's personality.[41] At its best, Kerouac's style attains this organic relationship with its content, a relationship basic to the style of *Portrait*.

Kerouac's best prose, however, is rarely his spontaneous prose. Perhaps his most ambitious single piece, "Old Angel Midnight," attempted, as Kerouac himself wrote, "to make a try at a 'spontaneous' *Finnegans Wake* with the Sounds of the Universe itself as the plot and all neologisms, associations, puns, word-mixes from various languages and non-languages scribbled out in a strictly intuitional discipline at breakneck speed."[42] The following lines typify the product: "Old Angel Midnight the swan of heaven fell & flew cockmeek, Old Angel Midnight the night onto twelve Year Tart with the long bing bong & the big ding dong, the boy on the sandbank blooming the moon, the sound wont let me sleep & since I found out time is silence Manjusri wont let me hear the swash of snow no mo in ole no po— O A M, Oh Om . . ."[43] However one reacts to Kerouac's puns and images, "Old Angel Midnight" holds no more of the material for a literary revolution than, say, Gregory Corso's poem "Marriage." Kerouac clearly has not created a new *Finnegans Wake*. At his best, Kerouac worked with less pretension and much greater intensity. Despite his theoretical commitment to spontaneous prose, Kerouac shaped *On the Road*, his own *Bildungsroman*, in a relatively traditional manner.[44] Kerouac struggled with the manuscript of *On the Road*, which he conceived in 1948, for nearly a decade before its publication in 1957.[45] In 1951 he actually composed a single-paragraph spontaneous prose version of the novel on sixteen-foot rolls of paper which he taped together so that he would not have to slow down to change pages in his typewriter. (Although Kerouac later implied that this was the final version of *On the Road*, it was in fact rejected by his editor, Robert Giroux.[46]) The published version of *On the Road* resulted from several subsequent reworkings and is a carefully structured critique of the nature and limitations of spontaneity.

On the Road differs from *The Bell Jar* and *Portrait* itself in that its protagonist, Sal Paradise, already considers himself an artist at the beginning of the book. Three times in the first chapter Sal declares, "I was a writer,"[47] and Dean Moriarity tells him, "Everything you do is great" (*OTR*, p. 7). After the first chapter Sal almost never mentions his creative aspirations. Rather than focusing on the problems and development of the young writer, Kerouac's *Künstlerroman* focuses on an interrelated set of characters shaping their experience on the same principles which Kerouac once hoped to use to shape his prose.

On the Road eulogizes Dean Moriarity and his tremendous spontaneous energy, but Dean is not the book's hero. He cannot see the sadness of his own self-inflicted alienation from even his closest friends. He never realizes, as does Sal, the limits of his own lifestyle. At the start of the novel, Sal shares Dean's willingness to proceed without specific design; a general direction—an image to blow on—will suffice. Pure emotional exhilaration propels Sal to Denver, on to San Francisco, and back to New York on his first trip. Part One of *On the Road* presents a complete and satisfying (though wearying) East-West-East cycle, a fully realized heroic quest.

But each subsequent part departs further and further from the complete cyclic pattern. As in *Portrait*, the prose rhythms reflect the thematic progression. Part Two, which presents only the East-West journey, fizzles out amidst bad feelings in San Francisco. Near the beginning of the second trip Kerouac's prose embodies the energy of the main characters: "In Missouri, at night, Dean had to drive with his scarf-wrapped head stuck out the window, with snowglasses that made him look like a monk peering into the manuscripts of the snow, because the windshield was covered with an inch of ice" (*OTR*, p. 112). The rhythms flow, the images provide humor and stress Sal's involvement in Dean's feelings, however strange and dangerous; but the intensity cannot be maintained. As Sal and Dean grow apart, Kerouac's prose "runs down." At the end Kerouac's style reflects Dean and Sal's lack of energy: "At dawn I got my New York bus and said good-bye to Dean and Marylou. They wanted some of my sandwiches. I told them no. It was a sullen moment. We were all thinking we'd never see one another again and we didn't care" (*OTR*, p. 178). The sentences are Hemingwayesque; there is no imagery. Part Three focuses on just half of an already aborted West-East journey—the characters lack the energy to travel past Chicago. By the end of the section Sal realizes that the road itself, the central symbol of spontaneity for spontaneity's sake, now bores him: "I realized I was beginning to cross and recross towns in America as though I were a traveling salesman—raggedy travelings, bad stock, rotten beans in the bottom of my bag of tricks, nobody buying" (*OTR*, p. 245).

The trip to Mexico in Part Four is Sal's final attempt to revive his enthusiasm for the road and to affirm Dean's principle of spontaneity. Fully aware that the East-West-East cycle of Part One can no longer nourish the traveler's emotions, Sal interprets the Mexican journey as a revitalizing change: "I couldn't imagine this trip. It was the most fabulous of all. It was no longer east-west, but magic *south!*" (*OTR*, p. 265). For a while the pure novelty of Mexico fascinates the travelers, but ultimately, in Mexico City, Sal and Dean reach their literal and spiritual destination: "This was the great and final wild uninhibited Fellahin-childlike city that we knew we would find at the end of the road" (*OTR*, p. 302). It is the end of the road in every sense. Dean deserts the dysentary-stricken Sal. Like Part One, Part Five contains no coherent sense of movement; only this final aimlessness is melancholy, rather than exuberant. All of the illusions of the "beat" generation collapse.

After Dean abandons him in Mexico City, Sal writes: "When I got better I realized what a rat he was, but then I had to understand the impossible complexity of his life, how he had to leave me there, sick, to get on with his wives and woes. 'Okay, old Dean, I'll say nothing'" (*OTR*, p. 303). *On the Road* breaks this vow. In essence, Sal rejects Dean. He has not regained the Garden of Eden; he has not found love or friendship; he has not discovered a principle (in spontaneity) which can nourish life or art. Contradictions, unreconciled oppositions, rule the novel. Like Kerouac, whose best work is carefully patterned rather than purely spontaneous, taking its lead from Joyce the traditionalist rather than Joyce the experimentalist, Sal and Dean remain victims of the clash between their dreams and the real world in which they dissolve.

If Kerouac's work implicitly recognizes the inevitability of Stephen Dedalus' return to Dublin, James Baldwin's *Go Tell It on the Mountain* demonstrates that Dedalus never really left. Like Joyce, Baldwin structures his *Bildungsroman* to emphasize the extent to which the very strength of the protagonist's desires for freedom from his society reveals him as an expression of that society. Just as Stephen Dedalus' final invocation reveals the extent of his continuing dependence on his many fathers (in church and family, in addition to those in art and myth whom he consciously invokes), John Grimes's salvation reveals his strong ties to the life of the streets which he apparently rejects.

Like Plath and Kerouac, Baldwin reacts to Joyce as if Stephen Dedalus had successfully separated himself from his environment. Baldwin sees clearly the impossibility of this type of dissociation—which resolves many American romantic novels. So even when Baldwin repudiates Joyce, his own practice parallels Joyce's. While paying homage to Joyce's sensibility, Baldwin suggests that Joyce endorsed dissociation from the past: "Joyce is right about history being a nightmare—but it may be a nightmare from which no one *can* awaken. People are trapped in history and history is trapped in them."[48] Stephen Dedalus, too, realizes the truth of Baldwin's observation (see the following section of this chapter). Like *Portrait*, *Go Tell It on the Mountain* demonstrates the inevitable involvement of the individual with the community which formed him. Like *Portrait*, it refuses to accept the situation quiescently and struggles for a new perception of the possibility of acting within the historical context. Accepting his historical context as a given, Baldwin insists that perceiving that context through arbitrary categories increases its dehumanizing pressure. Baldwin, like Joyce, accepts neither romantic dissociation from history nor naturalistic despair before history.

Just as Joyce unveils the insufficiency of the traditional Irish institutions to accommodate Stephen's ambitions and abilities, Baldwin criticizes the dichotomy of "Temple" and "Street" which the Harlem community uses to define John Grimes in *Go Tell It on the Mountain*. In his early essays, written concurrently with the novel, Baldwin stresses the necessity of abandoning perceptual categories which oversimplify experience: "I think all theories are suspect, that the finest principles may have to be modified, or may even be pulverized by the demands of life."[49] Insisting on the complexity of the individual, Baldwin resists viewing experience primarily in collective terms: "the reality of man as a social being is not his only reality and that artist is strangled who is forced to deal with human beings solely in social terms."[50] Still, Baldwin recognizes the impact of social forces on the individual character: "I don't think that the Negro problem in America can be even discussed coherently without bearing in mind its context; its context being the history, traditions, customs, the moral assumptions and preoccupations of the country; in short, the general social fabric."[51] In *Go Tell It on the Mountain* he expresses these personal and cultural positions more effectively than in any subsequent novel. Although John Grimes inevitably fails to escape the social context which binds him—as Stephen Dedalus fails to escape Dublin—he shows promise of coming to terms with the categories which make the context increasingly oppressive. Even at John's early stage of development (he is much younger than Stephen at the end of *Portrait*), he begins to comprehend his personal and cultural identity.

Rigid categories dominate John Grimes's Harlem environment —categories which nearly every character accepts uncritically. The most obvious and stifling categories are those establishing the Temple-Street dichotomy. The Temple of the Fire Baptized serves as a sanctuary of purity against the violence and immorality of the Street. The brothers and sisters of the Temple readily classify people, relegating wild children (such as Roy) to the Street and welcoming the apparently malleable (such as John) to the Temple. As George Kent notes, these categories fail to recognize adequately the complexity of the individual, and they inevitably oversimplify reality.[52] Gabriel—and his is only the most obvious case—belongs wholly to neither world. His apparent immersion in the world of the Temple results from the extremity of his sinful Street youth and does nothing to repress the violence of his personality. He merely expresses, through religious hypocrisy and intransigence, what he once expressed through sexual indulgence. Despite his weaknesses of the flesh, however, Gabriel cannot be reduced to a simple hypocrite. Until he is disillusioned by the mercenary older preachers, the young Gabriel feels a sincere religious vocation. His difficulty stems from his attempt to ignore a basic aspect of his character. His decision to marry the nearly asexual Deborah rests on his determination to elevate the spiritual-Temple aspects of his character over the physical-Street aspects. The attempt fails, leaving Gabriel a frustrated victim of his own attempt to simplify his complexity in order to fulfill the demands of an external category.

While Gabriel shows the dangers of accepting the definitions proposed by the dichotomy, he no longer possesses the potential to reject them. Baldwin transmits the "positive" message of *Go Tell It on the Mountain* through John, who hesitates between the poles of the dichotomy in the first part of the novel. Though at the outset he accepts the external definitions, John implicitly recognizes that the two worlds cannot be divorced. Even after John's attempt to scrub away the grime in the church, to obliterate any trace of the dirty Street in the pristine Temple, the narrative voice, which mirrors John's perceptions, recognizes the ineffaceable connection between the two worlds: "In the air of the church hung, perpetually, the odor of dust and sweat; for, like the carpet in his mother's living-room, the dust of this church was invincible."[53] This recognition, though only partially conscious, prepares John for the wrestling match with Elisha, with its dense sexual imagery (*GT*, pp. 63–65). The wrestling match plays a key role in John's development; it shows him that the Temple cannot be divorced from physical reality, and it initiates the emotional turmoil which leads to his vision on the threshing floor. During that vision he synthesizes the oppositions which torment him through the early stages of his development, and he recognizes his own complexity: "The light and the darkness had kissed each other, and were married now, forever, in the life and vision of John's soul" (*GT*, p. 277).

The crux of *Go Tell It on the Mountain* lies in the vision and not, as most critics have argued, in John's ensuing "salvation." Shirley S. Allen, Roger Rosenblatt, and Donald B. Gibson all contend that whatever hope the novel offers rests on the strength of John's emerging religious faith.[54] Gibson, who believes that faith to be much stronger than Rosenblatt does, states the basic logic behind this emphasis: "John is the force of love; Gabriel of evil. The plot affirms the victory of love over evil and the denouement of historical necessity."[55] But this formulation perpetuates the same kind of categorization which Baldwin undermines in the novel's first two parts. Gabriel maintains human feelings, particularly for his physical sons, and John's salvation itself—seen as an attempt to reject the Street—reveals a propensity for hypocrisy which parallels that of his stepfather. If Baldwin extends any hope, it rests on the vision's sense of human complexity which John's conscious flight back to the world of the Temple cannot deny.

Nothing in Baldwin's philosophical positions during the *Go Tell It on the Mountain* period of his career indicates his willingness to embrace the church as a solution to either individual or social problems; the progression of Baldwin's own life, which in many details parallels John Grimes's, led him away from the church and toward existentialism. Coupled with the opening sections of *Go Tell It on the Mountain*, which reject the church's simplistic vision of life, these facts encourage deemphasis on salvation in interpreting the novel's resolution. The most promising approach lies in seeing John Grimes as an incipient artist who, like Stephen Dedalus in *Portrait*, possesses the raw material needed for expressing the racial conscience, but who has not yet attained the maturity requisite to acting constructively on his perceptions. Like Stephen Dedalus' flight from Ireland, John Grimes's flight from the Street emphasizes that he has not yet recognized the implications of his recent experience.[56]

If, as many of his essays clearly imply, Baldwin sees recognizing the insufficiency of external definitions as the key element of artistic awareness, John's threshing-floor vision points to an artistic rather than a specifically religious vocation. The vision confronts John almost immediately with the disintegration of the familiar categories: "Nothing remained: all was swallowed up in chaos" (*GT*, p. 262). As the vision develops, Baldwin presents dialogue between John's Temple impulses and "a malicious, ironic voice [which] insisted that he rise—and, at once . . . leave this temple and go out into the world" (*GT*, p. 262). Neither impulse can destroy the other. Rather, they interact in a contrapuntal pattern, generating both "voices" of the dialogue and forcing John to recognize his own complexity. The main elements shaping this complexity are John's racial background and his relationship with his "father."

Although Gibson and Eldridge Cleaver, among others, attack Baldwin's early work for an alleged lack of social, political, and racial relevance, John's vision nevertheless culminates in an image of black history with clear political implications, particularly when juxtaposed with the story of Richard and Elizabeth presented in "Elizabeth's Prayer" (*GT*, pp. 212–35), which provides a realistic anticipation of John's symbolic experience on the threshing floor. Richard combines intelligence, racial awareness, and an ability to love; he seems very nearly a Baldwinesque saint. If *Go Tell It on the Mountain* in fact preached the individualistic gospel attributed to it by its ideological detractors, Richard would clearly have provided the "answer." Social pressures, however, destroy him (to the police he remains just another nigger in spite of his accomplishments), and legal pressures drive him to suicide. Richard Wright, frequently proposed as a "relevant" counterexample to Baldwin, could easily have endorsed the moral of the story: *no* black man in contemporary America can make it on his own without a hell of a lot of luck. Maintaining Richard as a point of reference, then, allows us to reach a clearer understanding of the implications of John's vision of black history.

After reaching a pit of existential isolation, after realizing the full extent of the chaos which initiated the vision in a place where "there was no speech or language, and there was no love" (*GT*, p.

271), John finds that the path back to reality leads him into contact with the pain and suffering both of his own life and of the black race as a whole. The sound which shatters the stillness of his confrontation with the grave, the sound which propels him toward his tenuous salvation, is a sound which "He had heard . . . everywhere, in prayer and in daily speech, and wherever the saints were gathered, and in the unbelieving streets" (*GT*, p. 272). The sound transcends the categories, recapitulating the suffering of all the Gabriels and Florences and Richards who join in an "army" which "moved on the bloody road forever, with no continuing city, but seeking one to come: a city out of time, not made with hands, but eternal in the heavens. No power could hold this army back, no water disperse them, no fire consume them. One day they would compel the earth to heave upward, and surrender the waiting dead" (*GT*, p. 278). This vision combines communal and personal, religious and secular elements. It insists that the ultimate confrontation, the day of reckoning for the violence done to black individuals such as Richard, must come from an "army," a group of individuals sharing a common cause. While perhaps not political in Wright's sense, the vision is surely no more individualistic than the slave songs which cloaked explosively subversive sentiments in spiritual terminology.[57] Although the city is ostensibly "heavenly," the vision emphasizes "blood" and a militantly demanding attitude on the part of the sufferers, an attitude which reflects their attitude toward whites rather than toward God. In terms of the structure of *Go Tell It on the Mountain*, Part One emphasizes individual perceptions, while Part Two emphasizes social pressures and racial history; the social and individual revolts blend in the apocalyptic imagery of Part Three.

The second focus of John's vision concerns his relationship with his "father." Baldwin's consistent use of the general phrase, rather than Gabriel's name, serves a dual purpose: to remind the reader that John never discovers that Gabriel is not his actual physical father, and that any action based on the inaccurate assumption remains subject to ironic revaluation; and to intimate the symbolic dimensions of the question of paternity, reminiscent of the layering in *Portrait*. While Stephen Dedalus rejects his physical father, who represents Ireland's decline into squalor and sentimentality, his attempt to become a creator (and therefore a father) himself reveals that he is actually following in the footsteps of the father who tells the story in the first paragraph of *Portrait*. Similarly, John Grimes can neither simply accept nor repudiate Gabriel's example. When the father in the vision accuses John of being "the Devil's son" (*GT*, p. 269), of belonging to the Street rather than to the Temple, John defends himself by penetrating the mask of paternal hypocrisy: "I hate you. I don't care about your long white robe. I seen you under the robe. I seen you" (*GT*, p. 269). In a desperate attempt to dissociate himself from crushing paternal repression, John turns to Jesus the son rather than to God the father for salvation. While necessary to John's self-awareness, the distancing carries with it a new threat of oversimplification. In an important sense, Gabriel *is* John's father; John potentially shares Gabriel's willingness to turn away from his Street self, a willingness which threatens to involve him in hypocrisy and self-delusion. On the realistic level, then, John must recognize his kinship with Gabriel to avoid becoming an analogously repressive figure himself. That John, at least subliminally, understands this situation is indicated by his attempt to communicate with Gabriel when he rises from the vision (*GT*, p. 281). By attempting to recognize their kinship and insisting that he has been freed not by the father but by the son, John attempts to forge an internal definition. John feels the importance of escaping the Street-Temple dichotomy and, unlike Gabriel, does not turn against the Street after his "salvation": "He was in battle no longer, this unfolding Lord's day, with this avenue, these houses, the sleeping, staring, shouting people, but had entered into battle with Jacob's angel, with the princes and the powers of the air" (*GT*, p. 296). Although John has no clear conception of the pressures which will encourage him to reenter the battle against the Street, he embarks with the essential information needed to attain a balanced understanding.

The resolution of the novel's symbolic dimension parallels this realistic denouement. Michel Fabre, in his excellent analysis of the question of paternity in *Go Tell It on the Mountain* as it relates to Baldwin's relationship with Wright, comments on "the multiplicity of metaphorical functions that the author imposes on John's story. His destiny is presented as a quest for identity and the entire episode as an initiation. The story reenacts the Oedipus myth of the lost father and the death of the king. It is articulated out of numerous Biblical tales, and through the expedient of the Bible it becomes a metaphor of race relations in the United States."[58] The racial symbolism, which I have discussed in connection with the social dimension of John's vision, demands particular attention. If John is the black son struggling for freedom from a white society which is at once repressive and paternalistic, then the solution to his dilemma lies in the same kind of measured distancing and engagement with which he approaches Gabriel. Clearly the black man must recognize his kinship, his permanent social relationship, with the white man. Simple separation poses insurmountable practical difficulties—Baldwin once astutely inquired where the Nation of Islam planned on attaining the capital to finance its autonomous black economy—and plunges the black man into the maelstrom of oversimplification. But a continuing acceptance of the repressive paternalistic relationship offers no solution, either. If the black man is to break down the rigid categories of American racial thought, he must, like John facing Gabriel, recognize the extent to which he participates in the very weakness which keeps him in chains. (In his essays Baldwin frequently condemns the susceptibility of the black middle classes to white materialistic values, a susceptibility which destroys Florence's relationship with Frank in *Go Tell It on the Mountain*.) He must understand that accepting the father's terms, attempting to turn his back on politics and attain salvation by concentrating solely on himself, can only perpetuate his physical and mental bondage. Only when he has understood these facts can he hope to forge his own solution in the absence of white encouragement, the absence of the father's answering smile (*GT*, p. 303).

Part Three of *Go Tell It on the Mountain*, then, combines realistic and symbolic resolutions. While John slips momentarily toward the Temple end of the polarity, he does not share its rigid vision of human simplicity. He has first envisioned and then, in his meeting with Gabriel, begun to act on a complex recognition of the hatred and love, the light and darkness, the Temple and the

Street, in his own mind. He has shattered society's categories without rejecting the social context. He appears to be well on his way to the responsibility which will allow him, like Baldwin and like Joyce, to father his own image, and that of his people, in the world.

Homer's Joyce: John Updike, Ronald Sukenick, Robert Coover, Toni Morrison

History begins where the rest ends. In *Ulysses* the rest ends early, leaving the characters, some of them somnambulists, to wrestle with their dreams. Stephen Dedalus proclaims in "Nestor" that "History . . . is a nightmare from which I am trying to awake" (*U*, p. 34). In "Aeolus" he knows that history is a "nightmare from which you will never awake" (*U*, p. 217). Histories—national, racial, personal, artistic, mythic—threaten to overwhelm the individual characters in Joyce's work. All histories are very real; all are dreams. None can safely be ignored or uncritically accepted.

Joyce creates a mosaic where his characters interact with their histories in a way which allows them to attain dignity without denying the histories which helped shape them, and without submitting themselves entirely to the repugnant aspects of those histories. The young Joyce's repudiation of the chains of history has been overemphasized; his mature attitude was one of reacceptance. When Frank Budgen suggested that Irish independence might "satisfy" history, Joyce simply asked why he "ought to wish to change the conditions that gave Ireland and me a shape and a destiny."[59] A far cry from the young Stephen Dedalus, who wishes to dissociate himself from the past. Joyce's ready acceptance of the Irish and English histories, once the focal points of his youthful rebellion, carried over into his attitudes toward other histories; he was the only one of the Joyce children to accept the familial history incarnate in John Joyce, and he subsumed a great deal of literary history in "Oxen of the Sun." But Joyce's acceptance should not be confused with complacence. His personal relationship with his histories involved shaping in addition to being shaped. In each case Joyce accepted history because, in effect, it created *him*. The stress portends much, because he then proceeded to re-create history in his own image. A symbiotic relationship develops between the artist, his characters, and the history which affects them all. Basing his creation on a public history, Joyce implicitly works against both the parasitic romantic elevation of the self projecting its solipsistic image onto reality and the destructively indulgent acquiescence to "real" history in its inhospitable immensity. Joyce attains this symbiosis largely by juxtaposing his characters against a mythic background which may serve to deflate characters with overblown self-images (Mulligan, Gerty McDowell) or to affirm those who realistically manifest heroic qualities (Bloom and, to an extent, Stephen). He carefully modulates his styles to control the significance of his juxtapositions.

American writers struggling with the nightmare of their own history, a history which now includes Joyce, frequently accept his emphasis on myth and stylistic variety. These emphases can, of course, result in many different types of work, not all of them seeking a "Joycean" balance. Robert Scholes argues that the growing awareness of myth as a literary device results in increasingly self-conscious "allegorical" performances which emphasize the disjunction between artifact and reality.[60] John Updike's *Centaur* and Ronald Sukenick's *98.6*, while sharing the desire for a constructive interaction between symbol and reality, veer off toward ultimate, though (at least in Sukenick's case) not unintentional, irresolution. Sukenick emphasizes the role of the artist as performer, as does Robert Coover in *The Public Burning*. But neither attempts to escape from reality through the type of allegorizing Scholes identifies. Rather, Sukenick manipulates the myth of Frankenstein in order to probe both the limits of conscious control and the nature of American society. Similarly, Coover adapts the myth of Uncle Sam and superimposes it on the "real" historical backdrop of the Rosenberg case, while analyzing the ways in which the American artistic tradition mirrors (and is in part responsible for) America's political immaturity. Toni Morrison's *Song of Solomon* first denies the entire structure of Euro-American myth, the structure which Joyce employed, in order to reconstruct a vision of a realistically and symbolically rich experience based on Afro-American history and myth. All of these writers demonstrate the impulse to reconcile levels of meaning; all follow Joyce in using myth as a focus; all attempt to soothe at least the most nightmarish American historical dreams into regenerative rest.

Manipulating the symbolic dimension of *The Centaur* in much the way Scholes analyzes, Updike invites an allegorical reading of his novel by invoking the myth of the wounded centaur Chiron, who offers himself to the gods as an atonement for Prometheus. This myth provides a backdrop for the realistic story of George Caldwell (Chiron) and his son Peter (Prometheus) in Olinger, Pennsylvania, in 1947. This is a familiar enough device—John O'Hara, for example, builds *Appointment in Samara* around a similar introductory parable. But Updike wants a great deal more than a general mythical analog commenting on the significance of the real experience. He varies his styles and redirects the focus frequently to create various juxtapositions of the levels of his work. Although Robert Martin Adams, following T. S. Eliot, claims that both Updike and Joyce use "the sense of mythical presences to give dignity and a sense of universality to a scene of deliberate meanness, ugliness and squalor,"[61] Updike refuses to endorse the position: "I've often wondered what Eliot meant in his famous essay on *Ulysses*. Does he mean that we are ourselves so depleted of psychic energy, of spiritual and primitive force, that we can do little but retell old stories? Does he mean that human events, love, death, wandering, certain challenges overcome or certain challenges which sweep us under, have already attained classic narrative form? I don't quite know what Eliot meant."[62] Updike seems uncomfortable with Eliot's insistence on the supremacy of myth. Unarguably, however, *The Centaur* resembles *Ulysses* in its portrayal of the juxtaposition of myth and reality in the minds of the two central characters.

Both of these characters, in their realistic and symbolic guises, derive from Joycean sources. Caldwell resembles Leopold Bloom in his role as both exile and everyman. Like Bloom, Caldwell leads an uneasy sexual and family life, is condescended to by his superiors, and maintains an active but seemingly absurd interest in intellectual matters. Like Bloom, he copes with the mundane problems (such as perpetual car breakdowns) of modern bourgeois life. As Chiron, Caldwell belongs to the mature and weary set of mythic heroes which Joyce actively preferred to the youthful and militant. As a developing son with creative drives seeking both artistic and sexual outlets, Peter plays a role similar to that of Stephen Dedalus. Peter's relationship to Prometheus identifies him as one of the many mythic-realistic artists who have followed Joyce's neo-Daedalus (himself part of an already lengthy column of rebellious creators).

Updike indicates at several points that he wishes these dual identities to form a Joycean middle ground between myth and reality. *The Centaur*'s epigraph, from Karl Barth, invokes man as this middle ground: "Heaven is the creation inconceivable to man, earth the creation conceivable to him. He himself is the creature on the boundary between heaven and earth."[63] But a later echo of this idea alters the terms significantly: "Indeed it was rumored that Zeus thought centaurs a dangerous middle-ground through which the gods might be transmuted into pure irrelevance" (*TC*, p. 27). Are we to identify man and centaur? Is the centaur an ideal? A reality? Is the mythic level meant to be more or less significant than the human? The point of the juxtaposition remains veiled. Doc Appleton, identified mythically with Apollo, implies that the centaur image refers to man's body-soul split, and that Caldwell sees the centaur's identifying characteristic as a link to subhuman rather than suprahuman reality: "You believe in the soul. You believe your body is like a horse you get up on and ride for a while and then get off. You ride your body too hard. You show it no love. This is not natural" (*TC*, p. 129).

But what *is* natural? Updike sidesteps the question. He superimposes mythic images on realistic passages, realistic images on mythic passages. His basic writing styles reflect the main foci of their material. When Updike shifts to a clearly mythic setting for the first time (*TC*, p. 21), he writes in lengthy, flowing sentences filled with natural rather than mechanical imagery. Emphasizing the altered setting stylistically stresses the disjunctions rather than the connections between the levels. Most chapters, in fact, establish one basic locale and employ a corresponding style. In these chapters (2, 4, 5, and 7 are realistically located, 3 and 9 mythically centered) references to the "other" world can easily be dismissed, as Adams dismisses the entire mythic dimension, as "decorative and dependent."[64] But the other, less clearly grounded chapters (1, 6, and 8) present more complex problems. The search for a middle ground, for a resolution of myth and reality, centers on the chapters which to various degrees attempt to yoke the realms without clearly identifying a primary locus. These chapters strain Updike's stylistic resources. Since each realm possesses a unique style, their convergence demands a synthetic style to communicate the implications of the meeting.

Updike further complicates the difficulty by opening the novel with one of its most complex stylistic passages. The first two sentences blend the levels: "Caldwell turned and as he turned his ankle received an arrow. The class burst into laughter" (*TC*, p. 3). As Updike proceeds, he identifies Caldwell with Olinger, Chiron with Olympus. But the arrow comes from Chiron's story. Often Updike employs images from the myth to describe the realistic action, but in this case the arrow appears to be real; Hummel removes it (*TC*, p. 9) and shows no surprise that the local science teacher has been shot by his students. Certainly Updike wishes to stress the grotesque elements of contemporary culture which average citizens accept unquestioningly. But he also implies that the two realms coexist in a quite literal way—that Chiron's problems cannot be clearly distinguished from Caldwell's. The remainder of the first chapter, however, offers different perspectives. Updike first shifts clearly to the mythic level (*TC*, p. 21) and then returns to a completely "real" Olinger (*TC*, p. 31) (without arrows). This seems to stress the divergence of the realms which are combined in the opening section.

Updike offers several possible explanations. The most obvious presents the arrow simply as Caldwell's delusion. When he returns to his classroom, Caldwell attempts to explain his absence by showing Zimmerman and the class his wound. No wound exists, at least physically, in Olinger. Caldwell appears to have imagined the opening pages; they affect his conscious behavior, and he apparently *has* gone to Hummel's. Apparently in his own mind he has gone there for an anodyne of some sort. But what, realistically, did he do or receive? Updike leaves the question unanswered. The realistically grounded chapter seven identifies the arrow with Hester Appleton's sexuality; she wears a "gold arrow on her blouse"

(*TC*, p. 195) when she speaks to Caldwell of his marital frustrations. This image reinforces the sexual torment motif which pervades the Olinger sections, but it does not provide a clear gloss on the use of the image in chapter one. This fluidity adds an unsettling and emotionally effective undertone to *The Centaur*, but it serves to identify the reader very closely with Caldwell's amorphous fears and minimizes the possibility of resolving symbolic and mythic significance.

Updike suggests at several points that Peter, rather than his father, holds the key to the juxtaposition. As a future artist, he possesses the least repressed sensibility in *The Centaur*. There are several indications that at least his own first-person chapters are being consciously composed in some nearly mythic future. After a highly traditional opening segment, chapter two (Peter's first chapter) evolves from the 1947 Olinger present, which has been described with diction and syntax perfectly appropriate to an adolescent boy. Updike breaks the "normal" flow: "And yet, love, do not think that our life together, for all its mutual frustration, was not good. It was good. We moved somehow, on a firm stage, resonant with metaphor" (*TC*, p. 70). This suggests that the mythic dimension originates in Peter's metaphoric sensibility, and that the various narrative styles in *The Centaur* mask Peter, who, as Edward R. Vargo suggests,[65] writes the entire novel. This would help explain the shifting mythic presence; since it is imposed by Peter on the story of his father's life, we need not worry about the nature of the mythic dimension which becomes a "decorative and dependent" symbolic device.

This schematizes well, but it doesn't work. Updike reveals that Peter does not, in fact, write the entire novel. The obituary, chapter five, includes an explanation of Caldwell's nickname "Stick" (*TC*, p. 152). While not particularly important to plot, theme, or character, this detail does remove one of the most inviting explanations of the relationship between the novel's levels.

Updike certainly perceives the difficulties posed by these discrepancies. Chiron comments, "A combination, my lady, often cancels the best of its elements" (*TC*, p. 24) and later thinks: "Monsters are most vulnerable in their transitions" (*TC*, p. 297). *The Centaur* is indeed a monster; its good elements threaten one another with cancellation. The resolutions of the two plot levels mirror the difficulties which result from Updike's failure to bring his diverse styles into clear relationship with one another.

In Olinger, Caldwell rejects the temptation of dissociation, of lighting out for the territories by quitting teaching and becoming a farmer. Peter describes his resolve as a "defeat" of his mother (*TC*, p. 292), hinting that Caldwell has realized the sexual source of his agony and is now able to overcome its stifling influence. This allows us to see Peter's approval of his father as a vital step in his development as an artist; he accepts the pain of his family life and sees Pennsylvania as the source of his future art (*TC*, p. 293). Interpreting the Olinger plot in this manner, however, increases the difficulty of comprehending the mythic dimension. Updike's myth, unlike *The Odyssey*, in which Ulysses and Telemachus effectively handle their problems, emphasizes victimization. Prometheus, who plays very little part in the mythic plot, explicitly embodies the mythic victim. Chiron "longed for death" and "died like any wearied man" (*TC*, p. v); he does not learn to cure the agony caused by the arrow, and ultimately he is dissociated entirely from his environment, when "Zeus sets him as a shining archer among the stars" (*TC*, p. v).

Updike resolves the mythic dimension with a retreat rather than a confrontation. Do we then see Caldwell's refusal of the farm as a retreat from his family? Or is he a victim whatever he chooses? Or, perhaps, do we see only a discrepancy between the symbolic and realistic resolutions of *The Centaur*? By ending the novel with a chapter and epilogue in purely mythic style, Updike deprives us of the stylistic guidance which Joyce provides to help relate myth and reality. In comparing his novel with *Ulysses*, Updike stresses simply that he altered Joyce's emphasis: "It seemed to me that there was something mythical about the events. It's an experiment very unlike that of *Ulysses*, where the myth lurks beneath the surface of the natural events. In a way, the natural events in my book are meant to be a kind of mask for the myth."[66] In the epilogue, Updike suggests that Chiron, constellated, "assists in the regulation of our destinies, though in this latter time few living mortals cast their eyes respectfully toward Heaven, and fewer still sit as students to the stars" (*TC*, p. 299). To the end, Updike insists on a significant potential relationship between myth and reality. Despite his more open presentation

of the myth, he clearly shares Joyce's desire to create a middle
ground between man and heaven. While *The Centaur* intimates
much, it leaves us studying the stars but confused by their lessons.

Although Ronald Sukenick has denied special interest in the
Joycean approach to myth as an organizing principle for fiction,
his most successful novel, *98.6,* employs the myth of Frankenstein to investigate the limits of human ability to create new
forms. Like many of the "Superfictionists" with whom he works
in the Fiction Collective, Sukenick is fascinated with the interaction of various levels of fictional reality. Unlike many Superfictionists, however, Sukenick rejects the conception of the novel as
a reality in itself. While accepting the idea that the novel is free to
reflect (as his does) personal fantasies—solipsistic as well as social realities—Sukenick insists that he wishes to avoid allowing
"people to escape . . . from reality . . . I want to bang them with
it!"[67] The myth of Frankenstein provides the vehicle for this confrontation between the artist, his work, and the surrounding social context.

Sukenick recognizes the existence of multiple realities and
strives to treat as many as he perceives. To do so, he believes, demands the technical versatility enabling him to cope with any
new perception concerning any level of experience. The primary
importance of Joyce to Sukenick lies in Joyce's demonstration
that new techniques can be generated to deal with new experiences and then combined with older techniques in cohesive aesthetic units. Innovative techniques, provided they confront readers with new realities, will create their own readers. Sukenick
observes: "A few years ago I had to make defensive explanations
about why I even put *Finnegans Wake* on the reading list; now
students respond to it as if it were mimesis itself."[68] If *Finnegans
Wake* is on the verge of accessibility, as Sukenick implies (an im-
plication which, sadly, probably reflects his own aesthetic more
than a general trend), then the modernist experiments have succeeded in granting the contemporary novelist as much technical
freedom as he can generate for himself. Sukenick comments:

> The "experimental novel" isn't experimental anymore. The ex-
> periment has been a success and we now have a large, solid,
> complex alternate tradition for fiction. . . . everywhere I go

young people are writing out of Joyce, Gertrude Stein, Genet, Beckett, in other words out of the Moderns and their successors. I agree that the Modern period is dead, but in the same sense that Symbolism is dead or Surrealism is dead—dead but not dead-end. It is the Moderns now to whom we look back and it is the problem they raised that we have to contend with.[69]

The primary problem bequeathed by the modernists is the demand that each novel forge its own unity out of its diverse techniques: "There is certainly no such thing as THE novel. Instead there are as many novels as there are authentic novelists, since in an exploratory situation, every form should be idiosyncratic. Fiction itself proceeds by digression and cannot be predicted or defined. Each novel is a unique definition, a definition of itself."[70]

The problem of finding methods which will allow the development of these organic forms dominates *98.6*. Fleeing the seeming chaos of American reality, a novelist named Ron founds a commune which he hopes will develop into an organic expression of its members. But like Sukenick, whose previous novels are entitled *Up* and *Out*, Ron has "tried up and he has tried out. Neither of them works."[71] He carries numerous aesthetic preconceptions to the commune. Though he claims he no longer wants to write (*N*, p. 79), Ron's retreat reflects more his disappointment over the limitations of his previous performance than any real disaffection with fiction. Sukenick, adapting the role of omnipotent narrator, "explains" Ron's newfound interest in life rather than art as another manifestation of his impulse toward "fiction": "He invents stories about his own life alter-careers led by alter-egos. Some of these are amusing some even touching. They all avoid the one identity he can't invent. His own" (*N*, p. 80). Ron hopes the commune will transcend this limitation; his decision to change his name to "Cloud" represents his search for what he naively hopes will be a new, more natural existence.

But the commune suffers from the same limitations as the novel. It cannot develop its own organic form freely because it inhabits the same world as numerous other groups, with their "organic" forms which sometimes require overlapping mental and physical space. Each representative of the "Krypton" group, the River Queen or the motorcycle gang that comes into contact with the commune, imports elements which deflect its internal development. Ultimately Ron finds himself involved in "search and destroy" missions, legacies of the very chaos the commune sought to escape. When the communal ideal dissolves into violence, Ron returns to the novel in his search for an inclusive form: "What chaos. Cloud clutches his head. Cloud no longer believes any of this is happening. This is not real life. What was happening is now all over. It lacks credibility. Cloud is writing a novel again. It's almost finished" (*N*, p. 147).

Though Ron seems unaware of the artificiality of the commune setting, the structure of *98.6* indicates that Sukenick understands that it exists only in contrived isolation from social reality. In fact, *98.6* suggests that creator, creation, and social context take part in a process of mutual shaping. Ron comments on the aesthetic level of the relationship: "Though this settlement was originally my idea as you know I've long since stopped being its creator he says. Instead we all invent it as we live it. And in very real ways it begins to invent us in return" (*N*, p. 98). But he fails to extend the principle to the relationship of the commune (or novel) and communard (novelist) to American society as a whole. Sukenick provides this connection.

Sukenick establishes this larger relationship of artist, work, and context through the myth of Frankenstein, which provides a perfect vehicle for investigating the limits of human ability to create new forms.[72] At once a re-creation of the classical myth of Prometheus and a part of American popular movie culture, the Frankenstein myth suggests the breadth of Sukenick's concern. Further, the myth blurs the distinction between creator and creation; the name Frankenstein belongs to the scientist, but in common use summons visions of the green-faced monster. This ambiguity parallels the tension which Sukenick sees between performer and performance in *98.6*.

Mary Shelley's link between the scientist Frankenstein and the creative spirit Prometheus surfaces several times in section one of *98.6*, which is entitled "Frankenstein." In addition, Sukenick draws on the pop culture image of Frankenstein as a horrifying anomaly in his use of Frankenstein as a synonym for the United States, which he represents as a chaos of crime, violence, and spiritual desolation. The second section—"The Children of Frankenstein"—focuses on Ron's attempt to escape the United States by moving to the commune. The commune's failure is evident in the description of the central building which Ron hopes will develop an organic form free from the taint of "Frankensteinian" reality: "The Monster is the building they'll move into when it's done they call it The Monster because it's gotten so fantastic. That is The Monster is what they call it lately they don't really have a name for it. Or for their group. Ron calls it Bjorsq but won't define it. Or can't" (*N*, p. 65). Ron hopes that the development of an organic form will allow him to bring the monstrous elements into his aesthetic grasp. But Sukenick, by superimposing the mythic reference on his fictional treatment of Ron's experience, insists on the impossibility of the attempted dissociation which motivates the communal enterprise. Though not as aesthetically aware as Ron, Ralph recognizes the underlying structure of the creator-creation relationship: "Ralph has a sense of imminence of new birth of a change beyond his doing. After all that's why you create a monster to do things you can't do. Isn't it? And then it does them to you" (*N*, p. 95). The danger for the commune, as for the original Dr. Frankenstein, consists of the impossibility of predicting the behavior of a new creation.

In fact, Ron's monster leads his creator to the familiar film fate of the mad scientist. Following repeated clashes with neighbors, culminating in the "search and destroy" missions, the sanctuary of the creator burns down: "That night The Monster catches fire. It's such a big fire that the Volunteer Fire Department of Stamperville comes to watch. By the time it's out The Monster is gutted. Then the Volunteer Fire Department of Stamperville pitches in to rip up the guts" (*N*, p. 159). The problem with the commune as an alternative to American society is that Ron's shaping imagination, paradoxically dedicated to non-interference with the organic development of the monster, cannot banish the chaos and violence of the surrounding society. Frankenstein the country invades Frankenstein the artist, subverting Frankenstein the creation. The social Frankenstein attacks the communal monster from within by forcing it to use violence because, as Wind thinks, "He wants to go back but he knows there's no point until our monster is bigger than their monster. Or more terrible. That's a possibility" (*N*, p. 141). This possibility undermines the integrity of the creation which the commune originally conceived as an

Antifrankenstein: "They don't even want to think about Frankenstein they want to create their own thing what they want to create is an Antifrankenstein. The Antifrankenstein is going to be the salvation of Frankenstein that's the only way to do it it's the last chance they've thought about it. Anything born of Frankenstein is of the nature of Frankenstein the only thing to do is stay completely apart everything else has been tried it doesn't work" (*N*, p. 140). The fate of the Antifrankenstein monster emphasizes the futility of the attempted dissociation.

This refusal to endorse dissociation connects Sukenick with those of his contemporaries who are forging a new tradition of the American novel. As his critical writings demonstrate, Sukenick knows a great deal about the historical development of the novel; in *98.6* he uses the images of the condor and the Missing Lunk to invoke the opposed metaphysical (romantic) and naturalistic approaches to experience. Characters react to the condor differently depending on their temperaments, but they always relate the condor image to some realm beyond either the United States or the commune: "Someone who has just seen one of these birds will grab you with pale face and glowing eyes without knowing exactly what he wants to say so what he says is I saw a Condor. What he really wants to say is something like I just saw a vision of universal death and eternal life but of course he doesn't believe in these things as tangible realities" (*N*, p. 84). Ron creates a complementary image relating to the people so immersed in tangible realities that they lack metaphysical awareness, the image of the "Missing Lunk:" "Some inconceivably subhuman but superanimal species preceding Pithecanthropus Erectus that might in fact have lived at the same time as the Condors which are very ancient. Some species intelligent enough to be free but too dumb to be unhappy" (*N*, p. 97). The Missing Lunk, concerned only with physical problems, lacks all awareness of the elements of mystery in reality. This state of opposition bothers Ron, who wishes to establish a framework within which apparently contradictory elements, Condors and Missing Lunks, can coexist: "Why are things always doubled in contradiction this way. Either way you choose you lose. It's always this or that when you need both Cloud is beginning to think there's something wrong with the whole culture. Body or soul. Dream or reality. Reason or feeling. Vision or sanity.

Love or power" (*N*, p. 119). Several times in *98.6* individuals or groups attempt to reconcile symbolic and physical actions, most notably in the communal basketball game (*N*, p. 89–91) and in Eucalyptus' garden work (*N*, p. 114). But these gestures are limited to the commune itself and have no effect on its interaction with the Frankensteinian reality which gradually takes over.

The resolution of *98.6* lies in the performance of Sukenick the novelist, rather than in the experience of Ron the character. Early in *98.6*, Ron attempts to compose a pangram, "a sentence that uses every letter in the alphabet but only once" (*N*, p. 26). Ron's best attempt at a pangram reads "Vex'd nymphs waltz jig fuck borq" (*N*, p. 26). "Borq," which should logically follow "fuck," simply doesn't work; the pangram collapses, and variations of "borq" haunt Ron throughout the novel. Similarly, Sukenick introduces the multitudinous elements of American reality in section one of *98.6*, attempts to shape them in the sexual-communal enterprises of section two, and fails to resolve them quite adequately in the "borq"-ish utopian vision of "Israel" in section three.

Jerome Klinkowitz suggests that Ron's arrival in "Israel" adequately resolves the novel: "It is the missing dimension which the author tried to bridge through love in Section One, through searching for the Missing Lunk in the wilderness of Section Two."[73] Klinkowitz, however, overlooks the fact that section three of *98.6* remains as much dissociated as the commune's monster. Sukenick has already demonstrated the futility of dissociation; he reiterates his position by placing "Israel" under the control of a Dr. Frankenstein whose German background merely underlines his inappropriateness as a savior. When a voice in section three asks: "Dr. Frankenstein do you plan to promote the kind of neoindustrialization with which you are identified in Europe and America here in Israel?" (*N*, p. 183), Dr. Frankenstein replies with a rambling monolog which includes an account of his fascination with pangrams. He seems a more highly aware manifestation of Ron who has not yet attained Sukenick's perspective. Recognizing the futility of attempts to create the perfect form in reality, he attempts to do so imaginatively. But Dr. Frankenstein's pangram, like Ron's, fails. "Bjorsq" is left over; the purely imaginative approach shares the weakness of the communal approach. Nature, the physical reality which exceeds the perceptive abilities of both Ron and Dr. Frankenstein, outperforms them. Mockingbirds sing in natural "words" which incorporate the disruptive elements of the pangrams. Their duets of "Bjorsqi, bjorsqi, bjorsqi" even add an element of non-assertive individuality—their "i" resembles that of cummings' poems—to the final elusive word. Even the Missing Lunks, totally ignorant of metaphysics but able to accept unquestioningly the multiplicity of physical reality, accept Bjorsq: "This language that people don't understand is extremely stupid and nonsensical and is the language The Lunk speaks. This language is called Bjorsq. While Bjorsq is obviously inconvenient for many purposes it has one great advantage when two Lunks meet and speak in Bjorsq they understand one another perfectly. It's more than understanding it's as if they're singing a duet" (*N*, p. 161). Although total acceptance allows both the mockingbirds and the Lunks to turn the apparently disruptive elements into communicative "duets," neither Ron nor Dr. Frankenstein comprehends the total language of reality; their level of awareness limits their performance to what they can unify at any given moment.

Dr. Frankenstein in section three, then, provides another image of Sukenick as performer, extending the motif established with Ron and Cloud in the earlier parts of *98.6*. At the end of the section Sukenick attempts to merge Dr. Frankenstein and Sukenick the novelist. The composite figure sits listening to music, thinking about the literary meaning of the Frankenstein figure, and attempting to balance the physical reality and symbolic influence of *98.6*:

> AT THE SAME TIME orchestrating the whole thing toward those Moments of Luminous Coincidence when everything comes together AT THE SAME TIME AT THE SAME TIME sorry to leave Southern California the sun the waves the mother tongue another bungled paradise AT THE SAME TIME happy to be heading for San Francisco another chance AT THE SAME TIME typing up my novel AT THE SAME TIME my life is unravelling AT THE SAME TIME the novel is bungled fragments stitched together AT THE SAME TIME everything is seamless perfect not because because but AT THE SAME TIME playing the blues letting it go it is as it is. Another failure. [*N*, p. 187–88]

The closing performance approximates the balance Sukenick seeks. It attempts to exclude nothing, to admit the "Bjorsqi." The very declaration-admission of failure strengthens the feeling that Sukenick represses nothing. Just as Joyce equated the organization of the sections of *Ulysses* with the organization of the human body and observed that the physiological condition of the body as it moves through the day in large part explains the progression of styles, Sukenick invokes physiology for his metaphor of simultaneity. The nightmarish climax of section one connects the many levels of performance in *98.6*. "Her temperature is ninety-eight point six. In a pensive mood they walk the young man to the station. All this takes place in Frankenstein" (*N*, p. 60). *98.6*, too, takes place within Frankenstein, within the country, within the artist. Sukenick's performance consists of establishing a forum for communication between his avatars and their society, giving them intimations of an inclusive language which will complete a pangram, uniting self and context: "Bjorsq is rhythmic the rhythm of your pulse and the rhythm of the surf" (*N*, p. 161). If Frankensteinian social reality does not provide the material for perfection, Sukenick, at once Frankenstein the artist and Frankenstein the creation, will generate a new organic language to comprehend his full perception of reality.

In his early works Robert Coover presented mythology as generated primarily by the individual imagination. Sukenick criticizes *The Universal Baseball Association, J. Henry Waugh, Prop.* for granting autonomy to the protagonist's imaginative sense of reality: "We have to stick to reality or the exercise of the imagination becomes meaningless, a delusion."[74] Sukenick continues, "With the plausibility of the actual game lost, the philosophical freight begins to take over. . . . The book descends into what I would call pseudo-myth, an attempt to synthesize one's own version of traditional myth and impose it on contemporary experience as if it explained something."[75] As *98.6* demonstrates, Sukenick does not reject the use of myth. Rather, rejecting the dissociation of myth and reality, he demands a closer synthesis of symbolic and realistic significance than Coover attains in his early works.

By focusing on external historical events and characters, the Rosenberg executions and Richard Nixon, *The Public Burning* attains this synthesis. While still bearing the impress of Coover's personal version of myth, *The Public Burning* "explains" a great deal. A mysterious sign, echoing Stephen Dedalus, states the problem: "The tradition of all past generations weighs like a nightmare upon the brain of the living."[76] The "solution," emerging through Coover's manipulation and analysis of the American creative style and his treatment of the myth of Uncle Sam, explains the origin of and link between the unresolved contradictions in American culture and America's tendencies toward self-victimization. It also explains the complexities which render it nearly impossible for the American writer—Coover includes himself—to totally escape these contradictions.

In *Ulysses* Bloom and Odysseus coexist quietly; Joyce functions primarily through understatement and suggestion. While positing a similar parallel between the mythic Uncle Sam and the avatar Richard Nixon, Coover approaches the subject through hyperbole and exaggeration. Bloom incarnates Odysseus unconsciously; Nixon incarnates Uncle Sam only after elaborate preparation based on conscious obsession. Uncle Sam himself is a composite figure. Part tall-tale hero—he once "pissed Old Faithful back down its hole, and thereby created the Hot Springs of Arkansas" (*TPB*, p. 337)—he takes on particular characteristics of each presidential incarnation (*TPB*, p. 171–72). Thus, to some extent, "real" individuals shape Uncle Sam.

At the same time, however, he shapes them. The Nixon chapters of *The Public Burning* concentrate largely on Nixon's desperate attempts to feel himself attuned to the myth. At times Nixon reaches "an intuitive awareness of everything happening in Uncle Sam's head" (*TPB*, p. 95), but he spends most of his time "trying to imagine what it felt like to be the incarnation of Uncle Sam, the physical *feeling* of it as the transformation comes over you" (*TPB*, p. 60). Nixon clearly expects to lose some degree of his individuality in the process; he does not expect to create Uncle Sam in his own image. In a passage which intimates the center of Coover's conception of the contact between myth and reality, Nixon, watching Eisenhower, argues that too strong a sense of self may in fact preclude incarnation: "I watched this short-tempered old man, Uncle Sam's new real-time disguise, and thought: the most important thing is that there be room for the Incarnation to take place. A man can't be solid and a mask at the same time. Yes, image—I knew all about that. The essence of power is paradox and ambiguity. Learning to live with this was the hardest of all—I was still too precise, too self-critical, too anxious to make everything perfectly clear" (*TPB*, p. 230). Despite his attempts to repress his personality and to understand Uncle Sam and incarnation, Nixon remains essentially ignorant until his actual incarnation, which takes place when he is sodomized by Uncle Sam (*TPB*, p. 530–34). The internal "room" for the incarnation, which Coover images as anal, originates in the individual's direct, though not necessarily willing, participation in degradation. Up until the final pages Nixon attempts to construct an interpretation of Uncle Sam as a force of good combatting an evil "Phantom." But, as Uncle Sam informs him, "You gotta love me, like I really am: Sam Slick the Yankee Peddler" (*TPB*, p. 531). He does not share Nixon's delusion of purity.

In his collective manifestation, then, Uncle Sam seems aware that he contains multitudes—angels and phantoms, victimizers and victims. An elaborate structure of doubling in *The Public Burning* reinforces this awareness. "The Clemency Appeals" identify Eisenhower as "Pris," Ethel as "Pres." Nixon clearly serves as a double for the Rosenbergs; he sees himself as a victim of political cliques and an unsympathetic family and frequently identifies his feelings and life with the Rosenbergs (*TPB*, pp. 55, 92, 145–46, 182). This culminates in his tearful claim of kinship preceding the rape of Ethel Rosenberg (*TPB*, p. 441). Overarching the entire novel, the specious dichotomy of Phantom and Uncle Sam distracts everyone but its perpetuators. The characters involved in the doublings adamantly refuse to acknowledge their connection with shadow selves. Judge Irving Kaufman, a Jew willing to ignore the anti-Semitic undertones of the trial and to condemn the Rosenbergs, senses the significance of the doublings. Recognizing "judge and judged: two sides of the same coin" (*TPB*, p. 427), he meditates: "but now it's suddenly come to him, thinking about that indivisible two-sided coin, that the one thing you could never understand was the thing you were intimately a part of; identity, they'd taught him (tried to), made modal and virtual distinctions impossibile" (*TPB*, p. 427). But an interruption keeps him from pursuing the thought to its logical conclusion, and he represses his sympathy in favor of political expedience.

Underlying this unwillingness to understand the complexity of experience lies an essential immaturity of character. Building on Leslie Fiedler's argument in *Love and Death in the American Novel*, Coover indicts America for its sexual immaturity, which expresses itself in political oppression and ultimately results in self-victimization. In the midst of a pageant of American humorists, Coover states his premise explicitly: "America Laughs. At much the same things everybody laughs at everywhere: sex, death, danger, the enemy, the inevitable, all the things that hurt about growing up, something that Americans especially, suddenly caught with the whole world in their hands, are loath to do" (*TPB*, p. 450). This unwillingness to mature leads to sexual alienation and frustration, which in turn expresses itself as political intolerance. Coover sees this intolerance as an attack on the unrecognized "phantom" side of the individual which is projected into a political enemy. On the morning of the execution, every leading male political figure wakes up with an erection, but none finds sexual outlet. Rather, the sexual energy feeds the hysteria surrounding the Rosenbergs. Ultimately, this energy leads to Nixon's rape of Ethel Rosenberg, which, he admits, "was what I'd been planning to do all along! Fuck all the phony excuses I'd made to myself, this was what I'd come all the way up here for" (*TPB*, p. 437). The rape, in turn, precipitates Nixon's public humiliation, a humiliation Coover sees as the inevitable result of self-delusion. Although, in the best American evangelist-huckster tradition, Nixon rescues the immediate situation by calling on the crowd to "drop its pants for America" (*TPB*, p. 482–85), he anticipates the later, unwilling, dropping of his pants for Uncle Sam.

When Nixon stumbles on stage with his pants down, his immediate sense of dislocation focuses on his "frazzled mind reaching out for the old catchwords, the functional code words of the profession, but drawing a blank" (*TPB*, p. 471). When he finds the words, they come not from the vocabulary of political rhetoric, but from the tradition of American humor, a tradition which Coover identifies as the root of both America's practical politics and its most profound literature. The coincidence raises several questions concerning the complicity of American writers in propagating the very failings against which they rage.

Numerous political figures with differing motives exploit the comic aspects of the tradition. J. Edgar Hoover (*TPB*, p. 15), Everett Dirksen (*TPB*, p. 51) and Eisenhower (*TPB*, p. 162) successfully mimic the frontier humorist's exaggerative style in the cause of persecuting the Rosenbergs while the Marx Brothers tacitly defend them: "it's simply the astonishing cartoon resemblance Groucho and Harpo bear to Julius and Ethel" (*TPB*, p. 453). Nonetheless, the Marx Brothers do participate in the public spectacle and, though to a lesser degree than the persecuting politicians, share the responsibility for its results. Morally responsible art and opportunistic political jargon blend and nearly merge in *The Public Burning*. Eisenhower and Hawthorne express a similar apprehension of the hand of fate guiding all events (*TPB*, p. 9); Uncle Sam quotes Poe, Whitman, and Emerson (*TPB*, pp. 87, 397, 496); a sadistic cabbie acts out a scene from Huck Finn while employing Twain's joke-telling style (*TPB*, p. 268); *Time* magazine writes in William Carlos Williams's American meter (*TPB*, p. 323); and a "misunderstood" William Faulkner attends the execution in person (*TPB*, p. 420–21). The Pentagon and *Time* frequently employ a stylized free verse to express their vision of reality (*TPB*, pp. 66, 217, 236) and the three intermezzo chapters, all of which employ self-consciously artistic styles, show that both persecutors and persecuted respond to their experience in clichés grounded in a simplistic sense of reality.

Perhaps the most significant connection between the political and literary traditions involves Whitman. Kaufman, Eisenhower, and Uncle Sam invoke the "good gray poet," and *The Public Burning* itself resembles a Whitman catalog in its abundance of detail.[77] Both Kaufman (*TPB*, p. 25) and Eisenhower (*TPB*, p. 151) use a Whitmanesque style to justify the condemnation of the Rosenbergs. Uncle Sam goes a step beyond and opens the "Singalong with the Pentagon Patriots" chapter by proclaiming, "I hear America singing, the varied carols I hear" (*TPB*, p. 54). Manipulating the general tendency of the Whitmanesque celebration of America and self, Uncle Sam endorses a smug complacency. While Whitman intended no such attitude, he provides the raw material for Uncle Sam's travesty: Uncle Sam does not even alter Whitman's words, he merely places them in a slightly different context. The American literary tradition, a victim (like Nixon) of its own excesses, plays a major role in exciting the public uproar: "It seems like no one can hold back from celebrating the Poets and Prophets this morning, least of all the American Superhero, who speaks by custom with the grandeur of a nation of runesmiths, from Davy Crockett to Longfellow, the Carnegies and Cranes to Hank Williams and the Whittier Poets" (*TPB*, p. 427).[78] Just as the political victimizers metamorphose into victims, literary rebels merge with tyrants.

Coover holds no illusions concerning his own involvement in this morass. Placing the "aesthetic" of *The Public Burning* in the mouths of Nixon, *The New York Times*, and *Time* magazine, he underlines the fact that his own rebellion occupies the obverse side of a coin impressed with the face of America's intolerance and immaturity. Rather than claiming special status for his own work, Coover admits that its very diversity, the diversity of a Whitmanesque America, places it largely beyond his control. Ostensibly describing *The New York Times*, Coover writes: "And perhaps that was why—the tenacious faith in the residual magic of language—this monument was erected in the first place: that effort to reconstruct with words and iconography each fleeting day in the hope of discovering some pattern, some coherence, some meaningful dialogue with time. But so enormous a shrine it is, so prodigious a task just to keep the translation of gesture into language flowing, that all consciousness of any intended search for transcendence must long ago have disappeared and been forgotten, leaving all visionary speculations to the passing pilgrim" (*TPB*, p. 191). Like *The New York Times*, *The Public Burning* participates directly in the reality it describes. Realizing that his own work necessarily belongs to the tradition he criticizes, Coover attempts to heighten the reader's consciousness of the interaction of art and reality. He refuses to claim a specious transcendence, preferring to seek a dialogue between artist, audience, and social context.

This is not to say that Coover believes that a novel should "accurately" re-create the details of life. He frequently denies the possibility of objectivity: "'Objectivity' is in spite of itself a willful program for the stacking of perceptions; facts emerge not from life but from revelation, gnarled as always by ancient disharmonies and charged with libidinous energy" (*TPB*, p. 191). Rather, as the national "poet laureate" *Time* argues, "Objectivity is an impossible illusion, a 'fantastic claim' ('gnostic' is the word on his tongue these days), and as an ideal perhaps even immoral, that only through the frankly biased and distorting lens of art is any real grasp of the facts—not to mention Ultimate Truth—even remotely possible" (*TPB*, p. 320). Indirectly Coover accepts aesthetic strategies and symbolic structures which "alter" reality for a particular purpose. Nixon, who speculates more on the theory of fiction than any character in any of Coover's works, explains that the specific purpose of distortion in historical fictions, such as *The Public Burning*, is "to make what might later seem like nothing more than a series of overlapping fictions cohere into a convincing semblance of historical continuity and logical truth— at least long enough to wrest a guilty verdict from an impressed jury" (*TPB*, p. 122). The paradox is not subtle. Coover distorts to support the Rosenbergs; Nixon, to damn them. Since Uncle Sam has coopted every previous American rebel-writer into his myth, he will no doubt consume Coover also. In A.D. 2100 Uncle Sam's incarnation may well quote Coover as Eisenhower quotes Hawthorne. As Uncle Sam taunts the "agents of the phantom": "If the Red Slayer thinks he slays boys, he know not well the sub-title ways" (*TPB*, p. 496). Coover, like Emerson, and like Uncle Sam, realizes the inevitable connection between the opposites. He offers *The Public Burning* not as a vicious rejection of the U.S., but as part of an ongoing dialectic, a dialectic in which symbolic distortions reflect on the political reality where spokesmen will distort the distortions, establishing a new context, initiating a new cycle of distortion and dialog, a new Uncle Sam, a new myth of a new American reality.

Blue wings blur the beginning of Toni Morrison's *Song of Solomon*. Though silk, the wings are real. Carrying Robert Smith to his death, they impress an image of American insanity on young Guitar Bains's mind. Guitar dreams better, but, like Smith, he becomes a vigilante, his wings clipped. His dream, once removed from his own reality, enters the larger reality only when Milkman Dead learns to fly. Reality becomes dream becomes reality. Men live myths. When they know what they're doing, they can triumph.

Morrison's novel resembles nothing in American literature as much as it resembles the "magic realism" displayed in the contemporary Latin American novels of Carlos Fuentes, Gabriel Garcia Marquez, Miguel Angel Asurias, and Guillerme Cabrera Infante. Magic realism is not a specific aesthetic theory, but a style. The magic realist emphasizes disorienting images which seem unreal projections of a particular character's psychic state. He then embeds the images within a reality the focal character shares with one or more additional characters. This may serve either to validate the first character's perception or to question the solidity of any perceived reality. The striking images serve realistic, as well as symbolic, purposes. As many of its practitioners acknowledge,[79] magic realism derives in part from Joyce's treatment of naturalistic details as symbolic entities (Bloom's potato talisman). Frequently the Latin American novelists follow Joyce in employing mythological systems to establish the links between the various levels of their work. Morrison, like Joyce and Fuentes, submerges a mythological reality beneath an "ordinary" realistic surface. In *Song of Solomon* she portrays the dominant Euro-American culture's attempt to distort the images rooted in Afro-American myth and folk culture. In order to demonstrate the significance of the repressed mythology in black life, Morrison balances dreamlike and realistic imagery. Characters see the physical world as a dream, only to find the dream elements confronting them in concrete forms. Magic colors reality. What Euro-American culture dismisses as superstition reflects a sense of myth necessary to the mental health of Morrison's characters.

The epigraph of *Song of Solomon* suggests the similarity of Morrison's and Joyce's thematic, as well as stylistic, concerns. Morrison introduces *Song of Solomon* with "The fathers may soar. And the children may know their names."[80] Fathers, flight, and names recur throughout Joyce's work, particularly in association with Stephen Dedalus. While sharing the Joycean concerns, Morrison revalues the Euro-American Daedalus, affirming the alternate myth of the Flying African. Maintaining contact with white and black mythic systems, Morrison synthesizes a new myth of a flying man, one who knows his name and can turn his knowledge to account. The magic reality of Solomon solidifies in his great-grandson Milkman.

Before synthesizing her new myth, Morrison undercuts the authority of the dominant Euro-American systems. She does not posit the Afro-American myth as a given (as does Ishmael Reed in *Mumbo Jumbo* and *The Last Days of Louisiana Red*) and focus on questions of incarnation, as do Updike, Barth, and Coover. This decision reflects her perception that Euro-American culture has established an "authority" for its own myths which dominate the surface in both Euro-American and contemporary Afro-American society. (The very names of the black characters in *Song of Solomon* transmit Euro-American mythology.) Still, as Morrison reveals, the domination is only apparent. A deeper understanding of the process which led to the naming of Pilate, First Corinthians, Magdalena, Hagar, and Reba reveals that the names subvert rather than support the Christian myth. While recent generations continue naming children out of nearly blind acceptance of a family tradition (*SS*, pp. 71, 147), the tradition originates not in respect for, but in bitterness toward, Christianity. When the midwife questions the first Macon Dead's choice of Pilate as his daughter's name—"You don't want to give this motherless child the name of the man that killed Jesus, do you?"—his response verges on blasphemy: "I asked Jesus to save me my wife" (*SS*, p. 19). The significance of the name to Macon Dead lies in its physical appearance rather than in its religious connotation, which itself has no impact on him. He selects "Pilate" because it is "a group of letters that seemed to him strong and handsome; saw in them a large figure that looked like a tree hanging in some princely but protective way over a row of smaller trees" (*SS*, p. 18). His naming impulse borders on the totemic.

A specific connection between names and the people or places they identify characterizes the Afro-American culture in *Song of Solomon*. Frequently, as with Pilate, the names openly mock the "official" Euro-American system. Morrison devotes the second paragraph of the novel to the story of the naming of "Not Doctor Street, a name the post office did not recognize" (*SS*, p. 4). The Afro-American community bestows the name "Doctor Street" on descriptive grounds—the only black doctor in town lives there— and changes it into a humorous and defiant comment on the dominant culture, which insists that the avenue "had always been and would always be known as Mains Avenue and not Doctor Street" (*SS*, p. 4). The south side's ready compliance indicates its deep respect for white commands.

Few of the characters in *Song of Solomon* actually understand the importance, or even consciously recognize the existence, of the alternate naming system. Guitar typifies the community attitude when he dismisses Milkman's dislike of his name: "Niggers get their names the way they get everything else—the best way they can" (*SS*, p. 88). Largely because he doesn't know the origin of his nickname and doesn't understand the reasons why his family keeps its grim last name, Milkman has a deeper sense of the importance of names. Still, he unintentionally insults the residents of Shalimar by neither asking their names nor offering his own (*SS*, p. 266). Only after the insult places him in repeated physical danger does Milkman piece together the story of Solomon, the first Macon Dead, a story which explains his own name. Solomon is not the biblical king, not a part of Euro-American mythology; rather, he is the flying African Shalimar (or Challeemone—the oral tradition leads to variety in spelling). Similarly, Milkman's grandmother's descendants, the Byrds, are the descendants not of the slaveholding Virginia aristocrats but of the Indian "Birds." When he is able to see names from the perspective of Afro-American rather than Euro-American culture, Milkman comprehends the nature of the insult and realizes that "Under the recorded names were other names, just as 'Macon Dead,' recorded for all time in some dusty file, hid from view the real names of people, places, and things. Names that had meaning. No wonder Pilate put hers in her ear. When you know your name, you should hang on to it, for unless it is noted down and remembered , it will die when you do" (*SS*, p. 329). Pilate fiercely protects her own name, which she carries in her earring until her death. A similar acceptance of his name and his heritage allows Milkman to fly at the end of *Song of Solomon*.

Just as he must dissociate himself from Euro-American preconceptions in order to learn his name, Milkman must move beyond Euro-American mythic images before he can "surrender to the air" (*SS*, p. 337). The dominant Euro-American mythic images of the flying man—particularly since Joyce—have been those of Daedalus and Icarus, the father and son whose flight to freedom leads to death and failure for one of them. The image of Smith plunging to earth dominates the opening of *Song of Solomon* and reinforces the Daedalus image. When he leaves Michigan to begin his quest, Milkman flies in an airplane. This flight is an attempt to leave real confrontations behind: "In the air, away from real life, he felt free, but on the ground, when he talked to Guitar just before he left, the wings of all these other people's nightmares flapped in his face and constrained him" (*SS*, p. 220). Even Susan Byrd's first telling of the story of Solomon and Jake emphasizes the Daedalian aspects of the tale. A free black woman, Heddy "was melting tallow when she looked up and saw this man holding a baby and flying toward the ridge. He brushed too close to a tree and the baby slipped out of his arms and fell through the branches to the ground. He was unconscious, but the trees saved him from dying" (*SS*, pp. 323–34). The image of melting tallow and the failure of the son's escape recall the Daedalus myth, but the basic context of the story differs significantly; the child lives, and the failure results from not flying high enough, rather than from flying too high. Most important, the legend counteracts the stereotypes of the happy slave and the black beast. Solomon deals with his bondage not by acquiescing (an approach largely adopted by Milkman's father) or by blindly striking out (like Guitar). Rather, he reclaims his dignity and returns to the Africa which nurtured him.

To Morrison, the recognition of African heritage is a psychological necessity. She emphasizes that African folklore has always survived in Afro-American life. Milkman's life begins after Pilate's love powder ends the sexual alienation of his parents (*SS*, p. 133). Milkman's life depends in a very real sense on African elements in Afro-American culture. His hopes of understanding his parents' emotionally complex relationship, and, by extension, his own immediate past, hinge on recognizing his complex heritage. Similarly, his understanding of Pilate develops only when he accepts and accurately interprets the message of the ghosts which motivate many of her actions. Although he has heard of the ghosts often (*SS*, pp. 110, 147), Milkman denies their reality until he reaches Shalimar (*SS*, p. 294). Only after accepting the reality of the ghosts can he recognize that they divulge the secrets of his ancestry and of flight. When Pilate casts him into the cellar, he "buys" his release with a correct explanation of the ghost's words: "You just can't fly on off and leave a body" (*SS*, p. 147), which Pilate thinks apply to the body of a white man left behind in a cave. Milkman yells: "He was talking about himself. His own father flew away. He was the 'body.' The body you shouldn't fly off and leave." Milkman then explains the ghost's use of the word "sing," which Pilate registers as a command: "Let me tell you what your father said. Pilate, he didn't even tell you to sing, Pilate. He was calling for his wife—your mother" (*SS*, p. 333).

The scene, which points to the depth of Morrison's complex vision, is an epiphany for both Pilate and Milkman. Until Pilate casts him into the cellar as retribution for the callousness which results in Hagar's death, Milkman uncritically apotheosizes Solomon's flight from Virginia; he accepts the symbolic African image without placing it in its realistic context. Only when he places it in perspective and connects it with his own actions does he understand the image clearly; only then can he fly. If Morrison had resolved *Song of Solomon* with the image of Solomon soaring, it would have been a typical American romance, solved through metaphysical dissociation. But she insists that Milkman recognize that, in flying away, Solomon abandons twenty-one children in American bondage and drives Ryna insane by leaving her alone. Prior to this realization, Milkman's response to Sweet's question about whom Solomon left behind rings with ecstasy: "Everybody! He left everybody down on the ground and he sailed on off like a black eagle. 'O-e-e-e-e Solomon done fly, Solomon done gone/Solomon cut across the sky, Solomon gone home!'" (*SS*, pp. 328–29). But his words echo a blues rather than a shout. Milkman recognizes their complexity only when he sees that he, like Solomon, has flown away, destroying his lady. Morrison withdraws the easy romantic symbolic resolution and restates it with qualifications. Milkman truly comes to terms with his name, his personal past, his ancestry, and his mixed cultural background only when he determines to face Guitar directly. Guitar, despite his "insane" involvement with the vigilante "Days," remains the only person who reacts to Milkman with a full emotional range: "Would you save my life or would you take it? Guitar was exceptional. To both questions he could answer yes" (*SS*, p. 331). In deciding to "fly" to Guitar at the end of the novel, Milkman makes both a symbolic gesture—he embraces Solomon's heritage—and a realistic commitment—for the first time he will accept emotional complexity of his own free will; he will no longer attempt to "fly" away from the real people with whom he must live or, if need be, die.

By placing the weight of the thematic resolution almost exclusively on Milkman, Morrison risks a great deal. Since we do not actually know the result of his decision, the ending flirts with evasiveness. It would be easy to dismiss the flight as purely symbolic; however, Morrison's writing style throughout *Song of Solomon* militates against such a reading. Where Updike's style tends to confuse the levels, Morrison's, like Coover's, insists on the interdependence of dream and reality. Though technically less flashy than *The Public Burning, Song of Solomon* balances levels even more effectively. While Morrison modulates her style to reflect different characters, she always balances her modes. When Ruth contemplates the water mark on her table, "she regarded it as a mooring, a checkpoint, some stable visual object that assured her that the world was still there; that this was life and not a dream. That she was alive somewhere, inside, which she acknowledged to be true only because a thing she knew intimately was out there, outside herself" (*SS*, p. 11). In this case a physical detail, meaningless in itself, takes on larger significance by connecting a dream-life with reality. Conversely, when treating Milkman, at the time overwhelmed by problems in the real world, Morrison shows him veering toward a purely symbolic mode of interpreting his problems: "Without the least transition and without knowing he was going to, he began to describe to Guitar a dream he had had about his mother. He called it a dream because he didn't want to tell him it had really happened, that he had really seen it" (*SS*, p. 104). The fact that Milkman describes a scene which apparently is a dream—of his mother being overwhelmed by tulips (a sexual dream pun?)—heightens the sense of cooperation between dream and reality.

Milkman's confrontation with Circe, a mythic scene with specifically Joycean reverberations, typifies Morrison's magic realistic technique. When Milkman sees a pair of eyes in the window of the abandoned mansion, he interprets them first as a symbolic self-projection, then as an innocuous optical accident: "And it did look like a murderer's house. Dark, ruined, evil. Never, not since he knelt by his window sill wishing he could fly, had he felt so lonely. He saw the eyes of a child peer at him over the sill of the one second-story window the ivy had not covered. He smiled. Must be myself I'm seeing—thinking about how I used to watch the sky out the window. Or maybe it's the light trying to get through the trees" (*SS*, p. 238). But the eyes belong to "a pack of golden-eyed dogs, each of which had the intelligent child's eyes he had seen from the window" (*SS*, p. 240). The dogs are real but are associated with Circe, who herself represents an even deeper symbolic image to Milkman. When he meets her, he panics, thinking that dreams have obliterated his reality:

> He had had dreams as a child, dreams every child had, of the witch who chased him down dark alleys, between lawn trees, and finally into rooms from which he could not escape. Witches in black dresses and red underskirts; witches with pink eyes and green lips, tiny witches, long rangy witches, frowning witches, smiling witches, screaming witches and laughing witches, witches that flew, witches that ran, and some that merely glided on the ground. So when he saw the woman at the top of the stairs there was no way for him to resist climbing up toward her outstretched hands, her fingers spread wide for him, her mouth gaping open for him, her eyes devouring him. In a dream you climb the stairs. She grabbed him, grabbed his shoulders and pulled him right up against her and tightened her arms around him. [*SS*, p. 239]

Again the event is real, but Morrison's style stresses the degree to which Milkman reacts to it on the basis of his dreams. In fact, Circe fulfills the role of the archetypal crone, providing Milkman with the magic information concerning his ancestors which allows him to find himself and fly. In effect, Morrison's Circe scene fulfills the same function as Joyce's in *Ulysses*, demonstrating that the path to realistic equilibrium leads through the subconscious world of dreams.

Unity, then, underlies *Song of Solomon*. Morrison strives for a synthesis of symbolic and realistic actions and styles, a synthesis of African and American traditions. Ultimately, she seeks a dynamic unity of man and his environment. Perhaps the strongest, the most magical statement comes in her description of the first

Macon Dead's attempt to make his dream real. Macon—or Jake—Solomon's son, the Icarus surviving his fall, "had come out of nowhere, as ignorant as a hammer and broke as a convict, with nothing but free papers, a Bible, and a pretty black-haired wife, and in one year he'd leased ten acres, the next ten more. Sixteen years later he had one of the best farms in Menteur County" (*SS*, p. 235). For a fleeting moment, before the whites murder him, he attains unity, his symbolic freedom realized in realistic accomplishment. At the peak of his achievement, he hears the earth speak:

> "You see?" the farm said to them. "See? See what you can do. Never mind you can't tell one letter from another, never mind you born a slave, never mind you lose your name, never mind your daddy dead, never mind nothing. Here, this here, is what a man can do if he puts his mind to it and his back in it. Stop sniveling," it said. "Stop picking around the edges of the world. Take advantage, and if you can't take advantage, take disadvantage. We live here. On this planet, in this nation, in this county right here. *No*where else! We got a home in this rock, don't you see! Nobody starving in my home; nobody crying in my home, and if I get a home you get one too! Grab it. Grab this land! Take it, hold it, my brothers, make it, my brothers, shake it, squeeze it, turn it, twist it, beat it, kick it, kiss it, whip it, stomp it, dig it, plow it, seed it, reap it, rent it, buy it, sell it, own it, build it, multiply it, and pass it on—can you hear me? Pass it on!" [*SS*, p. 235]

The sermon, its rhythms drawn from Afro-American culture, accepts the realistic battle; it does not reject the past. At the end of *Song of Solomon* Milkman is struggling to realize the sermon, committing himself to flight and to the battle. Morrison is passing it on.

Everybody's Joyce: Donald Barthelme, Raymond Federman, William Melvin Kelley, William Burroughs

Admitting that no one really comprehends *Finnegans Wake* invites the corollary that the book "appears to have been a dead-end"[81] in the history of the English novel. The corollary, however, overlooks the phenomenon of numerous writers happily reading and rewriting a *Finnegans Wake* which may or may not have much in common with the Joycean original. Most of the book's followers agree that it challenges the traditional conception of a novel as something standing "outside" reality, whether in a position of engagement or of dissociation. They see the *Wake*, and their own works, as components of reality, artifacts which must be encountered in the same way as "concrete" objects, such as buildings and tables. As a result, questions of fictional mode engage these writers' attention primarily as they influence the reader's perception of the works' reality. Frequently the writers manipulate traditional realistic or symbolic modes to demonstrate that both modes, far from embodying distinct and opposed visions, merely contribute to the reality of the printed page.

While the post-Wakeans agree on the novel's concrete reality, they share no consensus on the implications of their position. The clash over the *Wake*'s political significance was dramatized at the 1975 James Joyce Symposium in Paris. Philippe Sollers, whose association with the French New Novelists connects him with the mainstream of the international concrete movement, hailed *Finnegans Wake* as the "book on the barricades," a radical attack on bourgeois institutions as codified in standard linguistic forms.[82] Leslie Fiedler, however, advanced the thesis that because *Finnegans Wake*'s abstruse frames of references render it accessible only to a highly educated elite, the book reinforces the cultural hegemony of the bourgeoisie who possess the leisure necessary to indulge themselves in pointless aesthetic games.

In fact, several contemporary post-Wakeans seem to support Fiedler's claims. Donald Barthelme's and Raymond Federman's individual explorations of the parodic and self-reflexive aspects of *Finnegans Wake* touch only tangentially on political issues. Despite their pretense of shattering traditional conceptions of fictional modes, both display many of the strengths and weaknesses of the romantic mode which deemphasizes social concerns. The writers who share Sollers's belief in the political potential of post-Wakean fiction have avoided an analogous overemphasis on the realistic mode. William Melvin Kelley's applications of Wakean language and motifs to Afro-American culture demonstrate the necessity of resolving real and symbolic experiences. While William Burroughs seems less ready to endorse political approaches to either the *Wake* or his own work, *The Ticket That Exploded* both criticizes and employs a layered, nearly Wakean, language as part of its attempt to counteract a repressive sociopolitical entity.

The split among followers of the *Wake* should not be over-emphasized. Each author I shall consider in some way accepts the *Wake*'s de- or re-construction of language; each accepts the *Wake*'s conception of a more fluid idea of character, both fictional and "real," than Western culture has traditionally encouraged. But neither should the schism be ignored. For, far more than most novels, *Finnegans Wake* offers its followers the opportunity of determining to a large degree how it is to be read. If Barthelme and Federman signal the dominant trend, *Finnegans Wake* may well remain a "curiosity," influencing artists and scholars, communicating only with an elite. If Kelley and Burroughs prove indicative, *Finnegans Wake* may indeed be read increasingly, and by a wider audience, as a precursor of a revolutionary reorientation of social reality.

If *Finnegans Wake* is not primarily the paraph of Joyce's career, is Barthelme's *Dead Father* more paragoge than parallel, a paraphrase of a paragon? Apparently paradoxical, paradoxically transparent, does it simply provide a paradigm of the perils of parodying a master parodist? Anyone with a dictionary and a bit of mental agility can parse the terms of Barthelme's satiric judgment; the real interest lies in the purpose of the pursuit. Like the title character of his novel who admits that "Having it both ways is a thing I like,"[83] and like Joyce before him, Barthelme attempts to encompass both terms of a series of seeming dichotomies. In *The Dead Father* the most troubling dichotomy is that between Barthelme's impulses to both deflate and pay homage to *Finnegans Wake*.

Barthelme's essay "After Joyce," one of his earliest statements on the theory of fiction, acknowledges that Joyce never simply turned his back on the real world to engage in private aesthetic pursuits. Barthelme identifies *Finnegans Wake* as a concrete object directly challenging the reader's perceptions, rather than approaching them through a series of illusions:

> Satisfied with neither the existing world nor the existing literature, Joyce and Stein modify the world by adding to its store of objects the literary object—which is then encountered in the same way as other objects in the world. The question becomes:

what is the nature of the new object? Here one can see an immediate result of the shift. Interrogating older works, the question is: what do they say about the world and being in the world? But the literary object is itself "world" and the theoretical advantage is that in asking it questions you are asking questions of the world directly.[84]

Barthelme carefully avoids the pitfalls of denying the work's *interaction* with (as opposed to reflection of) reality, stressing the freedom from constraint which his conception of post-*Wake* writing offers: "Far from implying a literature that is its own subject matter, the work that is an object is rich in possibilities. The intention of the artist may range in any direction, including those directions which have the approval of socially-minded critics."[85] From the beginning, then, Barthelme has acknowledged the central place of *Finnegans Wake* in his personal literary history.

In the same essay, however, Barthelme cautions that "*Finnegans Wake* is not a work which encourages emulation."[86] Indeed, for the first prolific decade of his career, Barthelme avoided direct confrontation with Joyce except in a few minor sketches such as "Bone Bubbles." Nonetheless, Barthelme's early works provide an aesthetic which clearly mirrors the positions outlined in "After Joyce." Most of Barthelme's early works employ a fragmentary style, but, as Barthelme cautions, to reduce his aesthetic to a reliance on fragments oversimplifies his practice. Very little of Barthelme's work focuses on fragmentation as such; rather, it employs fragments as a parodic technique directed against the various forms of the debased languages and sensibilities of contemporary America. As Raymond Olderman observes, the intrusion of a fragment of "reality," a brand name, into an apparently symbolic landscape in *Snow White* serves to remind the reader that "any one part which appears fabulous may be as true as the part we have just recognized."[87] Barthelme perfects this technique in stories such as "Robert Kennedy Saved from Drowning," which has it "both ways," employing realistic and symbolic elements to shake the reader's comfort with either a political or an allegorical reading. The story's title and context intimate a political statement, but the Kafkaesque technique of identifying the central character only as "K" encourages an interpretation of the story as an allegory of alienation. On balance, the story "enforces the way [it] is to be read,"[88] a phrase Barthelme originally applied to *Finnegans Wake*. It demands that the reader focus on the juxtaposition within the work, rather than on an external political situation or a pre-conceived existential symbolism. As a result the reader's attitude toward either Kennedy or Kafka may change, but the original dialog has been carried out with Barthelme's work.

Barthelme succeeds best when he chooses his targets most carefully, parodying modes which have become decadent.[89] In *The Dead Father*, Barthelme loses sight of the appropriate (vulnerable?) satiric target and attempts to clear away not the debris, but the source of the novel's own style. Jerome Klinkowitz contends that *The Dead Father* attempts "to shake us back to our senses. . . . There's an energy which comes from rapid changes of context, the mixing of comic scenes and the fracturing of linguistic modes. It's the basic method which has made cinema the prime attention-getting medium of our time: montage, quick-cut, a whole repertoire of techniques which work as well for tragedy as for comedy—which have, indeed, become the tempo of our modern lives."[90] But the description applies at least as well to *Finnegans Wake*, and Barthelme's choice of "contexts" covers a far narrower range than either Joyce's work or Barthelme's own earlier stories. Perhaps the one insurmountable weakness in the novel is its failure to employ elements of a realistic mode to keep the reader from reading *The Dead Father* as a somewhat simplistic allegory. The weakness stands out so starkly because the book itself demands that we compare it with *Finnegans Wake*. Barthelme not only echoes numerous Wakean motifs, but also derives his own thematic concerns from the Joycean original.

The opening section of *The Dead Father* establishes *Finnegans Wake* as Barthelme's primary point of reference. Like Dublin's sleeping giant Finn, *The Dead Father* dominates the landscape: "No one can remember when he was not here in our city positioned like a sleeper in troubled sleep, the whole great expanse of him running from the Avenue Pommard to the Boulevard Grist" (*DF*, pp. 3–4). Barthelme's setting differs from Joyce's in that both his sleeping giant and his city remain nameless. This lack of specificity typifies *The Dead Father* throughout and contributes to the feeling that the novel is essentially an exercise in symbolism. Another direct allusion, oddly, reveals Barthelme's decision to direct his parody at the symbolic dimension of the *Wake*. Thomas's tale-within-a-tale concerning the Great Father Serpent concludes with his statement, "I was abroad in the city with murderinging in mind—the dream of a stutterer" (*DF*, p. 46). This alludes to the dream of the stutterer H. C. Earwicker, whose chief concern, like that in Thomas's fable, is the Oedipal threat posed by his sons. Significantly, Thomas identifies *himself* as the stutterer during a later confrontation with the Dead Father (*DF*, p. 56); like the Earwicker offspring, he takes on attributes of the father as he succeeds in carrying out his "murderinging."

This fluidity of character—the tendency of individuals to merge with one another and/or to exchange roles—occupies a major place in *The Dead Father*'s thematic structure. Just as Joyce's ALP and Issy, despite obvious differences, share a basic perception of men as children and/or tyrants, so Barthelme's Julie and Emma continually repeat each other's phrases, growing indistinguishable even while attacking one another (*DF*, pp. 23ff., 147ff.). But the primary focus of the fluid character motif concerns Thomas and the Dead Father. Gradually Thomas takes over the Dead Father's symbolic costume, appropriating buckle, sword, and passport (*DF*, pp. 47, 81, 157). The Dead Father complains, "When you are an old person you live in a small room small but neat and you don't have any cymbals any more they've taken your cymbals away from you" (*DF*, p. 150); clearly he no longer possesses the power to resist. The allegory seems transparent: in order to "bury" his father, Thomas must himself become his father. Because Barthelme has often demonstrated his sensitivity to the weakness of similar simplistic schemes, presumably *The Dead Father* attempts to "clear away the debris" of easy symbolic equations. In fact, Barthelme introduces just such a focus early in the novel, when Julie comments on the Dead Father's "slaying" fit as "Impressive . . . had they not been pure cardboard" (*DF*, p. 12).

Unfortunately, the statement becomes disturbingly self-reflexive when applied to the juxtaposition of *The Dead Father* and *Finnegans Wake*. While Joyce occasionally sets up cardboard targets, the success of his presentation of the concept of fluid character rests on his allusions to a "real" world. He presents the analogy between Earwicker and Isaac, for example, by providing precisely the kinds of disorienting fragments of reality which Barthelme employs so effectively in his stories but expunges almost entirely from *The Dead Father*. While occasional references to contemporary reality occur in *The Dead Father* (the surgeon on p. 44, for example), they are invariably general, invoking abstract notions of contemporary culture without reinforcing them with the particular "brand names" or personalities which jar the symbolic surfaces of *Snow White* and "Robert Kennedy Saved from Drowning." Only in the "Manual for Sons" section of *The Dead Father* does Barthelme achieve any real disorienting effects. And that section seems only weakly integrated with the main body of the work, functioning equally well when read as a separate story, its original mode of publication.

Barthelme compounds the difficulty by casting his penultimate chapter in *Wake* language. Although he comments on a "Great endifarce teeterteeterteeterteetering" (*DF*, p. 171)—i.e., his farce is on the verge of collapse—Barthelme seems intent on establishing the triviality of Joyce's language and themes. The two syllables which echo insistently through the chapter's three pages are "end" and "Pap," culminating in "Endeavoring to meet ends. To the bicker end. Endocarial endocarditis. Enewenewenew don't want to undertake the OldPap yet. Let's have a party. Pap in on a few old friends. Pass the papcorn" (*DF*, pp. 172–73). Perhaps Barthelme has overdone the passage intentionally—implying that Joyce's *Wake* language is too obvious (????). Perhaps he has simply crossed the fine line between parody and travesty. Or perhaps he employs the technique in an attempt to establish his own statement as equivalent in importance to Joyce's. Here, as in most of *The Dead Father*, Barthelme has been unable to force the reader to read the book on its own terms. Whatever its intent, the passage lacks the diverse frames of reference of even the most crystalline *Wake* passages. It degenerates into a dictionary game for the glossing of collapsing cardboard characters, leaving the reader with the feeling that he has confronted either a very un-Barthelmean allegorical failure or a parody which has failed to find its target.

Raymond Federman's total commitment to "concrete" art sets him apart from sympathizers such as Barthelme. Federman derives his conception of the concrete novel primarily from two groups: Samuel Beckett and the French New Novelists, and the concrete poets, particularly the Brazil-based Noigandres group. Significantly, both groups acknowledge Joyce's seminal influence, although the works they create reveal divergent readings of Joyce. The French group creates self-reflexive works which, if not symbolic, are romantic in that they evince little interest in social concerns except as they influence individual consciousness and/or the aesthetic surface. The Noigandres poets, conversely, repudiate all elements of what they refer to as "subjectivity" and claim to be thorough realists. Despite these areas of disagreement, both redefine the work of art as an object, a part of reality. Further, as Federman's *Double or Nothing* demonstrates, even their conflicting ideas can be reconciled in a single work.

Writing on *Finnegans Wake* while it was still *Work in Progress*, Beckett stated the attitude toward fiction which became a rallying cry for recent French novelists: "Here form *is* content, content *is* form. You complain that this stuff is not written in English. It is not written at all. It is not to be read—or rather it is not only to be read. It is to be looked at and listened to. His writing is not *about* something; *it is that something itself.*"[91] Federman has written on Beckett's work, and *Double or Nothing* contains numerous echoes of the preceding passage. While admitting that "The history of the novel is—one must admit it—nothing else but the succession of its efforts to 'appresent' a reality which always evades, always substitutes for vulgar mirrors finer mirrors, more selective mirrors," Federman claims that "the essence of a literary discourse—that is to say a discourse fixed once and for all—is to find its own point of reference, its own rules of organization in itself, and not in the real or imaginary experience, on which it rests."[92] This emphasis on the self-reflexive elements of the novel leads Federman, as it led Beckett in his trilogy, into the "counterpointing of different levels of discourse" which Vivien Mercier sees as a primary characteristic of the French New Novel.[93] This involvement with self-reflexive fiction clearly differentiates the French from the Brazilian proponents of concrete art.

The Noigandres' "Pilot Plan for Concrete Poetry," signed by Auguste and Harolde de Campos and Decie Pignatori, proclaims an aesthetic of "thorough realism. Against a poetry of expression, subjective and hedonistic," and cites Joyce's *Ulysses* and *Fin-*

negans Wake as major sources of the "word-ideogram, organic interpretation of time and space."[94] The emphasis in the Noigandres' work shifts from the self-reflexiveness of the New Novel to a concern with, as Mary Ellen Solt notes, "establishing [their] linguistic materials in a new relationship to space (the page or its equivalent) and/or to time (abandoning the old linear measure)."[95] Solt endorses Mike Weaver's subdivision of concrete poetry into "constructivist" and "expressionist" modes: "The constructivist poem results from an arrangement of materials according to a scheme or system set up by the poet which must be adhered to on its own terms (permutational poems). In the expressionist poem the poet arranges his material according to an intuitive structure."[96]

Federman combines these modes in *Double or Nothing.* Each page of the novel presents a different "constructivist" system, while Federman's "expressionist" intuition maintains control over the ordering and juxtaposition of the pages. The key to this expressionist order lies in the concern with levels of discourse and self-reflexivity derived from Federman's French sources. While blending these elements, Federman demonstrates much more effectively than Barthelme in *The Dead Father* that "realism" and "symbolism" can be seen as equally arbitrary manipulations of a concrete fictional reality.

Federman employs a variety of constructivist devices such as the shaping of words to create the visual images of noodles (*DN*, pp. 7, 11), stars (*DN*, p. 34.0) and an ocean voyage (*DN*, p. 97.1). Sometimes the devices are grammatical, such as the omission of verbs (*DN*, p. 140). Occasionally pictorial and linguistic devices are combined, as in the highly effective use of a jarring column of the phrase "ALARM CLOCKS" down the middle of a page focusing on early morning (*DN*, p. 131). Perhaps the most interesting constructivist devices are those which provide connections with the novel's expressionist dimension. The page separating the "This Is Not the Beginning" and the "Beginning" sections consists of a block of the word "noodles" with plus, minus, triangle, and inverted triangle signs formed by blank spaces. The page seems enigmatic, but Federman provides a key on page 129, where the symbols recur in the context of a discussion of the convergence of levels of discourse. Federman employs the constructivist device to intimate the final unity within an artistic structure of the novel's "four persons," each of whom possesses a separate "sign." This use of symbols resembles Joyce's use of sigla in connection with the characters in the *Wake*.[97]

Federman assigns specific roles to the "persons" in *Double or Nothing*. The "first person" is described (the passive voice is an absolute necessity in discussing a novel without a distinct narrator) as a man who "simply wanted *to record*, to the best of his ability and as objectively as possible, but for reasons that were never clearly stated (man is indeed inexplicable), the activities of the second" (*DN*, p. oo). The second person is determined to lock himself in a room for a year and "write the story of the young man who had come to America from France (by boat) and who had such a ROUGH time during the war and was now an orphan" (*DN*, p. oo). This young man is the novel's "third person." Federman extends the complexities in a final note on the juxtaposition of the persons:

> It should be noted here that overlooking the whole intramural set up described in the preceding pages obviously there has to be a fourth person Someone to control organize supervise if you wish the activities and relations of the other three persons Someone who can keep things going in an orderly manner who can resolve arguments smooth out difficulties Someone who like a father or like a supervisor but not necessarily like an inventor The second person is the inventor nor like a recorder That function belongs to the first person And of course not like a protagonist The third person will fit into that role eventually. [*DN*, p. oooooooooo.o]

But there is still another voice which explains the relationship of the fourth person to the other levels, a voice responsible for the actual writing of the "This Is Not the Beginning" section. Since every voice in the novel cautions against identifying any piece of writing with any actual human being, it seems safe to assume that we are not to attribute the explanatory section to an actual "Raymond Federman." Are we then to attribute it to the "fourth person," thereby necessitating the conceptualization of a fifth?

I think not, though of course nothing precludes such a pastime. The point both of the sign-page and of the discussion of the persons seems to me to be simply that the novel can neither entirely avoid subjectivity nor accurately encompass an actual author's reality. *Double or Nothing* (and in this way it closely resembles Flann O'Brien's *At Swim-Two-Birds*) frequently and purposefully confuses its levels. This happens most clearly in the juxtaposition of the second and third persons; the second person often "makes" the third person's experience resemble his own (*DN*, pp. 31, 41, 123). But it is equally clear that the second person is merely a creation of the first person, the "recorder" who despite his theoretical lack of involvement makes constant choices concerning what is "simple reality." Significantly, he chooses to record the second person's fantasies and thoughts, rather than limiting himself to the physical activity which traditionally commands the realist's attention. The relationship of first and second persons differs from that of the second and third persons only in that the first person is "silent." Of course, bringing the fourth person into consideration simply extends the pattern. The fact that the third person's experiences follow in general outline the course of Federman's life emphasizes the point that the "real" Raymond Federman stands in direct relationship to *each* of the persons in *Double or Nothing*. Together they provide a fuller indication of the reflected author than does any one separately; but they do not, and cannot, exhaust him.

Federman accompanies this redefinition of the role of author and personae with an analogous treatment of fictional modes. On the surface the first person appears to be a realist—he wishes merely to record what happens—while the second person is a romantic—a Beckettian solipsist, shutting himself off from society to explore his own artistic impulses. The distinctions, however, break down almost as rapidly as they are established. The first person's "record" includes practically no verifiable action. "What happens" to the second person is nearly nothing. At the same time, the second person concerns himself obsessively with the "real" events, which "happen" to the third person. Federman's point, of course, is that nothing has ever "happened" to any fictional person, that all happenings ultimately resolve into words on a page and that the mental events of the second person's story are every bit as real as the physical events of the third person's. Federman treats both realism and symbolism as fictional "ingredients" which may be used within, but can never supersede, the concrete fictional reality. Federman acknowledges the basic modes early in *Double or Nothing*: "SOME GUYS ARE DREAMERS/SOME GUYS ARE REALISTS" (*DN*, p. 5). The second person can at times remind himself that "every detail counts" (*DN*, p. 86) in his book; at other times he can decide that "the room or rooms will become symbolic after awhile" (*DN*, p. 127). The linguistic and pictorial image of the noodle, however, counterbalances all such arbitrary decisions and distinctions. The second person's decision to express his perceptions of American "reality" "symbolically" (*DN*, pp. 108–11) metamorphoses from a hilarious plan for "A NOODLE MAP OF AMERICA" (*DN*, p. 109) into a noodle-shaped philosophical reflection on symbolism as a means of dealing with intractable reality (*DN*, p. 111). The words "NOODLE REALITY" run sideways along the edge of the page, just as "NOODLE MAP" forms a rectangle around the border of the preceding page. The fourth person's manipulation of the typography and juxtaposition of "serious" discourse with playful disruption leaves the reader with a very strong impression of NOODLE and a very weak conviction of the seriousness of the debate over fictional modes. The second person's insistence that "you just can't mix reality and fantasy like that just for fun you just can't it doesn't work or else the whole system is all screwed up all fucked up etc" (*DN*, p. 62) clearly reflects his own paranoia, rather than Federman's aesthetic.

Double or Nothing, then, presents a consistent and entertaining, if at times exasperating, critique of fictional modes. I have attempted to treat it in the terms it suggests for itself. But a further question needs to be posed: is *Double or Nothing* a novel or a disguised aesthetic tract? Federman would almost certainly reject the question, claiming that words are words, that the experience should not be subjected to arbitrary categorization. Still, since my primary concern is with influence and the development of a genre, I believe the distinction to be real, if not desirable. Readers of novels, past, present, and almost certainly future, may accept and adjust to radical theories of reality when accompanied by a compelling fiction; very few have ever accepted a theory and then demanded fiction embodying that theory. If *Double or Nothing* simply presents a theory of the novel, it will almost certainly fail to compel a wide audience to accept its theory.

In fact, the book does provide something of the individual sensibility which enabled Joyce to create his own readers. Primarily through the experience of the third person, *Double or Nothing* grapples with the holocaust and the alienation of a young immigrant adjusting to racial and sexual reality in America. Federman, however, refuses to present a fully realized treatment of either issue; his persons avoid confrontations with the holocaust, often by covering their deepest concerns with rows of Xs (*DN*, pp. 7.1, 153). Ronald Sukenick's suggestion that this device indicates "that the experience of the Holocaust is more than language can comprehend or communicate"[98] seems correct, and Federman's perception may well be accurate. As a central novelistic focus, however, the perception fails to justify Federman's demands on his readers. The primary justification for a revolutionary technique lies in its ability to extend the sensibility of the writer and/ or reader further than have previous approaches. The controlling sensibility of *Double or Nothing*, and of Federman's second novel, *Take It Or Leave It*, remains well within the frontiers reached by practitioners of less difficult novelistic forms. To date, Federman's work provides a challenging, but only marginally compelling, exercise in aesthetic theory.

William Melvin Kelley's *Dunfords Travels Everywheres* recreates a Joycean dreamscape and demands that its readers wake up to political reality. Even while crafting an intricately textured novel, Kelley rejects the aesthetic emphasis common to Federman and Barthelme, implying that *Finnegans Wake* provides crucial weapons for the struggle of blacks against physical and cultural oppression. One of the three epigraphs to *Dunfords Travels Everywheres* quotes Stephen Dedalus' meditation on the English language: "The language in which we are speaking is his before it is mine. . . . I cannot speak or write these words without unrest of spirit. His language, so familiar and so foreign, will always be for me an acquired speech. . . . My soul frets in the shadow of his language."[99] The epigraph serves both as Kelley's acknowledgment of the Joycean influence on *Dunfords Travels Everywheres* and as an analogy between the cultural situation of the Irish and the Afro-Americans, both forced to adopt the culture and language of alien rulers. *Finnegans Wake* unambiguously asserts Joyce's freedom from (or, more accurately, within) the English language which he has claimed for his own purposes; unrest of spirit drove him to forge a language able to accommodate his own perceptions. Similarly, *Dunfords Travels Everywheres* attempts to liberate Kelley's people from the continuing "slavery" imposed by their failure to reject the condescension and manipulation of Euro-American language and culture, and to employ the resources of their own idiom.

Kelley's attitude toward Joyce combines almost awe-full appreciation with a strong note of defiance. Grace Eckley has catalogued Kelley's borrowings from *Finnegans Wake*, which include specific motifs, general thematic patterns, and particular Norse myths.[100] While such allusions and Kelley's adaptation of *Wake* language may be seen as an homage to Joyce, Kelley clearly believes in the independent importance of his own work: "Says I, if il (jam jey) peut do it, I conduit too, faire le well I'si raisen, for the tongue of the queen in the mouths of my mumble brothers, lessens d'Afrique in d'prisome across d'water."[101] The passage reveals Kelley's confidence that he can match Joyce as it reveals his didactic purpose, his concern with the lessons of African people in their American prison. As Addison Gayle observes, the chief lesson is that the black man must confront "the illusionary world" of Euro-American culture and abrogate "the contract which surrendered his culture, history and racial identity centuries ago."[102] Eckley notes that this abrogation necessitates a rejection of sexual exploitation of blacks by whites, and that the image of Africa as a beautiful woman, "the source of all emcergy" (*DTE*, p. 53), serves as Kelley's ideal. In *Dunfords Travels Everywheres*, Kelley attempts to bring this ideal into harmony with the social realities of the intellectual Chig Dunford and the street-wise Carlyle Bedlow.

Kelley addresses his "lessons" to a composite figure first identified as "Mr. Chigle" (*DTE*, p. 49). The name undergoes a multitude of changes but seems an amalgam of Chig (the reflective Afro-American), Carlyle (the active Afro-American), and Mr. Charlie (an idiomatic term for white people). So, while Kelley wishes to communicate first to Afro-Americans, *Dunfords Travels Everywheres* also contains lessons for Euro-American readers. Kelley shapes the dream segments of his novel to communicate more directly with Afro-American than with Euro-American readers; the latter are more likely to be committed to the standard English which, Kelley believes, embodies the oppressive Euro-American culture. Standard English is "Mr. Chigyle's Languish" (*DTE*, p. 49)—Mr. Charlie's language which leaves both Chig and Carlyle languishing as long as they unreflectively accept it. Later it is "the Langleash language" (*DTE*, p. 86)—a restraining leash binding Afro-Americans to the standards of "correct" language and attitudes. Despite his Ivy League education, Chig remains unaware of the power of language until late in the novel. Though his inability to remember the words of a patriotic song (*DTE*, p. 45) emphasizes his position as an outsider, he shocks himself by saying "No, motherfuckers" (*DTE*, p. 46) to white companions. Chig worries over his instinctive use of a phrase from the street language of Harlem: "Where on earth had those words come from? He tried always to choose his words with care, to hold back even anger until he found the correct words. Luckily, he had never suffered a pronunciation problem. His family lived in Harlem; he had grown up there but had no trouble saying that, they, these, those or them" (*DTE*, p. 46). He fails to appreciate either the importance of his refusal to play his social role or his deep affinity with Carlyle, who uses similar phrases without anxiety. Locked into Euro-American modes of thought, Chig learns only slowly. When Wendy calls him a nigger, he reacts to the word automatically, assuming that it embodies a rejection: "The nigger had hid behind all the words all that time. He simply never wanted to hear or see it" (*DTE*, p. 149). Only when it is too late to establish contact does he discover, and then only because the white girl Lynn tells him, that Wendy merely passed for white in order to serve the interests of a black political organization. Chig claims to have registered something strange in her voice which connected her with the black "Family": "He could not help smiling: Wendy came from Virginia, had worked for the Family, had died. He had heard it all in the nigger, but had not seen her through her skin" (*DTE*, p. 167). In fact, he has been as unable as the average educated white to penetrate Wendy's "mask." His acculturation alienates him from his heritage. Only in a dream can Chig articulate his uncertainty concerning Wendy. Her dream image reflects Chig's incorrect interpretation of her racial identity—she appears as a blonde. In the dream Chig realizes: "that whooshn't his windy near as he could reember her, though he knew its suckled meaning" (*DTE*, p. 93). When he wakes up, he ponders why his dream's Wendy had blonde hair. "Wendy's hair had hung long and black" (*DTE*, p. 94). But he fails to answer the question, and his failure contributes to Wendy's final "elimination" by the TYO slaver organizations.

Throughout *Dunfords Travels Everywheres* Kelley's dream language veils its meaning from those limited to Euro-American frames of reference. Eckley falls victim to this cultural limitation when she limits her discussion of mythology in *Dunfords Travels Everywheres* to the Norse tales. Her failure to recognize several Afro-American myths leads to slightly off-center interpretations of the dream in chapter 9 as a variation of the Uncle Tom story and of the dream in chapter 30 as an adaptation of a TV western. While both elements are present, neither is primary to Kelley's lesson. "Uncle Turtom" (*DTE*, p. 55) is more the tortoise of Afro-American animal fables than Uncle Tom; and, while "C. Turtom" and "S. Rabisam" in chapter 30 may be cowboys, they derive primarily from Brer Turtle (or Tortoise) and Brer Rabbit ("Brevtert" and "Brosrab"; *DTE*, p. 195). Like their predecessors in Afro-American folklore, Kelley's protagonists employ their wits to get the better of opponents with superior strength—"frerbare" or Brer Bear (*DTE*, p. 194), immoral cunning "Mr. Foxx" (*DTE*, p. 192) who also turns up as "Mr. Phox" (*DTE*, p. 93) in Chig's dream of Wendy. Throughout Afro-American folklore the larger hostile animals represent white attitudes and behavior. Their downfall reflects the black desire for vengeance which, not merely during slavery times or in the South, has been given relatively little physical expression.

Recognizing the primary references of the two sections clarifies their lessons. Brer Tortoise and Brer Rabbit rely not on the moral rectitude of the original Uncle Tom or on the six-guns of the contemporary TV cowboy, but on a careful manipulation of their antagonists' sense of reality. In *Dunfords Travels Everywheres* language provides the primary tool for manipulating perception. Kelley establishes several "false bottoms" within his *Wake* segments; the basic meaning often contradicts that implied by the obvious Euro-American references. As the dream voice warns: "Behind a manger a manager! Bind an image and doubt squeezes a man, a swomen up the same stream, and he macks it because he must, mike no mystic about the lesson, Mr. Chairlyle" (*DTE*, p. 59). Kelley extends the advice of the narrator's grandfather in Ralph Ellison's *Invisible Man* who says, "Our life is a war and I have been a traitor all my born days, a spy in the enemy's country ever since I give up my gun back in the Reconstruction. Live with your head in the lion's mouth. I want you to overcome 'em with yeses, undermine 'em with grins, agree 'em to death and destruction, let 'em swoller you till they vomit or bust wide open."[103] Kelley suggests merely that the black man be prepared to employ the weapon in the voice appropriate to his situation: "The answer's in saying Yeses? Ye in the Northeast, yup en la Oeste, yeas in the Ease, Yazza in the Zouth" (*DTE*, p. 199). Near the conclusion of *Dunfords Travels Everywheres* he states his determination to follow his own advice: "Oilready Ivbegin tshift mVoyace" (*DTE*, p. 201).

Kelley, unlike Federman, fully realizes his theoretical point within his novel. Balancing real and symbolic experiences, Kelley demonstrates the potential for employing masks for political purposes. Chig, through most of *Dunfords Travels Everywheres*, lives in a symbolic world which distracts his attention from the real conflicts shaping his life as a black man. Carlyle, conversely, copes perfectly well with immediate reality but lacks the capacity to generalize from his experiences, to teach his people the lessons he has learned. Gradually, through the mediation of the Wakean voice which forms a composite of Chig and Carlyle, Kelley brings the levels together in a powerful plea for Afro-American unity.

The dreamlike setting of the opening chapters delineates the dangers of Chig's naively romantic belief that he can live as an American expatriate just as his white companions do. The group spouts the rhetoric of human equality; Marion states a romantic creed: "Today we just have to throw ourselves open to all human beings. . . . We have to spread it in our art" (*DTE*, p. 5). Chig attempts to live as if this "brotherhood" has succeeded in establishing freedom from racial oppression. Similarly, the "color codes" of the imaginary European setting treat color barriers as arbitrarily determined, and ultimately tractable, results of free choice:

> On the right side of the ringing wire, the native men and women of that country wore suits, jackets, pants, dresses, skirts and shirts in hues and mixture of blue and red. On the left side, the

natives wore combinations of yellow and red. Neither side's colors appeared all bright, or drab, all new or all old; but when Chig squinted, the colors blended that way.

One of that country's oldest traditions, many foreigners found it difficult to understand. None of the natives on either side of the wire owned wardrobes composed of one side's colors. In the morning, each native in the country would pick an outfit for that day. He might choose blue-red or yellow-red, making himself for the day, an Atzeoreurso or a Jualoreurso.

In the street, each native lived the day his morning choice had dictated. [*DTE*, pp. 2–3]

Like the dream scenes, this passage contains a deceptive surface meaning. Kelley offers the reader, like Chig, the opportunity to interpret the custom as an allegory of the existential significance of American racial relations: all people share a basic humanity (the constant red color) and only arbitrary codes keep Americans from interacting freely on an individual basis as the natives do in their own homes. Color differences, while ancient customs, appear to be subject to fairly simple political solution: remove the arbitrary customs (the clothing) and no one will be able to maintain the old distinctions.

Chig's situation, however, does not parallel that of his white "friends" or of either group of natives. The result of American "color codes" is not simply to separate the races, but to condemn blacks to a social situation which denies their humanity. As long as Chig fails to perceive his realistic position, he can be used by whites as a symbol protecting their own position: "Our having Chig in the car showed them we weren't the kind of people they were against" (*DTE*, p. 16). As the ongoing battle between the Family and the TYO indicates, the color codes of the United States have generated what amounts to a war which has roots running far deeper than legislated customs and which is not going to be solved by simplistic humanistic rhetoric.

Carlyle's problem requires less explanation than Chig's. From the beginning he understands the realities of black life in America. When the black bourgeois dentist's wife complains of white hypocrisy, "The point is when I saw they lied about caring, I looked into everything they said, and you know what? They lied about everything," Carlyle responds simply, "Hell, I known that since I was seven" (*DTE*, p. 74). Nor does Carlyle hesitate to act on his awareness. Like the folk hero Stack-o-Lee, he outwits and overpowers "the devil" in the battle for Hondo's soul. He assumes a demonic power himself at the confrontation: "Carlyle threw the Devil a shrug, patted the lump in his pocket. 'If the Devil's me, you'll never make it. And if he's you, you still might not make it'" (*DTE*, p. 175). But he fails to understand either the significance of his own physical actions or the symbolic gesture of the dentist's wife who sends him a cryptic postcard from Africa hinting at the importance of the African heritage (*DTE*, p. 85). The final image of Carlyle emphasizes both his potential contribution to the Afro-American cause and his failure of articulation: "Without hair, without a voice, he could have come from anywhere. Dark enough to pass for an African, his clothes had a South American flair" (*DTE*, p. 186).

Kelley's resolution of Chig and Carlyle takes place only in the final chapter, the story of Brer Turtle and Brer Rabbit. Prior to the chapter, he brings the pair together in the Grouse Bar in Harlem. Chig's arrival in Harlem signals his return from the unreal, romantic Europe. As a result of his painful confrontation with the symbolic racial war between the white Tiwaz Youth Organization and the black Family aboard the "slave ship" on which he returns to the United States, Chig brings to the Grouse the precise awareness of the nature of the American racial conflict which Carlyle lacks. Realistic competence and symbolic awareness exist in the same room; it remains only for Kelley in the final dream chapter to unite them and to propose the weapons of racial unity and the manipulation of Euro-American perceptions of reality, the determination to "yes" the whites to death and destruction. Kelley's dream language sounds one alarm to awaken Afro-Americans to the danger of accepting the Euro-American culture embodied in a language which enforces a stifling vision of reality.

William Burroughs rejects ideological approaches to literature; he views *Finnegans Wake* primarily as a warning against excessive experimentation. Nonetheless, *The Ticket That Exploded* extends some of Joyce's techniques in an attempt to carry out what LeRoi Jones calls "the whole social reconstruction that should have taken place in order for one to write intelligent fiction after Joyce."[104] Like Barthelme, Burroughs parodies numerous fictional and social institutions; like Federman, he employs unusual compositional methods to force an apprehension of his words as autonomous objects; like Kelley, he demands a reconciliation of physical action and symbolic apprehension. Most importantly, as Marshall McLuhan observes, Burroughs, like Joyce, "was sure he had worked out the formula for total cultural understanding and control." [105]

Burroughs's attitude toward Joyce alternates between the position that Joyce only began to exploit his own techniques and the criticism that he carried them too far. Responding to the charge of obscurity often leveled against experimental fiction, Burroughs notes that "any writer who hopes to approximate what actually occurs in the mind and body of his characters cannot confine himself to such an arbitrary structure as 'logical' sequence. Joyce was accused of being unintelligible and he was presenting only one level of cerebral events: conscious sub-vocal speech. I think it is possible to create multilevel events and characters that a reader could comprehend with his entire organic being." [106] Burroughs's most famous attempt to create such multilevel fictional events is the "cut-up" method, involving the blending of two or more texts. In *The Ticket That Exploded* a machine carries out a similar procedure: "A writing machine that shifts one half one text and half the other through a page frame on conveyor belts—(The proportion of half one text half the other is important corresponding as it does to the two halves of the human organism) Shakespeare, Rimbaud, etc. permutating through page frames in constantly changing juxtaposition the machine spits out books and plays and poems." [107] In fact, Burroughs subjected Joyce's texts to a cut-up method as part of *Nova Express*. Despite this involvement with Joyce, Burroughs remains skeptical of *Finnegans Wake*, which itself goes well beyond merely transcribing sub-vocal speech; Burroughs comments, "I think *Finnegans Wake* rather represents a trap into which experimental writing can fall when it becomes purely experimental. I would go so far with any given experiment and then come back; that is, I am coming back now to write purely conventional straightforward narrative. But applying what I have learned from the cut-up and the other techniques to the problem of conventional writing. It's simply if you go too far in one direction, you can never get back, and you're out there in complete isolation."[108] Burroughs's social interests render isolation a totally unacceptable condition.

Despite Burroughs's reservations, McLuhan is correct when he argues that *"Finnegans Wake* provides the closest literary antecedent to Burroughs's work. From beginning to end it is occupied with the theme of 'the extensions' of man. . . . Joyce works out in every detail the sensory shifts involved in each extension."[109] *The Ticket That Exploded* too analyzes the sensory shifts induced by technological extensions of humanity. The source of Burroughs's doubts concerning *Finnegans Wake,* however, lies in his perception that such shifts often dehumanize the individuals they affect. In addition, he perceives the disquieting presence in experimental fiction of manipulative tools indistinguishable from those used by the forces it ostensibly resists.

The Ticket That Exploded posits that unnamed forces have established control over "reality" which Burroughs defines as "a more-or-less constant scanning pattern."[110] By juxtaposing segments of images or words from different sources, the forces create "ghost images" with no physical existence: "You can get the same effect by switching a recording on and off at very short intervals. Listen carefully and you will hear words that were not in the original text" (*TTE,* p. 26). The similarity to Burroughs's own cut-up method demonstrates the very tenuous separation of the forces of "good" and "evil" in his fiction.

The manipulation of sexual images in order to breed neurosis in the individual who finds himself stimulated by a ghost image characterizes the "evil" forces in *The Ticket That Exploded.* Within the confines of a sexual amusement park, individuals enter cubicles in which "screens permutate partners divided down the middle line until there is no way to distinguish film from flesh and the flesh melts" (*TTE,* p. 69). Burroughs embodies the ghost partner in the figure of Johnny Yen, "The Boy-Girl Other Half strip tease God of sexual frustration" (*TTE,* p. 53). Ultimately obsession with an unreal sexual partner leads to utter debasement: "The victim is seen abusing himself publicly while addressing some unseen presence with endearing terms—He becomes dirty and emaciated—In the final stages he is literally eaten alive by his invisible partner" (*TTE,* p. 96). *The Ticket That Exploded* portrays a series of such victims, including the young Monk dancing naked around his tape recorder (*TTE*, p. 43), and Kiki, whose lover dissolves into a cloth leaking dust (*TTE*, p. 109).

To the extent that the evil forces maintain control over communications systems, they can maintain power unchallenged. Since they have created a social system based on ghost eroticism, the individuals subject to the system naturally fear being isolated from even their debased pleasures. The system possesses great leverage which it turns to self-perpetuation:

> The film bank is empty. To conceal the bankruptcy of the reality studio it is essential that no one should be in position to set up another reality set. The reality film has now become an instrument and weapon of monopoly. The full weight of the film is directed against anyone who calls the film in question with particular attention to writers and artists. Work for the reality studio or else. Or else you will find out how it feels to be *outside the film*. [*TTE*, p. 151]

Burroughs argues that the misuse of communications has led to a situation in which "The word is now a virus. . . . The word may once have been a healthy neural cell. It is now a parasitic organism that invades and damages the central nervous system" (*TTE*, p. 49). Burroughs attacks the very phenomena which he identifies as the basis of Joyce's style: "Modern man has lost the option of silence. Try halting your sub-vocal speech. Try to achieve even ten seconds of inner silence. You will encounter a resisting organism that *forces you to talk*" (*TTE*, p. 49). In other words, man's stream of consciousness renders him susceptible to sexual manipulation. Joyce's presentation, while realistic, functions to perpetuate the phenomenon which is the rest of the problem.

Ihab Hassan sees Burroughs's primary reaction to this problem as an "icy rage against language."[111] Further, Hassan believes that Burroughs's "true aim is to free man by making him bodiless and silencing his language."[112] *The Ticket That Exploded* does not bear out the first claim, and it supports the second only in a limited sense. Far from endorsing a "bodiless" state, Burroughs urges physical sexual consummation as an antidote to ghost eroticism. Burroughs lyrically presents the apparently autobiographical story of Bill and John, who overcome their feelings of separation through sexual contact (*TTE*, pp. 112–17). Their relationship offers the only fully realized image of individual resistance to manipulation through image in *The Ticket That Exploded*. As Burroughs writes: "A street boy's courage exploded the word" (*TTE*, p. 136).

A large part of John's appeal stems from his ability to be silent. He tells Bill that "Maybe that would be the first step . . . yes if we could learn to listen and not talk" (*TTE*, p. 114). Sensitivity to another existence follows from silence rather than from noise, and to this extent Hassan is correct concerning Burroughs's goal. Burroughs states the concept more fully in an extended meditation on the necessity of fully experiencing physical reality:

> Your sound track consists of your body sounds and sub-vocal speech. Sub-vocal speech is the word organism the "Other Half." Spliced in with your body sounds You are convinced by association that your body sounds will stop if sub-vocal speech stops and so it happens. Death is the final separation of sound and image tracks. However, once you have broken the chains of association linking sub-vocal speech with body sounds shutting off sub-vocal speech need not entail shutting off body sounds and consequent death. [*TTE*, p. 160]

Silence attracts Burroughs only in the context of continuing bodily existence.

Burroughs also realizes that silence cannot serve as an immediate goal. First responsible individuals must develop techniques for countering the manipulation of communications systems: "Communication must become total and conscious before we can stop it" (*TTE*, p. 51). Burroughs proposes that the weapons of the manipulators be turned back against them. When confronted with an attempt at manipulation, Burroughs suggests, the best response is random noise which will disrupt the carefully modulated control attempt: "the use of irrelevant response will be found effective in breaking obsessional association tracks all association tracks are obsessional get it out of your head and into the machines stop arguing stop complaining stop talking let the machines argue complain and talk" (*TTE*, p. 213). Beyond mere disruption, Burroughs envisions a situation in which resisters "will learn to give the cues you will learn to plant events and concepts after analyzing recorded conversations you will learn to steer a conversation where you want it to go the physiological liberation achieved as word lines of controlled association are cut will make you more efficient in reaching your objectives whatever you do you will do it better" (*TTE*, p. 208). Significantly, the final source of resistance material lies within the body itself: "record their body sounds from concealed mikes the rhythm of breathing the movements of after-lunch intestines the beating of hearts now impose your own body sounds and become the breathing word and the beating heart of that organization" (*TTE*, p. 209). Only when the individual proves capable of disrupting the manipulative systems imposed upon him can he hope to attain Burroughs's ideal state of bodied silence.

Just as he expressed reservations concerning the implications of Joyce's style, Burroughs questions his own. After recommending response in kind as a method of protecting the individual's humanity, he poses the crucial question: "why stop there/why stop anywhere" (*TTE*, p. 211). No easy answer exists. Burroughs can only observe, "It would seem that a technique a tool is good or bad according to who uses it and for what purposes" (*TTE*, p. 21), and direct his own attention to responsible ends. To him the forces of evil are those who perpetuate unreconciled opposition, who follow the simple creed, "Always create as many insoluble counter-orders and alternative conflicts recordings to the explosion of a planet" (*TTE*, p. 170). The forces of good are those who use their techniques to resolve these disjunctions between reality and the distorted symbolic systems, those who "remember good is better than evil because its nicer to have around you. Its just as simple as that" (*TTE*, pp. 194–95). While Burroughs knows it's not that simple, he also knows that, given social reality, he will often be forced to act, to use ambiguously moral techniques, as if it is.

CHAPTER FOUR

Individual Encyclopedias:
In Search of the Big Novel

JOYCE CONTAINS MULTITUDES. *Ulysses* and *Finnegans Wake* transmit vast amounts of information about the world and, at the same time, explore individual existence in minute detail. In effect, they accept Walt Whitman's challenge to the modern writer to simultaneously sing the song of himself and that of the world. Joyce's works, like those of the very few consummate writers of world literature—Dante, Shakespeare, Blake, Dostoevsky, perhaps Melville and Whitman in their best moments—define themselves. Attempts to explain their greatness inevitably end in oversimplification. Contemporary writers of towering aspiration, such as Saul Bellow, Ralph Ellison, John Barth, and Norman Mailer, share with Joyce (and, in the American tradition, with Whitman) the impulse to tell the reader everything they know about the world— to write encyclopedias—and to encompass individual human personalities—to write supreme biographies.

Both of Joyce's masterpieces combine these impulses. *Ulysses* concentrates on several biographies—those of Stephen, Bloom, and Molly—as a method of providing Joyce's full range of information about their world. *Finnegans Wake* deemphasizes, although it by no means abandons, the interest in the individual; it catalogs Joyce's vast knowledge of the world in a more direct manner and then uses the encyclopedia to afford new perspectives on the Earwicker family biography. The very breadth of Joyce's knowledge and the detail of his characterizations establish him as the century's most imposing literary presence. Even those writers who feel the least direct affinity with Joyce's temperament strive to create works which will encompass as much and receive the same critical attention as *Ulysses* and *Finnegans Wake*.

Ronald Sukenick, who shares the aspiration, comments on precisely this emblematic aspect of Joyce's achievement and its effect on American writing:

> Fiction in the fifties was august and self-confident, not for any good reason, it just was. The novel was still the great symphonic form in the world of letters. There was the tradition of the "great novel." Fiction thought of itself as evolving periodically into imposing masterpieces that would justify the form. The important thing about *Ulysses* was not that it called into question the very fictive tradition it epitomized, but that it was a "great novel," one in a series. Only that could explain the awe in which it was held and the totality with which it was ignored by fiction in the fifties. Fiction at that time paid a great deal of lip service to Joyce, Kafka, Lawrence, Proust, Faulkner and literary modernism, but somehow all that had very little to do with us, with fiction in America.[1]

While Sukenick's attitude toward the 1950s—which produced William Gaddis as well as J. D. Salinger—is something less than just, he perceives one of the main differences in emphasis among the major post-Joycean American novelists. Bellow and Ellison write "great novels"; they craft their works carefully, relatively secure in their belief that traditional approaches to characterization provide the most effective means of transmitting their encyclopedic visions. *Herzog* and *Invisible Man* employ particular techniques pioneered by the modernists—there is no danger of confusing either with a Victorian novel—but they rarely seek to radically alter the reader's attitude toward the nature of fiction. John Barth's earlier work, culminating in *Giles Goat-Boy*, marks a more radical approach to the world. But later Barth novels, such as *Letters*, and the recent works of Norman Mailer directly challenge the conception of the consummate novel as "one in a series" of similar works. Seeing the essence of previous "big novels" in their ability to create forms able to encompass new visions, they emphasize the idiosyncrasy of their perspectives. Where Bellow and Ellison communicate their visions through the comparatively objective filters of traditional personae, Mailer and

Barth enter their works themselves. Admitting that their knowledge of the world derives ultimately from their own experience, they combine the individual and encyclopedic urges in "performances" which blend autobiography, essay, and whatever other forms seem appropriate with aspects of the traditional novel. For Mailer and Barth, the novel becomes one performance in an open-ended organic unit, rather than an addition to a moribund series of monuments.

The Individual Encyclopedias differ greatly, but all share a profound moral sense, a sense common to each of the consummate works of world literature. The idea of the moral sense should not be taken simplistically. Joyce is no Aesop; Dostoevsky doubts the existence of a moral base at times; the orthodox Dante cannot be reduced to platitudes. Perhaps Whitman best describes the moral function of the greatest art. The individual element, whether filtered through a persona or specifically autobiographical, is important because, as Whitman says, "all else in the contributions of a nation or age, through its politics, materials, heroic personalities, military eclat, etc., remains crude, and defers, in any close and thoroughgoing estimate, until vitalized by national, original archetypes in literature."[2] The individual must vitalize the encyclopedia in order to enable human beings to benefit from the multiplicity of the world. And, whether the work is conceived as one in a series or as an organic performance, Whitman continues,

> The true question to ask respecting a book, is, *has it help'd any human soul?* This is the hint, statement, not only of the great literatus, his book, but of every great artist. It may be that all works of art are to be first tried by their art qualities, their image-forming talent, and their dramatic, pictorial, plot-constructing, euphonious and other talents. Then, whenever claiming to be first-class works, they are to be strictly and sternly tried by their foundation in, and radiation, in the highest sense and always indirectly, of, the ethic principles and eligibility to free, arouse, dilate.[3]

The aesthetic beauty of Bellow and Ellison, of Barth and Mailer, of Joyce, rests finally on their radiation of the kind of moral sympathy which, though increasingly indirectly as the twentieth century progresses, still has the power to succor the human spirit.

The Writer as Craftsman: Saul Bellow, Ralph Ellison

Saul Bellow and Ralph Ellison write out of a profound ambivalence concerning individuality. Like Joyce, both perceive the limitations imposed by too narrow a focus on any individual's apprehension of reality. No one character, they feel, sees the full encyclopedic variety of reality. Simultaneously, however, they understand that to humanize the encyclopedia, to make it comprehensible to the individual reader, they must relate it to a "representative" individual sensibility. Employing the Emersonian position which views the individual as the focal point of the search for meaning in external reality, *Herzog* and *Invisible Man* present individual characters discovering the necessity of relying on their own perceptions, particularly when they defend the self's integrity against external definitions. They also warn of the danger of failing to place these perceptions in their realistic context.

Like Joyce, both Bellow and Ellison carefully establish ironic distance between themselves and their protagonists. They freely alter "facts" to strengthen the structures of their novels, structures which transform masses of chaotic information into coherent encyclopedias. This ironic distancing originates in the novelist's perception of the difficulty of attempting to forge links between external facts and intense individual experiences. As Tony Tanner argues, the overwhelming intensity and variety of American culture frequently leads novelists to "turn back to the self and the experienced authenticity and relevance of its specific responses."[4] Although neither Bellow nor Ellison ultimately returns to this romantic individuality, each focuses on a character who feels a strong pull in that direction. Fully aware of the tendency of external pressures to turn the individual back in upon himself, Joyce created a similar character in Stephen Dedalus. Such a dominating character poses the artist with the aesthetic problem of establishing a position distinct from that of the romantic protagonist. Joyce's solution in *Ulysses* was to impose a clearly authorial order on both the encyclopedia and the individual character reacting to it. The intricate interrelationship of the novel's eighteen episodes originates with Joyce the craftsman, not with Stephen Dedalus or Leopold Bloom. Bellow and Ellison follow Joyce in crafting intricate links between "the outward-looking assimilative fictional genre" and "the experienced authenticity" of individual response. Both employ their craft to avoid their protagonist's frequent romantic overvaluation of the self. Through imagistic patterns and structural juxtapositions, both reveal aspects of reality beyond their protagonist's comprehension. Though they differ in their final statements about the interaction of self and world, both Ellison and Bellow argue for a recognition that the self, ultimately, is *not* the world, but that living in the world requires an encyclopedic sense of self.

Saul Bellow's misreading of *Ulysses* could well serve as Exhibit A for the defense of Harold Bloom's theory of literary influence. Despite the numerous parallels between *Herzog* and *Ulysses*, Bellow insists that any connections are coincidental and that *Herzog*'s defense of the dignity of the average man contrasts sharply with Joyce's conviction "that what happened to the ordinary man, his external life, was not interesting enough to chronicle."[5] This curious statement about a writer who devotes over 700 pages to an ordinary (though certainly not in all respects typical) advertising salesman merely hints at the extent of Bellow's misapprehension of Joyce. Harold Bloom hypothesizes that many artists feel a psychological compulsion to misread major predecessors in order to create works which resemble those of the previous writer more closely than the descendant realizes. Although this phenomenon does nothing to reduce the stature of works such as *Herzog*, which apparently unconsciously "imitate" their predecesors, it helps explain Bellow's insistence that Joyce expresses contempt and despair.

Bellow admits his "special interest in Joyce"[6] and has alluded to Joyce throughout his career. His early novels frequently employ Joycean devices. An epiphany resolves *Seize the Day*, in which Tommy Wilhelm bursts into tears at the funeral of an absolute stranger. The Joycean influence, however, is strongest in *Herzog*, Bellow's finest defense of the beleaguered individual facing the chaos of modern civilization. In his excellent discussion of the relationship between *Herzog* and *Ulysses*, Harold Fisch argues that, in effect, Bellow merges the quests of Bloom and Stephen Dedalus in that of Moses Herzog, who both carries the weight of history—as does Bloom—and also possesses Stephen's potential for intellectual articulation.[7] This profound synthesis would seem enough of an "original" accomplishment to fully absolve *Herzog* from charges of simple imitation. Nonetheless, Bellow persists in misreadings of *Ulysses* which, if accepted, make *Herzog* a work which "discovers" areas already mapped by Joyce.

Basing his argument on the premise that *Ulysses* contributes to "the idea that humanity has reached a terminal point,"[8] Bellow sees the book as a purely literary exercise which reduces Leopold Bloom to the status of passive victim of the encyclopedia. Bellow argues that

> the modern masterpiece of confusion is Joyce's *Ulysses*. There the mind is unable to resist experience. Experience in all its diversity, its pleasure and horror, passes through Bloom's head like an ocean through a sponge. The sponge can't resist; it has to accept whatever the waters bring. It also notes every micro-organism that passes through it. This is what I mean. How much of this must the spirit suffer, in what detail is it obliged to receive this ocean with its human plankton? Sometimes it looks as if the power of the mind has been nullified by the volume of expe-riences. But of course this is assuming the degree of passivity that Joyce assumes in *Ulysses*. Stronger, more purposeful minds can demand order, impose order, select, disregard, but there is still the threat of disintegration under the particulars. A Faus-tian artist is unwilling to surrender to the mass of particulars.[9]

Opposed to what he sees as the Joycean passivity, Bellow advo-cates an attitude of affirmation in the face of a full awareness of the despair endemic to modern life: "One would have to be opti-mistic to the point of imbecility to raise the standard of pure Affirmation and cry, 'Yea, Yea,' shrilly against the deep back-ground of 'Nays.' But the sympathetic heart is sometimes broken, sometimes not. It is reckless to say 'broken'; it is nonsense to say 'whole and unimpaired.' On either side we have the black and white of paranoia."[10] A better description of the emotional impact of Molly Bloom's concluding "Yes" in *Ulysses* is difficult to imag-ine. Despite Bellow's critical position, *Ulysses* anticipates *Herzog* in its concern with finding human meaning in a world without well-defined metaphysical coordinates.

Bellow's heated reaction to his "despairing" Joyce raises a corollary suspicion concerning his denial that Moses Herzog's name derives from the minor Jewish character in *Ulysses*.[11] It is possible, of course, that identical names and similar situations were originally intended as an allusion which Bellow now wishes to conceal. Even if they are pure coincidences, however, the numerous similarities between Herzog and Leopold Bloom, which are far more important than the similarities between the two Herzogs, remain. Several critics, building from the coincidence of names, have cataloged similarities between the two protagonists. Fisch and Maurice Samuel focus on Bloom and Herzog as Jewish heroes in the process of assimilation. They note that both characters appreciate good food, have masochistic tendencies and reject force and violence in their search for love.[12] To these parallels could be added a list of the specific problems shared by Herzog and Bloom: adulterous wives, concern over sanity and finances, the ghosts of mothers and fathers. But these worries seem less proofs of influence than emblems of the similarity between Bellow's and Joyce's concerns.

Far more important than the specific parallels, whether they are actually allusions or not, are the major issues treated by both *Herzog* and *Ulysses*. *Herzog* is Bellow's individual encyclopedia, his attempt to come to terms with the situation of an average man confronting a reality at once overwhelming and stifling. Like Joyce, Bellow faces a universe characterized by "the apathy of the stars" (*U*, p. 734) and attempts to reach a point of equilibrium which Bloom reaches in "Ithaca." Herzog thinks of the body which "leaves its bones, and even the bones at last wear away and crumble to dust in that shallow place of deposit. And thus humanized, this planet in its galaxy of stars and worlds goes from void to void infinitesimal, aching with its unrelated significance. Unrelated? Herzog, with one of his Jewish shrugs, whispered, 'Nu, maile. . . .' Be that as it may."[13] But before Herzog can actually attain this mental peace, he must pass through an arduous learning process. John Clayton observes that Bellow's style in *Herzog* "combines the two major impulses in Bellow's fiction: realism and romance. . . . The combination is possible because this is not the novel of a sufferer in the city but of a sufferer who contains the city within him."[14] To reach this complex balance, to come to terms with the fact that the ordering of the encyclopedia is his own responsibility, Moses Herzog must learn first to place his romantic conception of self in realistic perspective and then to recognize the full extent of humanity's realistic potential. Like Tommy Wilhelm and Henderson before him, Herzog must escape narrow definitions of his reality. He exceeds his predecessors by articulating his discovery and by recognizing that transcending narrow definitions of humanity does not imply transcending reality.

Critics differ widely over how convincingly Bellow communicates this sense of balance. David Galloway finds Herzog's final situation, sitting in his garden in the Berkshires, an adequate resolution of modes, embodying a "state in which he can exercise the intention of his heart in full knowledge and presence of reality."[15] Several critics, however, read the conclusion as Bellow's return to a transcendental romantic stance. While M. Gilbert Porter approves of transcendentalism as a triumph over existential despair, Clayton sees it as a mark of Bellow's inability to connect the individual and social dimensions of his work. Keith Opdahl argues an almost diametrically opposed position, stating that Herzog "makes a complete decision for social service, finding his salvation in a practical, hardheaded manhood." Tony Tanner claims that the pastoral garden setting reflects the one aspect of reality which Herzog most frequently overlooks, the blooming regenerative aspect, and that the apparently transcendental setting completes his sense of balance and is actually not romantic at all. Each of these critics recognizes Bellow's desire to encompass both internal and external reality; the difference in readings reflects a crucial ambivalence, or perhaps limitation, in Bellow's vision. While *Herzog* brilliantly portrays a growing apprehension of the relation of self and reality, it avoids—in a way characteristic of the Chasean romance—the question of precisely how the individual is to use this knowledge in his future life within the newly conceived reality. This evasion generates the critical debate over *Herzog*'s resolution.

Throughout *Herzog*, Bellow employs a number of structural patterns which contribute to a sense of stability in the book's resolution. While Herzog reaches certain basic Bellovian philosophical conclusions concerning the necessity of human love and awareness, he remains unaware of several of the overreaching patterns of his experience, patterns which imply the need for a more comprehensive understanding than Herzog himself attains. These patterns involve the dichotomies between "Potato Lovers" and "Reality Instructors," and between Emersonianism and "Transdescendentalism." In each case, Herzog must recognize the validity of both positions without committing himself entirely to either.

The circular structure of *Herzog* poses an interesting question relevant to the nature of the protagonist's equilibrium: at what point does Herzog reach the position expressed by the first sentence: "If I am out of my mind, it's all right with me, thought Moses Herzog" (*H*, p. 1). Is this acceptance a point of departure for a revaluation of experience in a Bergsonian duration lasting some 400 pages? Or is it Herzog's point of arrival? Juxtaposing sentences from the second paragraph and the novel's final page indicates that Herzog by no means remains content with insanity, a contentment associated with Poe's extreme of the romantic tradition. Shortly after the opening sentence, Bellow observes that Herzog "wrote endlessly, fanatically, to the newspapers, to people in public life, to friends and relatives and at last to the dead, his own obscure dead, and finally the famous dead" (*H*, p. 1). This obsessive involvement with letterwriting fades gradually until, by the end of the novel, Herzog has "no messages for anyone. Nothing. Not a single word" (*H*, p. 341). This underlines both Herzog's movement toward a more realistic valuation of the self and the connection between the letters and his previous imbalance. It also hints at his inability to establish coherent communication with outside reality. Still, the rejection of the letters moves Herzog closer to mental health. Embodying Bellow's encyclopedic impulse, the letters—addressed to scientific, philosophical, political, literary, and personal figures—present the rush of unrelated information which forces Herzog to reexamine himself.

Unable to cope with either American or global society or his personal life, Herzog retreats into a contemplation of what Tanner calls "authenticity of personal response."[16] His letters have no impact on reality; they merely heighten Herzog's sense of isolation. Even when his ideas are sound, their disorganization and internalization render them futile. They react against, rather than integrate with, the world. Herzog dimly realizes the necessity of defending his mind against the assault of unrelated facts. Reacting to Ramona's offer of sexual security, "he understood that she was trying to teach him something and he was trying (the habit of obedience to teaching being so strong in him) to learn from her. But how was he to describe this lesson? The description might begin with his wild internal disorder, or even with the fact that he was quivering. And why? Because he let the entire world press upon him. For instance? Well, for instance, what it means to be a man. In a city. In transition. In a mass. Transformed by science. Under organized power. Subject to tremendous controls" (*H*, pp. 200–201). Like the letters, these perceptions remain fragmentary. But they point to Herzog's sense that his quivering insanity results from his failure to come to terms with the encyclopedia.

Further, Herzog understands the link between internal and external questions; he sees the necessity of reaching equilibrium rather than indulging himself in solipsistic personal response. Sensing that "the practical questions have thus become the ultimate questions as well" (*H*, p. 165), Herzog echoes Bellow's desire for a new sense of the value of the quotidian: "Resisting the argument that scientific thought has put into disorder all considerations based on value . . . Convinced that the extent of universal space does not destroy human value, that the realm of facts and that of values are not eternally separated" (*H*, p. 106). In order to unite these worlds, to forge values in concord with facts, Herzog must balance the terms of the dichotomies which surround him, which attempt to divorce harsh facts and human value. In this struggle, Bellow's craft suggests resolutions beyond Herzog's awareness.

Potato Lovers and Reality Instructors surround Herzog throughout the novel, embodying one important dichotomy. The Potato Lovers, including Eisenhower, who "won because he expressed low-grade universal potato love" (*H*, p. 66), react to experience with a cheap sentimentality which lacks intellectual depth. Grasping anxiously at any shared experience, such as that of rubbing against a subway turnstile, they strive for "a feeling of communion—brotherhood in one of its cheapest forms" (*H*, p. 176). Opposed to the Potato Lovers stand the Reality Instructors, who insist on the harshness of fact. Reacting to Simkin early in the novel, Herzog thinks, "He was a Reality Instructor. Many such. I bring them out. Himmelstein is another, but cruel. It's the cruelty that gets me, not the realism" (*H*, p. 30). Among others, Sandor

Himmelstein, Herzog's ex-wife Madeleine, and Luke Asphalter attempt to force Herzog to face life without human warmth. Herzog, however, adamantly refuses to accept their lessons, persisting in his belief that the Reality Instructors share his own mental unbalance without sharing his awareness: "A very special sort of lunatic expects to inculcate his principles. Sandor Himmelstein, Valentine Gersbach, Madeleine P. Herzog, Moses himself. Reality instructors. They want to teach you—to punish you—the lessons of the real" (*H*, p. 125). Herzog, somewhat out of place on the list, seems much closer to the "average lunatic" struggling to define what his principles actually are, if they exist. At no point does he attempt to force his own vision on another. There may well be a grain of emblematic truth to his claim that "the progress of civilization—indeed, the survival of civilization—depended on the success of Moses E. Herzog" (*H*, p. 125).

This claim reflects Herzog's basic romantic tendency. Taken as the resolution of the entire novel, it would omit a large area of Bellow's awareness. Still, Herzog tends far more strongly than Bellow toward romantic dissociation. As a scholar Herzog specializes in romanticism, and he thinks fondly of his high school speech based on Emersonian ideas. This predilection combines with Herzog's definition of realism as "nastiness in the transcendent position" (*H*, p. 229) to suspend him in his romantic agony through much of the novel. While Herzog never surrenders to what he calls "Transdescendence" (*H*, p. 176), he ultimately learns that resisting naturalism need not require a romantic response. Two near catastrophes, however, make Herzog realize that his agony is not of transcendental importance or intensity. The first catastrophe, which resembles a Joycean epiphany in its sudden attribution of meaning to an apparently trivial detail, occurs when Herzog resolves to take revenge on Madeleine and Valentine. Gazing through a bathroom window after he sneaks up to their house, Herzog sees his daughter Junie splashing Valentine with bathwater. Attempting to resist the human feeling inherent in the scene, Herzog observes: "The man washed her tenderly. His look, perhaps, was false. But he had no true expressions, Herzog thought. His face was all heaviness, sexual meat" (*H*, p. 257). Clearly Herzog longs to impose his own sense of meaning on the scene, an archetypally romantic desire. But his resistance to the realistic events crumbles as he registers the futility of violence, and he retreats, an important perception closer to self-awareness. Never an actor in his own melodramas, Herzog now ceases to dramatize his suffering.

The second crucial incident follows the auto accident on Herzog's excursion with Junie. Herzog, who has previously watched the activity of the New York court system, contemplates his own impending journey to the Chicago courts: "Is this, by chance, the reality you have been looking for, Herzog, in your earnest Herzog way? Down in the ranks with other people—ordinary life?" (*H*, p. 287). The answer is Yes, the Yes which Molly Bloom utters, the Yes which Bellow seeks to impose on the background of negation. While Herzog remains unaware of the implications of his question, the structure of the novel points to just such a resolution. Recognizing the link between himself and other *minor* sufferers, such as the driver of the truck which strikes his car, would allow Herzog to attain a balance between the Potato Lovers and the Reality Instructors. Unlike the feeling of potato love, his identification with those involved in the court system rests not on a cheap longing for contact, but on a reluctant perception of the real scale of individual problems. Herzog approaches such a balance when he thinks, "Our own murdering imagination turns out to be the great power, our human imagination which starts by accusing God of murder. At the bottom of the whole disaster lies the human being's sense of a grievance, and with this I want nothing more to do" (*H*, p. 290). At the same time, Herzog accepts the necessity of facing the harsh reality of Madeleine's arrival to pick up Junie. Whereas previously Herzog transformed his ex-wife into a witch figure from a romantic fairytale, he now simply recognizes her as an individual attempting to force him into the role of victim. His solution is simple: "I reject your definitions of me" (*H*, p. 299). Previously he had accepted Madeleine's definition of Moses Herzog as an inadequate husband and a professional failure. By dissociating himself from this vision of reality, he frees himself for self-discovery.

Throughout the novel Herzog struggles against limiting definitions of reality, but his struggles never generate more than abstract suggestions that "perhaps a moratorium on definitions of human nature is now best" (*H*, p. 129). He never articulates the one basic perception for which the two epiphanies prepare him. Having freed himself from Madeleine, Herzog goes to the Berkshires and prepares for recovery. His final letters, to his dead mother and to God, state his detemination to regain his balance, his rejection of the insanity he embraced at the start of the novel. To the extent that he recognizes the necessity of stepping beyond limiting definitions, Herzog articulates Bellow's themes. Bellow certainly shares Herzog's desire to transmit his complex love for those close to him, expressed in his letter to his mother: "I want to send you, and others, the most loving wish I have in my heart. This is the only way I have to reach out—out where it is incomprehensible. I can only pray toward it. So . . . Peace!" (*H*, p. 326). Similarly, Bellow endorses Herzog's resolve to "do no more to enact the peculiarities of life. This is done well enough without my special assistance" (*H*, p. 340). And Herzog's defense of average life, the point of departure for his closing ruminations, contains Bellow's basic beliefs (the beliefs which underlie his "quarrel" with Joyce): "We must get it out of our heads that this is a doomed time, that we are waiting for the end, and the rest of it, mere junk from fashionable magazines. Things are grim enough without these shivery games. People frightening one another—a poor sort of moral exercise. But, to get to the main point, the advocacy and praise of suffering take us in the wrong direction and those of us who remain loyal to civilization must not go for it" (*H*, pp. 316–17). Like Bloom confronting the Citizen-Cyclops, Herzog is talking about love.

But Bellow's presentation of Herzog implies a good deal more than these relatively simple truths. Herzog never articulates or acts on the principles of balance which Bellow's structure, neatly balancing Potato Lovers and Reality Instructors, Emersonian and Transdescendental ideas, implies. Herzog is more willing to express his love of family at the end, but he fails to connect that love with the realistic sense of common humanity he experiences after the accident. More important, he cannot express the love directly to his brother, and he cannot emotionally comprehend the difference between Madeleine, with her limiting definitions, and Ramona, whose sexuality encourages an expansion of Herzog's sense of *actual* human possibility. While he rejects both transcendentalism and transdescendentalism as inadequate, Herzog remains in a position which can be interpreted in terms of either. Like the romantic transcendentalist, he sits amidst nature and does nothing; like the transdescendental (naturalistic) victim, he has been forced to adopt his position by massive social forces. Bellow clearly implies the necessity of a return to the circumstances of everyday life to escape this impasse. Only there can potato love be convincingly transformed into mature love; only there can the individual maintain equilibrium, confronting harsh facts without becoming a "lunatic" Reality Instructor.

In order to defend the average man in his normal circumstances against the indifference of the art of twentieth-century giants such as Joyce, Bellow brings his average man to a dawning awareness. But it is difficult to see how Moses Herzog attains any more understanding of his situation than does Leopold Bloom, and Herzog is *less* able to act on what awareness he does attain. The fullest awareness in *Herzog*, as in *Ulysses*, belongs not to the ordinary character but to the extraordinary structuring agent, the artist. The salient difference between the two works is that where Joyce presents the interaction of Bloom's mind and his normal context, Bellow merely implies that Herzog, mentally reconstituted, must eventually participate in a similar interaction. Bellow recognizes reality; he does not confront it. His misreading and reconstruction of *Ulysses*, as Harold Bloom would certainly have anticipated, results in an equally ambitious but ultimately less comprehensive encyclopedia.

Ralph Ellison's reservations concerning Joyce—which, unlike Saul Bellow's, evidence very little anxiety—involve curiously diffuse issues. In "Society, Morality, and the Novel," Ellison expresses his concern that the works of the great modernist writers, including Joyce, lack public accessibility and, whatever their intent, serve an anti-democratic function.[17] In *Invisible Man*, however, Ellison's argument with Joyce proceeds in a different direction. The narrator observes that Joyce in effect overemphasized the representative aspect of Stephen Dedalus' quest and that "Stephen's problem, like ours, was not actually one of creating the uncreated conscience of his race, but of creating the *uncreated features of his face*."[18] In fact, Ellison believes that the fully aware individual, capable of expressing both his realistic and symbolic perceptions in publicly accessible form, in effect *is* the conscience of his race. Ellison implicitly denies the distance between artistic and folk awareness, arguing that integrity and social function are not incompatible artistic goals. Where Joyce, feeling much less faith in the congruence of artistic and folk sensibilities, separates the artist-hero psychologically from his society, Ellison embodies historical trends in his hero's experience, working equally in folk and "elite" cultural modes. Ironically, Joyce offers his artist-hero no physical separation from his social circumstances, while Ellison allows his a strategic withdrawal on the understanding that "a hibernation is a covert preparation for a more overt action" (*IM*, p. 11). Whatever their differences, Ellison and Joyce share the desire to help redeem their people, individually and collectively.

Ellison freely acknowledges Joyce's influence on *Invisible Man*. Remembering that he "had read *Portrait* any number of times" before writing his own novel, Ellison accepts the presence of several parallels which critics have noted between the two novels. He cautions, however, that a scene such as Barbee's sermon is not simply a transfer of Joyce's retreat sermon to an Afro-American setting.[19] While the thematic similarity of *Invisible Man* to *A Portrait of the Artist as a Young Man* is striking—both books focus on the development of the consciousness of a prospective artist—the technical similarities reveal a more profound and deeply assimilated influence. The progression of styles in *Invisible Man*, which, Ellison observes, moves from naturalism through expressionism to surrealism,[20] resembles the evolution of style in *Portrait*. Reflecting Ellison's determination to avoid the implicit limits of vision implied by narrow allegiance to any one fictional mode, *Invisible Man*'s shifting style expresses, as Tanner notes, "both the state of mind of the narrator and the society he is involved in."[21]

In addition, Ellison adopts the Joycean epiphany, complete with the Joycean technique of revealing each epiphany as a necessary but incomplete stage of a progression leading to a new level of awareness. The invisible man must certainly be able to experience the epiphany, eating the yam (*IM*, pp. 199–200) in an action which marks his acceptance of racial heritage. But when he attempts to return to the epiphany, he finds himself plunged back into the harsh reality of the frost which, like the narrator, bites the yam (*IM*, p. 202). Like Joyce, Ellison insists that each epiphany forces the hero to an increased awareness of his ability to interact with his society, directly or through his art.

The most profound points of connection between Joyce and Ellison involve *Ulysses* and *Finnegans Wake*, rather than *Portrait*. Indeed, Ellison prefers that the lessons he learns from predecessors not express themselves directly through allusion but penetrate deeply into the texture of his novel:

> It is best of course when they don't show themselves directly, but they are there in many ways. Joyce and Eliot, for instance, made me aware of the playful possibilities of language. You look at a page of *Finnegans Wake* and see references to all sorts of American popular music, yet the context gives it an extension from the popular back to the classical and beyond. This is just something Joyce teaches you to do, and you can abstract the process and apply it to a frame of reference which is American and historical.[22]

In an earlier interview Ellison commented on another lesson learned from Joyce and Eliot: "When I started writing, I knew that in both *The Waste Land* and *Ulysses* ancient myth and ritual were used to give form and significance to the material; but it took me a few years to realize that the myths and rites operating in our everyday lives could be used the same way."[23] Indeed, Joyce's deepest influence on Ellison lies in his demonstration of the possible ways of expressing combinations of mythic, popular, and high cultural elements.

Ellison's application of these lessons rarely seems Joycean. Several critics have traced particular myths, including that of Odysseus, through *Invisible Man*, but Ellison's insistence on his protagonist's near anonymity clearly distinguishes him from either Stephen Dedalus or Leopold Bloom.[24] As George Kent observes, Ellison's acceptance of both classical and folk mythological systems as equally valid emotional and intellectual structures distinguishes him from both classical white and contemporary black novelists.[25] Ellison feels little need to *defend* the dignity of the individual or the folk tradition; in his democratic framework— and Ellison is perhaps the most staunchly democratic writer since Whitman—both are givens. Rather, Ellison demonstrates the capacity of his synthetic approach to folk and high culture to encompass the encyclopedic experience of his protagonist. To achieve this Ellison turns to black music, first to blues but finally to jazz, which for him embodies private aesthetic richness, modernist ideas of complexity, folk experience, and public political potential.

As Gene Bluestein demonstrates, Ellison believes "that the roots of high culture lie in the expression of the common people"[26]—in spirituals and the blues. Writing on the application of blues to literature, Ellison defines the form as "an impulse to keep the painful details and episodes of a brutal experience alive in one's aching consciousness, to finger its jagged grain, and to transcend it, not by the consolation of philosophy but by squeezing from it a near-tragic, near-comic lyricism. As a form, the blues is an autobiographical chronicle of personal catastrophe expressed lyrically."[27] Because of the ability of the blues to accept and express seemingly contradictory emotions, the narrator must accept them before advancing an awareness which transcends "autobiographical" experience and recognizes the connections of those experiences with a wider reality. The narrator must recognize his link with the folk culture before he can move on to the synthetic richness of jazz.

The invisible man's first stage of development involves his acceptance of his racial background. This acceptance focuses on the narrator's response to the blues. The wise Vet at the Golden Day, Jim Trueblood, and Peter Wheatstraw participate in the blues level of black folk consciousness in a way which eludes the narrator. The narrator is more horrified than impressed by Trueblood's acceptance of his incestuous relationship with his daughter, an acceptance which is absolutely necessary to Trueblood's continued ability to cope with the real problems of his life. When Trueblood, a blues singer, says, "While I'm singin' them blues I makes up my mind that I ain't nobody but myself and ain't nothin' I can do but let whatever is gonna happen, happen" (*IM*, p. 51), the narrator is "torn between humiliation and fascination" (*IM*, p. 52). He is unable to understand the Vet's meaning when he speaks of "things . . . most peasants and folk peoples almost always know through experience, though seldom conscious thoughts" (*IM*, p. 70), and when he meets the archetypal jiver Peter Wheatstraw he feels "uncomfortable. Somehow he was like one of the vets from the Golden Day" (*IM*, p. 132). Nonetheless, as the first step of his development, the invisible man progresses rapidly from his removed comment that blacks "are a hell of a people" (*IM*, p. 135) to his identification with the "poor robin" who has been "picked clean" in Wheatstraw's rambling song (*IM*, p. 147).

While this identification is necessary, it is not sufficient. Early in the novel Ellison indicates that the blues/spiritual tradition has a limited range of effectiveness. The fairly narrow range of the spirituals is emphasized as the narrator listens to the music rising from a black church. He thinks of "sun-shrunk shacks at the railroad crossing where the disabled veterans visited the whores, hobbling down the tracks on crutches and cane; sometimes pushing the legless, thighless one in a red wheelchair. And sometimes I listen to hear if music reaches that far, but recall only the drunken laughter of sad, sad whores" (*IM*, p. 28). Mary Rambo's song, the "Back Water Blues," reaches farther and the narrator draws strength from it: "I lay listening as the sound flowed to and around me, bringing me a calm sense of my indebtedness" (*IM*, p. 226). But the narrator cannot fall back on this comfort under extreme stress. His attempt to escape from the riot and return to Mary's leads only to his plunge into the lower darkness (*IM*, p. 423).

Ellison presents the folk tradition embodied in the spirituals and blues as a necessary but insufficient element of the invisible man's cultural framework. Ultimately he turns to jazz, which embraces the strength of the folk tradition but has a wider range of reference and is therefore more effective as a political tool. Larry Neal has observed that jazz, specifically the music of Louis Armstrong, provides the constituting structural principle for *Invisible Man*.[28] Ellison has argued that Armstrong belongs with the pioneers of innovative twentieth-century art. In *Shadow and Act* Ellison writes: "Consider that at least as early as T. S. Eliot's creation of a new aesthetic for poetry through the artful juxtapositioning of earlier styles, Louis Armstrong, way down the river in New Orleans, was working out a similar technique for jazz."[29] Ellison argues that jazz has appropriated a wider range of ideas than European music: "From the days of their introduction into the colonies, Negroes have taken, with the ruthlessness of those without articulate investments in cultural styles, whatever they could of European music, making of it that which would, when blended with the cultural tendencies inherited from Africa, express their own sense of life."[30]

Ellison perceives the adaptive possibilities of jazz as equal to those which Joyce sees in European cultural traditions. The narrator's vision, while listening to Armstrong's music in the prologue to *Invisible Man*, compresses a large number of artistic possibilities into one extremely dense passage reminiscent of the "Circe" section of *Ulysses*. For the sake of simplicity I have divided the passage into four sections, but much of their emotional impact derives from their rapid flow in the text:

1) That night I found myself hearing not only in time, but in space as well. I not only entered the music but descended, like Dante, into its depths.

2) And beneath the swiftness of the hot tempo there was a slower tempo and a cave and I entered it and looked around and heard an old woman singing a spiritual as full of *Weltschmerz* as flamenco,

3) and beneath that lay a still lower level on which I saw a beautiful girl the color of ivory pleading in a voice like my mother's as she stood before a group of slaveowners who bid for her naked body,

4) and below that I found a lower level and a more rapid tempo and I heard someone shout: "Brothers and sisters, my text this morning is the 'Blackness of Blackness'" (*IM*, p. 7).

In section 1 (and the portion of the text immediately preceding it) Ellison presents the "realistic" level of jazz on which it is primarily important as a part of the narrator's environment. But, under the influence of a reefer, the narrator perceives new levels of artistic significance, all implicit in Armstrong's rendition of "What Did I Do to Be so Black and Blue?" In section 2, the hot jazz is transformed imagistically into its folk roots. It has become a vehicle for the spiritual's expression of the racial unconsciousness, the calming strength which the narrator draws from Mary Rambo's song. As the narrator descends further in section 3, jazz takes on symbolic significance. In a kind of Jungian transformation of opposites, the slave-pain of the spiritual metamorphoses into a sublimated expression of racial hostility. The ultimate level in section 4, which extends for several pages beyond the citation, brings the narrator face to face with the ambiguous reality of "blackness," paralleling the whiteness of the whale in *Moby-Dick*. Rather than ending with a romantic immobility in the face of metaphysical conflicts, the narrator, who has passed through several "reassuring" levels of folk experience to reach the ambiguities, is able to accept the contradictions and use them for his own purposes. In the epilog the narrator explicitly embraces the contradictions implicit in his blackness and says: "In order to get some of it down I have to love. I sell you no phony forgiveness, I'm a desperate man—but too much of your life will be lost, its meaning lost, unless you approach it as much through love as through hate. So I approach it through division. So I denounce and I defend and I hate and I love" (*IM*, pp. 437–38). He by no means surrenders to ambiguity. Rather, he resolves to use it in carrying out an explicitly political plan to play "a socially responsible role" (*IM*, p. 439). Even while recognizing the symbolic implications both of his blackness and of his invisibility, the invisible man remembers that his particular perception of them remains rooted in his specific circumstances as a black man, as an American, and as an intellectual. His use of the perceptions seeks to interact with each of these realities.

The significance of the narrator's various experiences has been analyzed numerous times, but I would stress that his practical success in any given situation relates directly to his control of the surrounding "rhythm." This idea derives from the jazz principle that if the instrumentalist controls the perception of time, the tempo of life, he will very likely control his audience and, at least in an existential sense, his own and his environment's momentary destiny. Ellison draws a physical analogy in the prolog when the narrator describes an inferior boxer's victory which results from his momentary control of rhythm. "Once I saw a prizefighter boxing a yokel. The fighter was swift and amazingly scientific. . . . He hit the yokel a hundred times while the yokel held up his arms in stunned surprise. But suddenly the yokel, rolling about in the gale of boxing gloves, struck one blow and knocked science, speed and footwork as cold as a well-digger's posterior. . . . The yokel had simply stepped inside of his opponent's sense of time" (*IM*, p. 7). Not coincidentally, this analogy leads directly to the vision based on Armstrong's music. Jazz is not merely an aesthetic experience; it is a potential physical weapon.[31] But only after a lengthy initiation does the invisible man comprehend the *political* implications of this level of his artistic ability.

The narrator lacks control of the rhythms of his life in the early sections of *Invisible Man*. During the Battle Royal he is merely one of a mass of thrashing bodies. Similar situations recur at the Golden Day and at Liberty Paints, where, amidst the throbbing of the basement machinery "things were speeding up" (*IM*, p. 171) and, paradoxically, "movements seemed too slow" (*IM*, p. 174). As a result of the ensuing explosion, which lands him in the hospital, the narrator comes to an inarticulate recognition of the importance of rhythm: "I listened intensely, aware of the form and movement of sentences and grasping the new subtle rhythmical differences between progressions of sounds that questioned and those that made a statement. But still their meanings were lost in the vast whiteness in which I myself was lost" (*IM*, p. 181).

Gradually he develops an understanding of speech rhythms and is able to manipulate the crowd with his effective orations at the eviction scene and the first brotherhood rally. But, where the rhythmical threat in the earlier sections of the novel related to his lack of identification with the black cultural tradition, it now stems from too much identification. The narrator is victimized by the attempts of whites to impose stereotypes upon him, either positively or negatively. A white woman at a brotherhood party tells him his voice is "primitive . . . at times you have tom-toms beating in your voice" (*IM*, p. 312). Though inverted, Brother Jack's refusal to let the invisible man sing reflects the same racially conditioned response. Despite his apparent control at times, the narrator still lacks confidence and, especially in times of transition, finds himself lost amidst the rhythms of New York. "A ragged rumba rhythm" (*IM*, p. 243) accompanies his departure from Mary's for his career with the brotherhood. On his return to Harlem from downtown exile, "The uptown rhythms were slower and yet were somehow faster" (*IM*, p. 320).

The invisible man approaches a full appreciation of the importance of life rhythms only when he becomes aware of the zoot-suiters, the "men out of time" (*IM*, p. 333). He wonders whether "they were the saviors, the true leaders, the bearers of something precious" (*IM*, p. 333), posing the question specifically in terms of jazz: "Was this the only true history of the times, a mood blared by trumpets, trombones, saxophone and drums, a song with turgid inadequate words?" (*IM*, p. 335). Rinehart raises the zoot-suiters' approach to a fine art and operates, among his many businesses, a jazz church. But the zoot-suiters' limited concept of jazz, their inarticulateness reflected in the inadequate words which accompany their music, renders their approach inappropriate for the culturally minded invisible man. When he attempts to mimic Rinehart, he once again loses control of his life's rhythm, ending up in a bar fight with Brother Maceo.

If Rinehart is Ellison's final warning against too much individual fluidity, Ras the Destroyer is his final warning against excessive identification with the racial community. Rinehart is free from all external definition; Ras is defined totally by his blackness. Rinehart is an existential, Ras a communal nightmare. Caught between the two during the riot, the invisible man, once again rhythmically confused, can only flee with the hope of retreating to Mary's. His flight fails. But his headlong descent into the darkness of his burrow parallels his descent through Armstrong's music in the prologue and is similarly rich in possibilities. He tumbles through the simultaneously realistic and symbolic destruction of his personal past (*IM*, p. 429), through a politically charged dream vision (*IM*, pp. 429–30), to awake "in the blackness" (*IM*, p. 431).

Despite his claim that "gin, jazz and dreams were not enough" (*IM*, p. 433), the narrator relates his final resolution to return to the surface world (and play a political role) directly to Armstrong. He accepts the contradictions and the possibilities generated by his experiences, insisting on their social importance: "With Louis Armstrong one half of me says, 'Open the window and let the foul air out,' while the other says, 'It was good green corn before the harvest.' Of course Louis was kidding, he wouldn't have thrown old Bad Air out, because it would have broken up the music and the dance, when it was the good music that came from the bell of old Bad Air's horn that counted. Old Bad Air is still around with his music and his dancing and his diversity, and I'll be up and around with mine" (*IM*, p. 438). When faced with the threat of paralysis in the face of ambiguity, the narrator consciously restrains his perception: "to see around corners is enough. . . . But to hear around them is too much; it inhibits action" (*IM*, pp. 10–11). The narrator, like Ellison, promises to play a "socially responsible role" at least partially through the creation of "music" based on both his own "dancing and diversity" and the "good music" coming from the bell of old "Bad Air's" classical culture.

Invisible Man, then, recognizes the necessity of symbolic awareness of the contradictions of invisibility, as well as the need for realistic action. To the extent that he focuses on the links between the awareness and the action, Ellison balances his fictional modes as effectively as does Joyce; Ellison never attempts to deny the validity of either type of experience. But to the extent that he overestimates the political power of individual awareness, Ellison shares Bellow's difficulties in resolving *Herzog*. Like Bellow, Ellison clearly indicates the need for a return to society; like Bellow, he fails to portray the return. While Ellison seems much more certain of the nature of the return—which aspires to a much wider political effect than does the return of either Bloom or Dedalus to Dublin—many critics feel that he simply recommends what are in effect romantic transcendentalist politics.[32] Tanner notes the connection between the invisible man's final position and the tradition of the hero in the American romance: "The narrator has discovered what many American heroes have discovered, that he is not free to reorganize and order the world, but he can at least exercise the freedom to arrange and name his perceptions of the world. He cannot perhaps assert and define himself in action, but sometimes at least he can assert and create himself in some private space not in the grip of historical forces."[33] Ellison believes the ordering of perceptions inevitably interacts with historical forces: "It is not within the province of the artist to determine whether his work is social or not. Art by its nature is social. . . . If it is to be more than a dream, the work of art must simultaneously evoke images of reality and give them formal organization. And it must, since the individual's emotions are formed in society, shape them into socially meaningful patterns."[34]

Clearly, then, Ellison does not conceive of the resolution of *Invisible Man* in quite the way Tanner reads it; he intends the ending to embody the realistic social, as well as the symbolic individual, truth of experience. His failure to establish this balance unambiguously reflects in part his commitment to the ambiguity which he sees as an inevitable component of reality, and in part a common American tendency to focus on metaphysics when society presents seemingly insoluble problems. Even with this weakness, which parallels that of *Herzog, Invisible Man* remains a great synthetic work. Ellison's sense of the metaphysical does not develop out of direct romantic revelation; it does not require a leap of faith on the part of the audience to establish its credibility. Rather, it grows out of Ellison's scrupulous meanness of observation, his minute examination of the everyday reality which, like that of Joyce's Dublin, gradually opens up to reveal its intricate connection with all of the diverse realities, public and private, accessible to human perception.

The Writer as Performer: John Barth, Norman Mailer

Performance does not necessarily imply power. A good performance may exercise power over the mind of an audience, but a weak performance may create an impression of an egotistic performer celebrating his own questionable ability. Richard Poirier, tracing the roots of performance in twentieth-century literature to Joyce and Eliot, denies that their involvement with their own artistic processes amounts to a claim of omnipotence: "Hesitancy about the place of the artist in the work, even though it is he who is assembling it, hesitancy about the value of literature even while the writing of it is the dedication of a lifetime—these are attitudes consistent with the reaction by Eliot and Joyce against the promotion of the artist by Pater." In effect, Poirier sees as a mark of uncertainty what many have viewed as arrogance. Joyce and Eliot, writes Poirier, "treat literature, in its effete exclusivity, as a kind of enemy,"[35] opening their work to the influence of numerous styles previously excluded from Western "high art." The power of their performances derives in large part from the fact that they feel less confident of their ability to determine what is and what is not significant and therefore present an extremely broad range of reality. Creating encyclopedic works which report the processes of gauging significance, they attempt to involve their readers directly in the process of sifting through reality. To the extent that they succeed in gaining this involvement, their performances bear out Poirier's claim that, in modern art, "Performance is an exercise of power, a very curious one. Curious because it is at first so furiously self-consultive, so even narcissistic, and later so eager for publicity, love, and historical dimension. Out of an accumulation of secretive acts emerges at last a form that presumes to compete with reality itself for control of the minds exposed to it."[36]

The Individual Encyclopedias of contemporary novelists aspire to just this kind of control. Almost all of them can be considered performances in Poirier's sense. Certainly the craft of a Bellow or an Ellison involves a great deal of concentration on the secretive acts of the artist shaping the reality of his work. But, since performance in the large sense has become nearly ubiquitous, general discussions tend toward futility. Performance today implies a much more direct involvement of the author in his own work. The primary proponents of performance in the contemporary novel are those writers, such as John Barth (especially in his recent *Letters*) and Norman Mailer, who enter directly into their works as participants in the fictional reality. Just as the idea of performance originated in Joyce and Eliot's rejection of Pater's elevation of the artist, Mailer's and Barth's heightened emphasis on themselves as performers rests on their doubts concerning the ability of any one mind to encompass the encyclopedia, to impose an individual style on the reality with which it competes. When they succeed in fusing the secretive individual and historical encyclopedic dimensions of their works, they establish their authority on solid bases. When they fail, they destroy the foundations of their own work, leaving themselves in the position of tightrope walkers dancing on a void.

Near the end of *Letters*, one of the many characters who first appears in an earlier John Barth novel suggests that we imagine "an artist less enamored of the world than of the language we signify it with, yet less enamored of the language than of the signifying narration, and yet less enamored of the narration than of its formal arrangement."[37] This writer clearly enough is John Barth, but it is a John Barth who is not yet aware enough of himself as a performer to resolve the tension between his formal creation and the world which it reflects. It is the Barth who performed in *Lost in the Funhouse*, *The Sot-Weed Factor* and, above all, *Giles Goat-Boy*. Each of these performances, however, remains distanced. None explicitly recognizes that Barth, carrying his burden of personal history, is himself the performer. Only in *Chimera* and, much more openly and successfully, in *Letters* does Barth enter directly into his works, generating forms appropriate to his peculiarly introverted vision. Accompanying the new emphasis on performance comes the recognition that, as the character in *Letters* observes, the formal obsession of the "Barthian" artist may ultimately enable him to "love the narrative through the form, the language through the narrative, even the world through the language" (*L*, p. 650). Where the formalist of *Giles Goat-Boy* remains apart from the world, torn by irreconcilable oppositions, the performing formalist of *Letters* struggles to participate in both the artistic and the historical "worlds."

Always an extremely allusive writer, Barth has utilized a variety of Joycean techniques and motifs throughout his career. As he has grown more interested in performance (and the relationship of author and character), he has concentrated more on the textual disputes and generational conflicts of *Finnegans Wake*. In his earlier work Barth focused on adapting the mythic parallels pioneered by *Ulysses*. (See "Homer's Joyce," in the previous chapter.) During the early and middle phases of his development, Barth openly rejected Joyce's "synthetic" approach to the treatment of myth and reality:

> I always felt that it was a bad idea on the face of it, though there are beautiful counter-examples, to write a more or less realistic piece of fiction one dimension of which keeps pointing to the classical myths—like John Updike's *Centaur*, or Joyce's *Ulysses*, or Malamud's *The Natural*. Much as one may admire those novels in other respects, their authors have hold of the wrong end of the mythopoeic stick. The myths themselves are produced by the collective narrative imagination (or whatever), partly to point down at our daily reality; and so to write about our daily experiences in order to point up to the myths seems to

me mythopoeically retrograde. I think it's a more interesting thing to do, if you find yourself preoccupied with mythic archetypes or what have you, to address them directly.[38]

In *Giles Goat-Boy*, Barth attempted to address myth directly, ultimately creating an uneasy tension with his work's realistic implications.

It would be an oversimplification to dismiss *Giles Goat-Boy* as a disembodied allegory with no relationship to reality. Robert Scholes argues: "In *Giles Goat-Boy*, John Barth has forged an allegorical instrument that enables him to piece together our fragmented world and explore the possible ways of living in it."[39] Raymond Olderman expands on the nature of the understanding *Giles Goat-Boy* seeks to instill, pointing to Barth's attempt to redefine the terms of our perception: "We are forced to admit that both [current history and Barth's allegory] or neither are possible, and that contemporary history is fabulous, distinguishable from fiction only because the author has made his contrivance obvious."[40] This seems to be precisely the premise underlying Barth's understanding of his own sensibility: "A different way to come to terms with the discrepancy between art and the Real Thing is to affirm the artificial element in art (you can't get rid of it anyhow), and make the artifice part of your point instead of working for higher and higher fi with a lot of literary woofers and tweeters. . . . If you are a novelist of a certain type of temperament, then what you really want to do is reinvent the world. God wasn't too bad a novelist, except he was a Realist."[41] Even while rejecting one of the terms, Barth admits his desire to relate art, which at this stage of his work implies a symbolic or romantic focus, and reality.

In *Giles Goat-Boy*, George argues that traditional definitions of symbolism oversimplify the separation of symbol and reality. When Bray says, "But do you really think it's worthwhile to take WESCAC so seriously? It's only a symbol," George responds: "This assertation I might have quarreled with: had Mother been impregnated by a symbol? Was it a symbol that had EATen the Amaterasus and G. Herrold, and would in all likelihood soon EAT me, if not the entire University? That incorporated in its circuitry all the dreams and definitions that tricked studentdom into believing in its own existence, and in the reality of its flunkage? Some symbol!"[42] Throughout *Giles Goat-Boy* Barth attempts to re-create our entire perception of the terms of various dichotomies, not merely that of symbol and reality. As Scholes observes, Barth structures the book dialectically; George presents a thesis (absolute acceptance of opposites; *GGB*, p. 420), antithesis (absolute denial of opposites; *GGB*, p. 553) and finally a synthesis (recognition of paradoxical complexity which entails a focus on the full breadth of reality in any situation; *GGB*, p. 650). Within this superstructure numerous individual details evolve similarly. Giles first struggles to act like a Grand Tutor, accepting an external definition (*GGB*, p. 108); in rebellion against this pressure, he adopts an entirely internal definition of Grand Tutorhood (*GGB*, p. 160); eventually it grows clear that Grand Tutorhood lies in the inevitable, though not necessarily intentional, convergence of the two definitions.

Philosophically, then, there appears to be little difference between Barth and Joyce in their attempts to resolve apparent opposites. But inevitably Barth's allegorical emphasis generates significant differences in practice. While Joyce's stylistic variety allows him to treat a wide range of histories effectively (the "Oxen of the Sun" style perfectly reflects literary history in a way that the "Circe" style could not), Barth's single style handles some histories much more effectively than others. As long as it focuses on mythological or philosophical histories, Barth's style succeeds. When it treats national and political history, Barth's style collapses.

Peter Greene, Barth's emblem for the American character, illustrates this collapse. Scholes considers Barth's presentation of Greene "a masterful job in the dimension of history, sociology, and psychology."[43] Nonetheless, the treatment of Greene reveals the very serious limits of Barth's historical perception and his allegorical method. Always an entertaining figure, Greene perfectly reflects an America in many ways at odds with itself. Both America's democratic aspirations and its repressive tendencies shape Greene's character: "So at odds was he with himself, he would bribe the campus police to put down a demonstration, then find himself marching unrecognized among the demonstrators, in his old forester's clothes, and take a beating he himself had paid for"

(*GGB*, p. 237). In fact, he can be seen as an emblem of the American artistic tradition: "In sum, he was so utterly of two minds about himself and his connections with things that he seemed rather a pair of humans in a single skin: the one energetic, breezy, optimistic, self-assured, narrow-minded, hospitable, out-going, quick-thinking, belligerent, and strong; the other apathetic, abject, pessimistic, self-despising, indulgent, rude, introspective, complacent, uncouth, feckless, and flabby" (*GGB*, p. 245). These two aspects of Greene form the basis of the dialectic through which he passes. When George first meets him, Greene constantly reassures himself with the complacent refrain: "I am okay, and what the heck anyhow" (*GGB*, p. 240). When disillusioned about Anastasia's "purity," however, he sounds an antithetical refrain of "No durn good" (*GGB*, p. 538). To this point, Greene, suspended amid contradictions, effectively supports the larger structure of *Giles Goat-Boy*. Barth's attempted resolution, however, fails to transfer the philosophical synthesis to the historical level. Rather than combining the first two levels, Barth simply returns Greene to his original state of complacency. George provides an insubstantial statement of synthesis: "New Tammany College, as best I could judge from much reading and a little observation, was neither a Graduate School on the one hand nor a Dunce's College on the other; in its history and present state there was much to wince at—and much to take pride in" (*GGB*, p. 567). But in its application to Greene, all elements of criticism recede. Not only does George convince Greene that he was "right in the first place" (*GGB*, p. 568), he also cooperates in Stoker's creation of yet another unresolved dichotomy between "virginal" Anastasia and her imaginary "whore" twin Stacey. Apparently Greene, who plays a very small role in the final reel, can function only on the basis of delusions and unreconciled (but clearly self-destructive) oppositions.

Barth's difficulty in resolving this particular historical current would not necessarily flaw *Giles Goat-Boy* were it not for the fact that Barth so closely resembles Peter Greene in his cultural perspective. In fact, the philosophical-mythological and historical-realistic levels of the book are so interdependent that a structured weakness in one inevitably precipitates a collapse in the other. While Barth claims to deal with universally relevant mythic patterns and images, in *Giles Goat-Boy* he in fact embodies only an extremely limited American, and in large part academic, version of the universe.

Despite his claim that he deals with his mythic materials "directly," Barth obviously constructs his allegory along lines dominated by the history of America in the early 1960s. When Barth seeks objective correlatives for the eternal conflict of opposites, he chooses the USA and the USSR (WESCAC and EASCAC). His synthesis demands an acceptance of these terms, but the terms demonstrate Barth's limitation much more than his inclusiveness. Far from embodying any significant opposition, "west" and "east" in the narrow political sense may be only slightly differentiated aspects of one term in a larger opposition of white and nonwhite in world history. (There are, of course, numerous possible formulations of the larger conflicts; the point is that Barth's terms reflect a particular political arrogance which the intervening fifteen years have done much to unveil as naive.) The boundary dispute (Berlin Wall), which Barth employs as a symbol for eternal conflict, may indeed serve better as a symbol of the battleground for undifferentiated urges to power.

Throughout, Barth reduces aspects of political reality which could conceivably disrupt his allegorical formulation to cardboard stereotypes with their origins firmly rooted in Euro-American (not "universal") mythology. Just as Peter Greene sees "Old Black George" and his daughter alternately as comic darkies and as black beasts, Barth presents Croaker (Africa) simply as an expression of unchanneled sexual energy desperately in need of white guidance. The converse side of this stereotype pictures the black man, George, as mysterious guide—Nigger Jim without humanity. In effect, black people to Barth amount to nothing more than expressions of the unrecognized shadow side of the white man's psyche. There, as in his treatment of Peter Greene, and despite his grand claims to dealing with myth in a "pure" form untainted by "realistic" limitations, Barth reveals his inability to step outside the boundaries of the American cultural tradition. His allegorical style, inextricably built on unrecognized historical biases, fails to redefine adequately the terms of our perception of the relationship of "art" and "the real thing." Far from recognizing the significance of artifice, Barth has merely ignored the significance of reality. In *Giles Goat-Boy* he "wanted to have it both ways": he has it neither. History dreams him.

Barth does not remain content with this irresolution. In *Letters* a character suggests, "If history is a trauma, maybe the thing to do is redream it" (*L*, p. 107). Barth accepts the advice by creating a performance which recapitulates and extends each of his earlier books and ultimately leads to a revaluation of his attitude toward the history of the "real" world. A virtuoso performance, the novel presents Barth under a multiplicity of guises, but most directly as "The Author," "John Barth." In a letter to a character from his first novel, Barth comments on his own earlier infatuation with artifice. Referring to himself in the early 1950s as a "budding irrealist," Barth notes, "I wanted no models in the real world to hobble my imagination. If, as the Kabbalists supposed, God was an Author and the world his book, I criticized Him for mundane realism." But, he continues, "I approach reality these days with more respect, if only because I find it less realistic and more mysterious than I'd supposed" (*L*, pp. 189–90). While myth continues to play a role in Barth's apprehension and presentation of reality, it no longer dominates it. Rather, he shifts his attention to the relationship of written performance, historical pattern, and personal identity.

Both directly and indirectly, Joyce is a much larger presence in *Letters* than in any of Barth's previous works. Frequently Barth alludes directly to Joyce (e.g., *L*, pp. 11, 39, 40, 72, 74, 232, 354, 418), mostly in connection with Lady Amherst, the only "new" major character in *Letters*. At one point Barth quotes the opening of *Finnegans Wake* (*L*, p. 68). But more important, echoes of Joycean motifs occur throughout the work. Some of these, such as Jacob Horner's list of cuckolds, which recalls the "Ithaca" section of *Ulysses* (*L*, p. 428), simply amuse the reader who recognizes them. But others relate directly to Barth's central thematic concerns.

The most important of these echoes involves generational patterns. Jerome Bray, descendant of the Harold Bray of *Giles Goat-Boy*, concludes a letter with an invocation directed to his "Lost Mother, old articifrix" (*L*, p. 427), echoing the conclusion of *A Portrait of the Artist as a Young Man*. The following letter, written by Ambrose Mensch from *Lost in the Funhouse*, begins with the invocation of an "Old messenger" (*L*, p. 428). Todd Andrews, engaged throughout the novel in a dialog with his dead father as he was in *The Floating Opera*, recalls Stephen Dedalus by addressing a letter to his "Old father" (*L*, p. 457). The numerous references to the tension between twins, particularly but not exclusively between the descendants of Ebenezer Cook of *The Sot-Weed Factor*, recall the Joycean portrayal of the battles between Shem and Shaun. Just as Joyce pictures the twins involved in such intricate interchanges of identity that they themselves may no longer be sure who is who, Barth demonstrates that the machinations of the Burlingames and Cooks result in a situation where ambiguity becomes the only constant element. Rather than using ambiguity to vindicate an extreme allegorical style, however, Barth suggests that the ambiguity reflects "an age in which the Real and the Romantic are, so to speak, fraternal twins" (*L*, p. 490).

In *Giles Goat-Boy* the "romantic" Anastasia-Stacey split serves to distance the text from the "real" world. In *Letters* the familial struggles reflect very real historical struggles. Rather than allegorically reflecting what the character Barth refers to as "a nameless university which encompasses and replicates the world" (*L*, p. 531), *Letters* reflects history through numerous Whitmanesque catalogs of real events (cf. *L*, pp. 98, 232, 411, 569). These range throughout human history but concentrate on the Napoleonic Wars; the early "parental" conflicts between the United States, Great Britain, and the indigenous Native American peoples; and the political upheavals of the late 1960s. In each case Barth chooses the historical patterns for their emblematic value, much as Joyce chose the Napoleonic conflicts for use in the *Wake*. No longer establishing a personal-public hierarchy, Barth argues that public and private, real and symbolic, histories mirror the same processes.

In this context, the writing of history, as Joyce too realized, takes on special significance. A sufficiently skillful writer in control of the historical text may control the impact of history on future events, though it is important to recognize that the historical conflict may in fact determine who writes the history. Therefore it is not *simply* a matter of the romantic power of the imagination over reality. Neither Barth nor Joyce subscribes to Shelley's vision of poets as unacknowledged legislators of the world in any immediate sense. This intricate interplay between history and the artistic process accounts for the importance of letters—most prominently those written by ALP and Shem—in *Finnegans Wake*. It also accounts for the fact that every plot strand of *Letters* (a title which invokes both the Richardsonian and the Joycean epistolary traditions) involves a character making an artistic statement analogous both to *Letters* as a whole and to the *Wake*. Andrew Cook VI (a.k.a. Andrée Castine) attempts to control the political beliefs of his son by composing a letter which ultimately only increases the ambiguities. Andrews struggles to come to terms with his past by writing to his dead father; Horner engages in "scriptotherapy." Jerome Bray sets up a computer which he hopes will write the ultimate revolutionary NOVEL which gradually degenerates into a work of "numerature," but not before spouting an increasingly Wakean set of multilingual, cabalistically organized comic sequences (*L*, pp. 325ff., 525ff., 641). Ambrose Mensch ultimately provides the design for *Letters* itself. In addition, each of the characters appears to be planning Barth's *Chimera*, images from which permeate each plot.

   Not content with simply creating their own fictions, the various characters struggle to dominate "Barth's" (and Barth's) work. Barth manipulates the conceit (derived in part from the experiments of post-Joycean writers such as Flann O'Brien) of characters living independent lives. So when "Barth" writes to each requesting permission to "use" them in his latest novel (*Letters*), some accept and some refuse. Nearly all claim that Barth has plagiarized either their writing or their experience in creating his earlier novels. The most extreme case of this claim is Bray's determination to charge "Barth" with both plagiarism and distortion in the case of *Giles Goat-Boy* (*L*, pp. 27ff.); it is also echoed by Cook in relation to *The Sot-Weed Factor* (*L*, pp. 405ff.). Ambrose Mensch appears to be perfectly happy with "Barth's" use of "his" ideas, but he claims credit both for *Chimera* and for the development of "Barth's" aesthetic.

   All of this obviously brings Barth to a position where his text could easily have disintegrated into what "Barth" calls "Middle-Modernist affectation" (*L*, p. 191). But it does not disintegrate, for the simple reason that Barth is now deeply aware of the serious questions posed by his virtuoso performance. In *Giles Goat-Boy* Barth presented his allegory as if it reflected reality in an "unmediated" manner. In *Letters* he perceives that, given his aesthetic disposition, the question of mediation is of primary importance. He no longer attempts to deny that his individual performance, his control of the text of *Letters*, may significantly affect, even distort, the nature of his encyclopedia. Barth takes his cue from the Joyce who constantly reminds those who read *Finnegans Wake* of the relatively simple masculine and feminine principles lying behind the encyclopedic chaos by scattering the initials HCE and ALP throughout. In *Letters* Barth reminds us of the continual presence of John Barth by repeating the initials J. B. in the names of Jerome Bray, Jean Blanque (*L*, p. 110), Joseph Brant (*L*, p. 135), Jerome Bonaparte (*L*, p. 240), Joseph Bacri (*L*, p. 288), and many others. Characters whose names use one of Barth's initials (Harold Bray, Henry Burlingame, Merope Bernstein, Marsha Blank) are even more numerous. Certain other initials—A and C, for example, which complete the ABC pattern which Joyce used to invoke the alphabet and hence the elements of reality—also recur frequently. Each character competing for control of the text also attempts to suffuse the "universe" with his personality, but it is clear that the presence of J. B. dominates *Letters*.

Of course, Barth dominates *Giles Goat-Boy*, too, and the mere fact of greater recognition and manipulation of this control says nothing about its significance. Ultimately what makes *Letters* a superior work is that Barth now uses his performance to bring about a more profound apprehension of the world in both its symbolic and its realistic aspects. In terms of his individual life, his romantic persona, Barth like Mensch has forged an instrument, a formalistic and romantic instrument, which ultimately "liberate[s him] to be (as he has after all always been, but is enabled now more truly, freely, efficaciously to be) in the world" (*L*, p. 651). And his instrument works not only inward toward the romantic self, but outward toward the realistic elements of the encyclopedia. Near the end of the performance Barth addresses the reader directly, as he does near the beginning (*L*, pp. 42–45). He comments on the impossibility of encompassing a constantly changing reality in a fictional "universe" which is bound inextricably to the realities of its period of conception, composition, revision, and publication. J. B.'s individual performance may therefore control the reality of his text; it cannot control the reality of the world. His text can, however, lead the reader, like the author, to participate more freely in the world by heightening his perception of the encyclopedia as it exists at the moment of reading. After providing final catalogs of reality at the times of the final "fictional" moment, and during the "actual" outlining, drafting, and typing of the text, Barth asks the reader to "supply date and news items" relevant to the day of reading (and perhaps of commenting on) the text. All of which ultimately serves as a reminder that "our concepts, categories, and classifications are ours, not the World's, and are as finally arbitrary as they are provisionally useful. Including, to be sure, the distinction between *ours* and *the World's*" (*L*, p. 648).

Born a performer, Norman Mailer has played more roles than any other member of his literary generation. Novelist, Criminal, Philosopher, Playwright, Celebrity: with a multitude of roles to choose from, one of Mailer's favorites has always been the role of untutored American genius. Through his portrayal of Sergius O'Shaughnessy in *The Deer Park*, Mailer implies his independence from Joyce's sophisticated European influence. Sergius reads a poem in Wake language entitled "The Drunk's Bebop and Chowder" (a poem Mailer claims as his own in *Advertisments for Myself*). When Sergius presents the poem, a reader responds:

> "I didn't realize how much you're under the influence of Joyce."
> I knew I was going to make a fool of myself, but for once I didn't care. "Who's Joyce?" I asked.
> "James Joyce. You've read him, of course?"
> "No. I think I heard his name though."[44]

The passage is a typical Mailer performance; Sergius may be a native genius, but Mailer has certainly heard of, and read, Joyce. On occasion Mailer's performances include appreciation of Joyce as writer and symbol. Contrasting Joyce and Beckett, Mailer observes:

> I do not mean that one has to read all of Joyce to understand the style of Joyce's mind and the dialectical beauties of his spirit. But so far, it has been mainly the academicians who have attempted to grapple with the Hip intricacies of Joyce's mysticism of the flesh as it suffered and was mutilated and elaborated against the social anvil of Christianity.

Nor do I mean that I am an expert on Joyce—like many of you who will read this, I have read perhaps half of "Ulysses" and fragments from "Finnegans Wake"—but then it is not necessary to read all of Joyce in order to feel or not feel the meaning of his language and the reach of his genius. He is after all the only genius of the twentieth century who has written in the English language.[45]

Mailer very rarely apotheosizes anyone, particularly another writer, without claiming similar stature, at least potentially. (The creation of some future super-Mailer serves to "justify" many of Mailer's most outrageous performances, such as stabbing his wife in order to provide an authentic base for a future novel.) His appreciation of Joyce corresponds to this pattern. In *Advertisements for Myself*, Mailer describes his plans for an eight-volume sequence revolving around Sergius, who would "travel through many worlds, through pleasure, business, communism, church, working class, crime, homosexuality, and mysticism." Mailer admits the arrogance behind the project: "Not a modest novel—one would need the seat of Zola and the mind of Joyce to do it properly."[46] Even while admitting that the sequence will never be written, Mailer presents himself as a potential Joyce capable of handling a wider, Zolaesque mass of life.

Joyce, then, is Mailer's image of the encompassing literary talent. Despite abandoning the Sergius cycle, Mailer has never surrendered its encyclopedic ambition; continually performing through the protagonists of his novels, he grapples with the contradictions of American society. Gradually his performances, which in *The Naked and the Dead, Barbary Shore*, and to an extent *The Deer Park* resemble those of Bellow and Ellison, have become more personal. Far from proving the extent of Mailer's arrogance, his growing willingness to focus on himself as participant indicates exactly the hesitancy which Poirier identifies as the driving motivation behind literary performance. Mailer comments: "God can write in the third person only so long as He understands His world. But if the world becomes contradictory or incomprehensible to Him, then God begins to grow concerned with His own nature. It's either that or borrow notions from other Gods."[47] Only by understanding the nature of his own involvement with his material, Mailer reasons, can the artist hope to forge an aesthetic whole out of a chaotic reality. The culmination occurs in *The Armies of the Night*, where, for the first time, Mailer successfully integrates his symbolic and realistic perceptions.

During the early stages of his career Mailer felt relatively little drive to unite the conflicting elements of his vision. Many critics (Mailer on the whole has attracted the highest-quality critical attention of any contemporary American novelist) have commented on his relationship to Chase's concept of the American romance.[48] For the moment, it is sufficient to note that Mailer both recognizes the existence of "a war at the center of American letters"[49] and desires to create a work which will exercise a direct influence over the quality of American life:

> After [Dreiser's] heroic failure, American literature was isolated—it was necessary to give courses in American literature to Americans, either because they would not otherwise read it, or because reading it, they could not understand it. It was not quite vital to them. It did not save their lives, make them more ambitious, more moral, more tormented, more audacious, more ready for love, more ready for war, for charity and for invention. No, it tended to puzzle them. The realistic literature had never caught up with the rate of change in American life, indeed it had fallen further and further behind, and the novel gave up any desire to be a creation equal to the phenomenon of the country itself; it settled for being a metaphor.[50]

The Armies of the Night reflects both Mailer's perception of the problem and his determination to escape the "metaphorical" trap. As Laura Adams argues, *The Armies of the Night* first presents the contradictions of American experience and then attempts to resolve them through acts uniting symbolic and realistic significance. Adams, whose fine chapter in *Existential Battles: The Growth of Norman Mailer* anticipates several of my arguments, believes that "Mailer has taken upon himself the task of making our most basic myth, the Adamic myth, exist on a literal level, in order to synthesize the thesis and antithesis present in much of our literature."[51] While I would agree with Adams's position, I would also suggest that Mailer extends the principle of individual resolution to a collective level. The formulation of the "aesthetic" in book two of *The Armies of the Night* connects the individual existential performance, culminating in Mailer's arrest, with that of the American middle class which manages momentarily to unite its symbolic and realistic actions during the "battle of the wedge."

Images of irresolution abound in *The Armies of the Night*, establishing an atmosphere of "working-day good American schizophrenia."[52] By amassing images of individual Americans—police, hippies, blacks—at odds with each other and with themselves, Mailer creates a sense of imminent disaster such as that which overtook F. Scott Fitzgerald: "Yes, how much of Fitzgerald's long dark night may have come from that fine winnowing sense in the very fine hair of his nose that the two halves of America were not coming together, and when they failed to touch, all of history might be lost in the divide" (*AN*, pp. 157–58). The primary images of opposition in *The Armies of the Night* are external, but they gain force when juxtaposed with Mailer's sense of internal contradiction. While claiming "a complex mind of sorts" for Mailer the character, Mailer the novelist criticizes his avatar's tendency to oversimplify (*AN*, p. 5) and images him as a cathedral constructed over a period of centuries by mutually antagonistic orders of the church (*AN*, p. 17). The social and individual contradictions coalesce in Mailer's description of the march on the Pentagon, partially a symbolic confrontation over America's self-image and partially a real meeting of "armies" charged with potential physical danger. As Adams observes, Mailer attempts to bring these elements into balance by creating an image of effective heroism and generating an effective literary style.[53] The first of these goals focuses attention on the performance of Mailer as character, primarily in book one, the second on that of Mailer as writer, primarily in book two.

Both of these goals have been present in Mailer's work since long before *The Armies of the Night*, and, as Tanner argues, his solution to the stylistic issues appears nearly complete in *An American Dream*. In that novel, Tanner notes, "Mailer walks a stylistic edge. He touches continually on two worlds—the inner and the outer, the demonic and the political, the dreaming and the waking, the structured and the flowing—and tries to be stylistically adequate to all without being trapped by any one."[54] In *An American Dream*, as in *The Armies of the Night*, Mailer alternates passages concentrating on realistic details with extended metaphorical explorations of issues or images suggested by the details. When Mailer sees the helicopters observing the march on the Pentagon, the original description fits well within the conventions of realistic fiction: "In any event, up at the front of this March, in the first line, back of that hollow square of monitors, Mailer and Lowell walked in this barrage of cameras, helicopters, TV cars, monitors, loudspeakers, and wavering buckling twisting line of notables" (*AN*, p. 113). But soon his style fades into what Tanner calls "demonized documentary":[55]

> He was, in fact, by now even virtually in love with the helicopters, not because the metaphors of his mind had swollen large enough to embrace even them! no! he loved the helicopters because they were the nearest manifestation of the enemy, and he now loved his enemy for the thundering justification they gave to his legitimate—so he would term it—sentiments of pride in himself on this proud day, yes, the helicopters ugliest flying birds of them all, dragon in the shape of an insect, new vanity of combat, unutterable conceit, holy hunting pleasure, spills and thrills of combat on a quick hump and jump from the down-home Vietnam country club, symbol of tyranny to a city man, for only high officials and generals and police officers flitted into cities on helicopters this small in size—Mailer, General Mailer, now had a vision of another battle, the next big battle, and these helicopters, press, television and assorted media helicopters hovering overhead with CIA-FBI—all others of the alphabet in helicopters—and into the swarm of the chopper would come a Rebel Chopper in black, or in Kustem-Kar Red, leave it to the talent of the West Coast to prepare the wild helicopters; it would be loaded with guns to shoot pellets of paint at the enemy helicopters, smearing and daubing, dripping them, dropping cans of paint from overhead to smash on the blades of the chopper like early air combat in World War I, and Fourth of July rockets to fire past their Plexiglass canopies. [*AN*, pp. 114–15]

Mailer's style demands that we recognize both the realistic and symbolic dimensions of the experience.

While stylistically similar to *An American Dream*, however, *The Armies of the Night* marks an advance on the earlier novel's treatment of heroism. Tanner argues that Rojack in *An American Dream* attains "the area of imagination—a territory not already marked out by contemporary society, but created by a personal energy of style."[56] But Rojack's accomplishment is symbolic; in reality he achieves nothing, lighting out for the "Yucatan territory" after his descent from the crow's nest of the parapet. In *An American Dream* Mailer's vision remains subject to the irresolution which his style apparently denies. Arguing that Mailer's heroism in *The Armies of the Night* is at once less spectacular and more convincing than Rojack's in *An American Dream*, Adams notes the new sophistication of Mailer's heroic ideal:

> It centers around his perception that one is not permitted to confront the power at the top in the United States as Rojack could confront Kelly in *An American Dream*. Who, then, was the potential American hero to confront and attempt to defeat: a couple of terrified National Guardsmen, a United States marshal, a commissioner who would teach him a lesson by confining him to jail, the press who inevitably misquote him? Taken separately these opponents hardly approximate a Barney Kelly. Even combined they are scarcely fit foes for a romantic hero.[57]

The point, of course, is that heroism rarely resembles romance. In *The Armies of the Night* the writer Mailer undercuts the character Mailer's original sense of himself as romantic hero, a process which, ironically, elevates him from mock-heroism to an authentic, if limited, heroism.

The Armies of the Night opens with an image which criticizes Mailer the character's romantic self-indulgence and prepares the reader to accept Mailer the novelist's vision of the March on the Pentagon. Quoting from *Time* magazine's report of a pre-march rally, Mailer presents an image of himself as obscene buffoon. *Time*'s report bears little resemblance to Mailer's first-person report of the events, but both make it clear that Mailer lacked rapport with his audience and ranted to little purpose. Telling his audience of his adventures in a dark bathroom, Mailer loses track of the fact that pissing on the floor, even for forty-five consecutive technicolor seconds, has little symbolic or realistic value. He faces a long march to his ultimate heroism. Still, Mailer insists that *Time* is part of a distorting medium which contributes to the national schizophrenia. Confronting a member of the American Nazi party after his arrest, Mailer reflects:

> If the Nazi started trouble, and there was a fight, the newspaper accounts would doubtless state that Norman Mailer had gotten into an altercation five minutes after his arrest. (Of course, they

would not say with whom.) This is all doubtless most paranoid of Mailer, but then he had had nearly twenty years of misreporting about himself, and the seed of paranoia is the arrival of the conviction that the truth about oneself is never told. (Mailer might have done better to pity the American populace—receiving misinformation in systematic form tends to create mass schizophrenia.) [*AN*, p. 141]

Only by providing better information can Mailer counter this tendency.

Mailer attempts to establish the authority of his information by presenting himself as at once a representative man and a consummate performer.[58] By describing himself first as the Historian (*AN*, p. 13) and the Novelist (*AN*, p. 26), Mailer claims the observational and recording roles. But as the work progresses he expands his roles to include those of the Beast (*AN*, p. 30), the Existentialist (*AN*, p. 40), the Citizen (*AN*, p. 55), the Ruminant (*AN*, p. 96), and frequently simply the Participant (*AN*, p. 133), the everyman figure caught up in events. At the same time that he is claiming these roles, Mailer admits he is performing, consciously shaping his image. Mailer-the-character believes "that taken at his very worst he was at least still worthy of being a character in a novel by Balzac" (*AN*, p. 8); Mailer-the-novelist comments on the implications of his choice of styles (*AN*, p. 133); Mailer-the-historian insists that history can make no claim to anything resembling objectivity (*AN*, pp. 254–55). Combined, these admissions create the impression that Norman Mailer's subjective report promises more insight into events than other sources simply because it knows its own limitations.

Similarly, Mailer's attempt to merge realistic and symbolic actions in *The Armies of the Night* revolves around the perception (a new one in Mailer's work) of the limitations of both purely symbolic and purely individual resistance to totalitarianism. Mailer understands, both as character and as novelist, the limitation of purely symbolic action. While he finds the attempted levitation of the Pentagon amusing as theater, he finds it an ineffective performance because it holds no real hope of success (*AN*, pp. 119ff.). On the other hand, he refuses to conceive of the march as a simple physical action, insisting that its effectiveness hinges on its ability to locate and strike at the Pentagon symbol. In fact, he believes that the Pentagon's primary defense lies in its seeming vulnerability to physical attack because "it was impossible to locate the symbolic loins of the building—paradigm of the modern world indeed, they could explore every inch of their foe and know nothing about him" (*AN*, p. 229). Mailer can accept neither abstract gesture nor simple action.

On the individual level, he solves the dilemma by getting himself arrested. Speaking to the rally, Mailer praises the march which "will be at once a symbolic act and a real act" (*AN*, p. 47). His original decision to be arrested so "the papers can't claim that hippies and hoodlums were the only ones guilty" (*AN*, p. 84) parallels his conception of the march as a whole; it is a real action calculated for maximum symbolic impact. But when the moment nears, Mailer reveals that he still sees the gesture in part as a pose which implies no serious commitment: "On the way, they agreed again that they would be arrested early. That seemed the best way to satisfy present demands and still get back to New York in time for their dinners, parties, weekend parts" (*AN*, p. 118). Only after his imprisonment does Mailer begin to recognize the importance of the gesture which leads to a series of confrontations—with the Nazi, with other prisoners, with his jailers—forcing him to see the limits and importance of his own action.

Mailer comes to an understanding of his arrest as a real and symbolic moral action, but when forced to come to terms with Tuli Kupferberg's refusal to sign a promise not to return to the Pentagon, an action which forces Kupferberg to serve his full jail term, Mailer revalues his own action. On the surface, Kupferberg appears simply to extend Mailer's logic: he will back up his symbolic resistance to the Vietnam war by accepting a physical incarceration which itself will provide a symbol potentially capable of motivating further realistic actions. Mailer reflects, "Seen from one moral position—not too far from his own—prison could be nothing but an endless ladder of moral challenges. Each time you climbed a step as Kupferberg just had, another higher, more dangerous, more disadvantageous step would present itself. Sooner or later, you would have to descend. It did not matter how high you had climbed" (*AN*, p. 195). Still, Mailer feels driven to justify his own choice of a cutoff point. Why go as far as he did? Why not go a step farther? Mailer the character's performance ends before he answers these questions. Mailer *has* attained a form of heroism which combines reality and symbol, but the larger resolution lies in the performance of Mailer the novelist in book two.

Book two fares badly with most critics. Adams finds it less impressive than book one, and Robert Solotaroff, rejecting the middle-class "rite of passage" which forms the climax of the book, considers it quite simply "a mistake."[59] The rite of passage, however, provides *The Armies of the Night* with its final unity and follows inevitably from Mailer's treatment of his own character. From its origins in contradiction to its resolution in a half-understood act of resistance, the experience of the middle class in book two follows the experience of Norman Mailer in book one.

Mailer sees the political left which conceived the March on the Pentagon as subject to numerous internal contradictions. Mailer insists that the march originated almost entirely in the white middle-class left, either excluding or being excluded by working-class and black radicals. Within the middle-class left, Mailer identifies a serious schism between the "Old Left" with its roots in 1930s Marxism and the internally divided "New Left," its affinities with academic liberalism on one side and hippie nihilism on the other. "Unity," Mailer comments, "had obviously not been encouraged" (*AN*, p. 224). Locating the origins of the middle-class political stance in a hatred of its own involvement with technology, Mailer the character frequently treats the other participants in the march with something bordering on contempt.

Mailer the novelist, however, understands the connection between this attitude and Mailer the character's inability to accept his own middle-class origins. Perhaps the most important passage in *The Armies of the Night* involves Mailer's attitude toward his own performance:

> Watching himself talk on camera for this earlier documentary, he was not pleased with himself as a subject. For a warrior, presumptive general, ex-political candidate, embattled aging enfant terrible of the literary world, wise father of six children, radical intellectual, existential philosopher, hard-working author, champion of obscenity, husband of four battling sweet wives, amiable bar drinker, and much exaggerated street fighter, party

giver, hostess insulter—he had on screen in this first documentary a fatal taint, a last remaining speck of the one personality
he found absolutely insupportable—the nice Jewish boy from
Brooklyn (*AN*, p. 134).

The nice Jewish boy from Brooklyn shares more with the middle-
class left than Mailer the Existentialist or Mailer the Beast find
comfortable. In fact, the middle-class boys who burn their draft
cards risk far more than Mailer the Celebrity at the Pentagon
rally: "By handing in draft cards, these young men were committing their future either to prison, emigration, frustration, or at
best, years where everything must be unknown, and that spoke of
a readiness to take moral leaps which the acrobat must know
when he flies off into space—one has to have faith in one's ability
to react with grace en route, one has ultimately, it may be supposed, to believe in some kind of grace" (*AN*, p. 74). Mailer attains
this state of grace only when he recognizes the profound similarity between his own gesture and that of the middle-class left
which accepts the brutality of the "battle of the wedge" as a symbolic and realistic rite of passage. For Mailer-the-novelist, the
greatest existential challenge lies in admitting those aspects of
his own character which discourage existential confrontation.
Mailer's limitations and possibilities parallel those of the other
participants at the Pentagon, those who find Kupferberg's rigorous
morality beyond their grasp. For the first time in his work Mailer
cedes the role of ideal hero to a character placed in contrast with
Norman Mailer; Mailer claims for himself, quite convincingly,
the role of representative man raised to something very near maximum awareness.

Mailer's decision to view the actions of the middle class at the
"battle of the wedge" as an "aesthetic" clinches the resolution of
The Armies of the Night. The term links Mailer the character, the
middle class of which he is a part, and Mailer the writer. Just as
Mailer the writer resolves the manifold contradictions embedded
in his book, so the middle class in book two, like Mailer the participant in book one, accepts "a physical and spiritual transaction
whose emotions are, at worst, so little agreeable as the passage of
the dentist's drill toward the nerve canal of a tooth" (*AN*, p. 278).
The middle-class protestors have overcome their deeply embed-

ded propensity to seek comfort at the cost of existential integrity and have passed through a physical and spiritual dark night which earns them the same limited, but real, heroism as Mailer. Mailer's final act of heroism is his admission that his own secretive acts can embody the essence of an unromanticized moment of history.

CHAPTER FIVE

Recognizing Reality, Realizing Responsibility: Joyce, Gaddis, Pynchon

LIKE YEATS'S ROUGH BEAST, our awareness slouches slowly toward an apocalyptic birth. Things have fallen apart; the center cannot hold. All together now, we can get down to the hard work of cleaning up the debris and reordering the ranks.

The modernist movement, various and versatile, perceived the collapse and recorded the accompanying pain. When writers such as Joyce offered constructive suggestions, they were treating the agony of a passing era. Sharing the modernist interest in the causes and impact of that agony, William Gaddis and Thomas Pynchon nevertheless prescribe anodynes of a new kind. Suspicious of attempts to restore the health of an anachronistic social order, Gaddis and Pynchon turn their attention to the birth pangs of a new age.

Joyce, Gaddis, and Pynchon share an awareness that the collapse manifests itself in literature through an increasing disjunction of symbolic awareness from social and personal reality. On one side, any individual quixotic enough to seek a synthetic meaning at all finds a bewildering welter of facts, discrete disconnected bits of actuality. On the other, he finds an equally bewildering variety of symbolic systems intended to explain why the facts don't appear to make sense. To make the struggle for synthesis even less inviting, literary synthesizers have become increasingly aware that their own books may in fact mitigate human contact with the sense of unity they propose.

Joyce partly reflects and partly rejects the modernist tendency to create alternate worlds which transcend the collapsing old reality. Joyce's works certainly reflect Stephen Dedalus' aesthetic, which concentrates on the "unity, harmony and radiance" of the work of art reaching out to an ideal stasis. But his work also comprehends the advertising aesthetic of Leopold Bloom, which seeks "to arrest involuntary attention, to interest, to convince, to decide" (*U*, p. 683). As a supreme example of modernist art, *Ulysses* forges an imaginative order which radiates an impressive aesthetic wholeness. As a pioneering work of the new order, it seeks to convince us that rich human experience remains decisively possible. Despite its recognition of the collapse of traditional support for the sense of human importance, *Ulysses* convinces us of the worth of Bloom's struggle to unite his real and symbolic actions toward Stephen and Molly. In many ways *Ulysses* remains a profoundly reassuring book.

In a sense William Gaddis is even more committed than Joyce to the modernist ideal of an encompassing artistic achievement. In his struggle to both describe and create a work revealing the comprehensive spiritual reality behind the fragmented world, Gaddis appears a quintessential follower of T. S. Eliot. But Gaddis also expands the modernist universe until it collapses in upon itself. Taking the concept of the "vocation," in the religious sense, of the artist much more seriously than did Joyce, Gaddis questions art's capability of embodying truly religious apprehensions of reality. Disconcertingly, the attempts of Stanley and Wyatt in *The Recognitions* to realize their art in the real world result in the destruction of either the work of art or the artist. Gaddis confronts a religious reality which renders traditional artistic constructions obsolete, however well they may link more accessible realities.

Thomas Pynchon assumes the insufficiency of literature, which is simply one of many methods of imposing order on a recalcitrant and recondite reality. Claiming no authority for his own perspective, Pynchon places squarely with us, the readers, the responsibility for determining what (if any) actions *Gravity's Rainbow* suggests. If we wish to accept entropy, to sit horrified by the collapse of structures which even in the old world lacked the authority they claimed, *Gravity's Rainbow* allows us to indulge our fear. If we feel driven to struggle against acquiescence, *Gravity's Rain-*

bow provides the materials for a new conception of human value in the era of the rough beast. The nature of the era may ultimately depend on how we make the choice, how we react to Pynchon's vision of life in a zone without authoritative texts.

While Joyce, Gaddis, and Pynchon weave a particular strand of twentieth-century literary history, each moves freely among the styles of previous literary eras. At the same time, each reveals particular historical affinities which shape the stylistic design of his works. Joyce, as the title of *Ulysses* suggests, aspires to a radically reconstructed classicism. Just as the Greeks approached the world with what the twentieth century interprets as a boundless confidence in their perceptual ability, so Joyce aspires to a supreme clarity of vision. If uncertainty enters Joyce's work, he intends that the reader see the uncertainty as a mark of Joyce's understanding of randomness. The carefully balanced chart of the structures of *Ulysses* reflects Joyce's classical tendencies. Gaddis, whose title alludes to a theological treatise, questions the classical ideal of clarity and insists that if inclusive art exists, its roots must lie in a late medieval or early Renaissance apprehension of the mystery of life, a mystery comprehensible not to the mind of man, but only to an inscrutable God. Mirroring this affinity, *The Recognitions* rests its style on a complex web of philosophical and theological speculations which aspire less to embodiment than to intimation of an ultimate aesthetic unity. Pynchon, whose title probably doesn't allude to literature at all, seeks an entirely different literary approach, that of the Victorian novelists. Both Joyce and Gaddis chose stylistic ancestors who worked within relatively well-defined aesthetic systems; Pynchon turns, or returns, to the "loose, baggy monster," the instrument of an era concerned more with social than with aesthetic forms of unity. Joyce's and Gaddis's stylistic variety can be explicated in terms of particular self-created or willingly accepted "rules"—variations of style can always be justified as effective ways of dealing with particular aspects of the aesthetic whole. Pynchon refuses to accept any similar rules. He will address us directly, use epigrams at chapter beginnings, splice in essays, shift interest to various grotesques and employ whatever else comes to hand, whatever participates in the social maelstrom with which he is most concerned. Denying the validity of aesthetic unity, Pynchon refuses to employ a style which in any way implies such validity. In confronting Pynchon's "style," as in confronting his "themes," we must accept the responsibility for the implications of whatever order we find.

Despite these important stylistic differences, Joyce, Gaddis, and Pynchon share the impulse to press both realistic and symbolic modes to extremes, revealing them as tools of a vision reaching beyond any arbitrary limitations. All three immerse their characters in landscapes where realistic details demand attention; characters' mental states interact continually with the minute details of their environments. Determining which details are "significant" is the central issue of the novels if we interpret them from a realistic perspective. The increasing unfamiliarity of the realistic settings in *The Recognitions* and *Gravity's Rainbow* reflects Gaddis's and Pynchon's heightened sense of the dislocations caused by America's migratory social patterns and the World War. Joyce's Dubliners live in one city most of their lives and can at least name familiar people and places. Gaddis's characters, most of whom live on Manhattan, grew up elsewhere and feel threatened even by familiar inanimate landscapes or buildings. While Pynchon's Zone contains as many real objects as Joyce's Dublin or Gaddis's New York, it lacks even potential familiarity—it has been constructed brick by shattered brick. Reduced to fragments by the war and to namelessness by the collapse of social structures such as language, the Zone merely provides fragmented material for attempts at reconstruction.

Similarly, the proliferation of symbolic systems in the three works reflects the increasing extremity of our situation. Joyce shows his awareness of a huge range of symbolic structures ranging from those of Aristotle to the newspapers of the Irish nationalist movement, from Aquinas to Eisenstein. While his knowledge may seem recondite, it remains well within his shaping power: Joyce implicitly reassures us that, at least in his mind, the symbols take on manageable dimensions. Gaddis offers a similar reassurance but seems more aware of the likelihood that even his own sensibility may not be able to forge an order which can withstand direct comparison with the reality it purports to comprehend.

Just as his realistic details lack names, Pynchon's symbolic references often lack clear physical or historical application. They appear to be cosmic jokes, random manifestations of the human shaping impulse. Pynchon's juxtaposition of abstract concepts from mathematics and science with symbolic systems originating in movies and comics creates an atmosphere of absolute overload. No one (and we suspect this includes Pynchon) can understand all of the systems alluded to in *Gravity's Rainbow*. Where Stephen Dedalus and Wyatt Gwyon seem to possess the potential for understanding the books in which they are characters, none of Pynchon's characters has even heard of all of the systems surrounding their fictional existence. The symbolic systems seem so far removed from human reality as to be absurd. How the hell do we even know benzene rings exist?

Because they let us build rockets.

And the rockets explode.

The extension of realism and symbolism ultimately forces a return to reality. Not to the modernist reality of the book, but to whatever reality it is out there that makes us worry about the rocket exploding. Unless we love the explosion, as Pynchon fears we may, we have to renew our senses of humanity. Joyce knew and took a first step. Gaddis and Pynchon stumble on. Fearing the solipsistic isolation of a Samuel Beckett, they share a sense that the key to recovery lies in our ability to connect our symbols and our realities with a sense of human responsibility, even if we're standing on a Bethlehemic void.

William Gaddis

William Gaddis haunts the corners of his theater, observing his actors dissolve. While nearly every character in *The Recognitions* claims center stage to declaim his agony, Gaddis eventually watches each echo Ed Feasley's despair when he admits, "I feel like I've left little parts of me all over the place. Like I could spend the rest of my life trying to collect them and I never could. These pieces of me and pieces of other people all screwed up and spread all over the place."[1] Reduced to pieces, the characters retreat further into solipsistic self-dramatization. Gaddis, adopting the Joycean role of God of his own creation with supra-Joycean seriousness, progresses from modernism through nihilism to mysticism in his attempt to force a recognition of the unity behind the chaos. Despite his elevated perspective, Gaddis, like his "protagonist" Wyatt, avoids the temptation of romantic individualism, with its solipsistic elements, by accepting myriad viewpoints: "There isn't any single perspective, like the camera eye, the one we all look through now and call it realism, there . . . I take five or six or ten . . . the Flemish painter took twenty perspectives if he wished, and even in a small painting you can't include it all in your single vision, your one miserable pair of eyes, like you can a photograph" (*TR*, p. 251). As Wyatt's statement intimates, Gaddis seeks an artistic form which will both embody his vision and force his reader to recognize a reality in which his characters live, and advances a theory of the larger reality. While the work of art, the Flemish painting or *The Recognitions* itself, must communicate the connections between photographic reality and the mystical reality he endorses, Gaddis does not view the work of art as a final answer. Wyatt confronts the insufficiency of the modernist idea of art as religion; he nearly succumbs to nihilism before recognizing that the insufficiency of art does not entail its lack of value. Far from denying the presence of meaning in the photographic world, Gaddis simply remarks the shortcomings of human understanding.

Following both Joyce and T. S. Eliot, Gaddis juxtaposes his contemporary setting with mythological patterns; in fact, Gaddis's early notes reveal that only after he read *The Golden Bough* did he decide that *The Recognitions* would be more than a brief satirical treatment of the Faust story.[2] Throughout the novel Gaddis, using an apparently reliable authorial voice, stresses the mythological patterns lying behind the realistic action. Transformed by Gaddis's commentary, a fly bothering Otto becomes "a goddess, a princess, and a devil" (*TR*, p. 203); later Gaddis comments directly on the parallel between the Harlem drag ball and the ancient Dionysian processions (*TR*, p. 311). In addition, Reverend Gwyon's sermons provide a compendium of mythological arcana linking contemporary Christianity with religions as diverse as those of the Australian aborigines whose Boyman corresponds to Christ (*TR*, p. 268) and the gnostics whose Mithra preceded Christ (*TR*, pp. 703ff).

The most effective presentations of the connection between myth and reality rely on the perceptions of the individual characters rather than on Gaddis's direct statements. Both the Gwyon family servant Janet and Wyatt's grandfather, the town carpenter, greet Wyatt as a mythic hero when he returns home after a long absence. Janet sees Wyatt as Christ resurrected "from the tomb" (*TR*, p. 407) and the town carpenter hails him as a hero come to harrow the contemporary hell by revealing its nature in "the great mirror in which you can see all that goes on in your kingdom" (*TR*, p. 410). While the town carpenter and Janet are among the least articulate characters in *The Recognitions*, they share a desire to elevate the secular world, to find meaning in their realistic surroundings.

The combination of Gaddis's commentary, Gwyon's speculations, and the inchoate urges of characters like Janet and the town carpenter creates an impression of a "fallen" world desperately in need of a sense of its own value. Like Eliot, Gaddis posits a universe of meaningful patterns which exist in contemporary life only in attenuated forms. The Christmas Eve setting of the double *Walpurgisnacht* of Esther's party (*TR*, pp. 568–642) and Recktall Brown's showing (*TR*, pp. 653–94) serves an ironic purpose, parallel to Eliot's use of the Easter season. No miraculous birth occurs on Christmas Eve; indeed, the "Christ figure" Wyatt attempts to murder Valentine, symbolically repudiating the structure of the savior myth. Even as a *Walpurgisnacht*, the evening aborts. Where Joyce's "Circe" chapter and Mann's *Walpurgisnacht* in *The Magic Mountain* leave their readers and participants with a sense of psychic purgation, of important issues confronted and at least partially resolved, Gaddis's scene leads only to increasing confusion. A character refers to the events as "A real Walpurgis . . ." (*TR*, p. 751), but his description, like the purgative experience, disintegrates before completion. Throughout *The Recognitions* Gaddis initiates patterns with redemptive mythological undertones, only to truncate or invert them.

While the mythic framework of *The Recognitions* derives more directly from "The Waste Land" than from *Ulysses* (although it is always possible, if not probable, that Gaddis shares Eliot's reading of *Ulysses*), the structure of the novel and many particular motifs allude directly to Joyce. Bernard Benstock notes the relationship between Wyatt and Stephen Dedalus, which involves numerous parallel events such as early illness, involvement with and rejection of the priesthood, guilt over a mother's death, and the search for a creative father. The fatherhood motif and the intricate development of the image of artist as counterfeiter pervade both *The Recognitions* and Joyce's fiction. When Wyatt accepts Sinisterra's offer of "Stephan" as a new name, the connection between Gaddis's and Joyce's artist-heroes seems unarguable.[3]

If *The Recognitions* alludes to Joyce frequently, it does not "copy" him, even in the sense which Gaddis finds admirable. *Ulysses* explores the idea of the average man as a heroic figure. Conversely, Gaddis hints often that, like Thackeray, whose satirical touch resembles Gaddis's, he has written a "novel without a hero" (*TR*, p. 247). Wyatt refers to his sense of life as a hypothetical novel in which "the hero fails to appear" but is still "there all the time. None of them moves, but it reflects him" (*TR*, p. 263). *The Recognitions* is this novel; like Wyatt's Spain, it contains "a whole Odyssey within its boundaries, a whole Odyssey without Ulysses" (*TR*, p. 816). More immediately, *The Recognitions* is *Ulysses* without Bloom.

Although Gaddis, in his authorial voice, warns that "this manic phase of a reality . . . would, left to itself, blow itself out in senselessness. Therefore, to redeem these absurd extravaganzas, which is after all the way of a hero, requires a worthy goal" (*TR*, p. 415), his novel suggests few "realistic" heroic goals. While he seriously considers aesthetic solutions to the problem of redeeming reality, he offers nothing to the Leopold Blooms of the world. Gaddis in fact viciously attacks postwar American society on all levels, at times seeming nearly willing to sit back and contemplate the senseless destruction. Americans, Gaddis indicates, willingly accept distortion of reality because they fear integrity. Again in his authorial voice, he comments on the origins of American isolation: "Tragedy was foresworn, in ritual denial of the ripe knowledge that we are drawing away from one another, that we share only one thing, share the fear of belonging to another, or to others, or to God; love or money, tender equated in advertising and the world, where only money is currency, and under dead trees and brittle ornaments prehensile hands exchange forgeries of what the heart dare not surrender" (*TR*, p. 103). Forswearing their human reality, intellectual Americans hide behind aesthetic argot and unintellectual Americans hide behind shallow materialism. Joyce, too, condemns both intellectual and unintellectual shallowness. But while Joyce balances his condemnations with "positive" portrayals of the intellectual Stephen and relatively unintellectual Bloom, Gaddis provides well-developed positive portraits only of artists. His dismissal of the average man reveals the comparative chill of his temperament and is part of his larger devaluation of "mundane" reality, despite his theoretical commitment to it as a necessary subject and component of redemption.

The Manhattan of the central section of *The Recognitions* at times seems to share the density of Joyce's Dublin. Characters wander streets, travel by urban transportation, encounter and fail to encounter one another much as they might have in the "Wandering Rocks." But even when their physical environment affects them most, they interact with it in a way which emphasizes symbolic rather than realistic details. In *Ulysses*, the loss of a wallet would clearly become a recurring concern for either Stephen or Bloom, like the loss of a key. In *The Recognitions*, Otto does lose his wallet (*TR*, p. 508), but Gaddis loses it too, never mentioning the loss after Otto meets Sinisterra. Part of this deemphasis of minor realistic events results from Gaddis's decision to employ stream-of-consciousness techniques only sparingly. What might well be important to a character holds little interest for Gaddis, the artistic shaper. Indeed, very little "noise" clutters *The Recognitions*, compared to *Ulysses* and *Gravity's Rainbow*. Both Joyce and Pynchon emphasize their characters' difficulties in determining which realistic details deserve close attention. They force the reader to participate in the realistic process of sorting through irrelevant facts to find the ones with human meaning. In *The Recognitions* the mere presence of a detail guarantees its significance. Gaddis simplifies this aspect of the realistic dimension of his novel in order to underline his own ability to resolve the apparent chaos of his material. As in Joyce's and Pynchon's work, the characters in *The Recognitions* feel overwhelmed by reality. Prior to her suicide attempt, Agnes writes:

> Have you ever thought about this, that right now this instant every one of them is somewhere being real? The Pope and the

President and also certain surviving kings, the people whose secrets we know and the ones of whom we know no more than the newspaper confides, all the people you have met and all the people you will meet, and you have never met and will never meet, all of them they are somewhere now right this instant being real. Even when you are not talking about them, not thinking about them perhaps not even remembering them in spite of these insults they are somewhere being real. As though they did not care! It is too much to comprehend that, still they dare it, but it is too much. [*TR*, p. 762]

Too much for Agnes, too much for the other characters, but not too much for Gaddis, who, as David Madden observes, attempts to resolve the novel's numerous strands through a symbolic structure which fits the multitudinous details into a coherent pattern.[4]

Gaddis's dismissal of realistic problems deeply influences the entire social level of *The Recognitions*. Viewing the difficulties of his characters as "interchangeable disasters" (*TR*, p. 315), Gaddis lacks sympathy with the realistic circumstances which determine their decisions. His satirical portrayal of Mr. Pivner—in many ways a Leopold Bloom figure seeking a lost son eventually found through a symbolic adoption—lacks all traces of Joycean sympathy and understanding. Rather than unconsciously sharing the virtues of a heroic prototype, Pivner retreats from even a debased manifestation of myth: "The names AJAX and HERCULES borne in gold thundered by at an arm's reach, but Mr. Pivner did not appear to read. He stepped back, respectful as all ages of the expedition of heroes" (*TR*, p. 282). Where Joyce sees Bloom's concern with financial security as a part of his attempt to protect the human warmth he shares with his family in a world teetering on a void, Gaddis condemns Pivner's financial life as an avoidance of the confrontation: "Here was no promise of anything so absurd as a void where nothing was, nor so delusive as a chimerical kingdom of heaven: In short, it reconciled those virtues he had been taught as a child to the motive and practices of the man, the elixir which exchanged the things worth being for the things worth having" (*TR*, p. 499). Throughout Pivner's futile search for his son, Gaddis neither evinces sympathy nor explains either the realistic reasons for or emotional impact of the separation. Pivner's eventual arrest for counterfeiting (*TR*, p. 743) and lobotomization (*TR*, pp. 933–34) defy credibility. Of course, Gaddis intentionally treats Pivner as a satiric emblem, rather than as a rounded character.[5] But his failure to provide a realistic base for the satire conflicts with the treatment of the intellectual victims of Gaddis's satire. This lack of warmth creates an impression that Gaddis simply does not understand any character not immediately concerned with the theological and aesthetic issues which command his own interest.

Gaddis's treatment of science in *The Recognitions* reveals a parallel limitation. Especially in comparison with Pynchon, who perceives the high metaphoric content of scientific thought, Gaddis appears to have drawn his image of science from a bad junior high school textbook. Apparently believing that science strives for absolute, mathematically demonstrable certainties, Gaddis condemns it: "Science in magnitude, biology and chemistry as triumphantly articulate as subordinates are always, offer no choice but abjure it in frantic effort to perfect a system without alternatives, the very fact of their science based on measurement; and measurement, designed to predicate finalities, refusing the truth which shelters in possibility" (*TR*, p. 469). Several passages throughout the novel (cf. *TR*, pp. 287, 414, 566) develop the same theme, and Gaddis never seriously entertains a scientific perspective on experience. As with his social satire, he declines consideration of the actual roots of science, preferring to proceed directly to abstract philosophical discourse.

What renders Gaddis's limitations so intrusive is his insistence that the conception of art developed in *The Recognitions* does not involve a devaluation of reality. Gaddis argues that art can, or at least should, bring us into closer contact with reality. As Joseph S. Salemi observes in his excellent analysis of the aesthetics of *The Recognitions*, Gaddis's ideal art does not abandon reality but seeks to suggest "a reality marked by breadth of vision, chaste dignity, and controlled intelligence. . . . [Wyatt's aesthetic] cherishes a personal piety (whether religious or secular) that invests reality with numinous, even mystical significance."[6] While Salemi's contention that " 'reality' and 'art' are interchangeable metaphors for each other"[7] is generally accurate, it overlooks Gaddis's doubt concerning art's capability of reaching the highest levels of mystical significance, the ultimate reality.

Beyond question, debased art serves as a metaphor for debased life and vice versa. While the true artists in *The Recognitions* "forge" older styles with a full awareness of their deeper significance, the shallow artists simply copy the superficial attributes of whatever kind of art will bring them social approbation. Max's "whole God-damned novel is lifted" (*TR*, p. 350), and he later publishes a translation of Rilke under his own name (*TR*, p. 622); Otto's play—composed of lines lifted from conversations which Otto fails to understand—seems plagiarized to Agnes (*TR*, p. 296); Feddle carries a copy of *The Idiot* in a book jacket with his own name and picture (*TR*, p. 937). In each case, the plagiarist intends to exalt his own image through his "work"; while Max and Otto claim superior intellectual ability, their conception of art parallels that of the Hemingwayesque laborer Jesse, who insists that the only good novel is one which reinforces his own self-image (*TR*, pp. 156–57). Totally committed to their own importance, none of the plagiarists can sustain even a tangential interest in the reality of another person.

In stark contrast, both of the "true artists," Wyatt and Stanley, base their work on feelings toward others, although their own intense commitment to their art prevents them from accepting new emotional contact. Stanley dedicates his work to his dying mother, and Wyatt's genius expresses itself most strongly in works expressing what he feels as his mother's reproach (*TR*, p. 548). While Wyatt "forges" the Flemish paintings and Stanley composes music in a baroque rather than modern style, their plagiarism strives not to elevate their own importance but to express their recognition of the connections between human and spiritual realities. They plagiarize, but Wyatt believes that "Pythagoras Socrates Plato Homer & Hesiod, all plagiarized from Moses" (*TR*, p. 393), and "that the saints were counterfeits of Christ, and that Christ was a counterfeit of God" (*TR*, p. 483). Plagiarism therefore supports the highest possible aspirations.

Esme's letter to Wyatt, which expresses his ideas more clearly than he can ever do himself, provides the clearest statement of the underlying aesthetic of *The Recognitions*. The purpose of art is "to recognize, not to *establish* but to *intervene*" (*TR*, p. 472), to reach out to establish contact between God and reality. The ideal painting will at once reflect the artist's fullest sense of reality and help shape that reality: "It does not seem unreasonable that we invent colors, lines, shapes, capable of being, representative of existence, therefore it is not unreasonable that they, in turn, later, invent us, our ideas, directions, motivations, with great audacity, since we, ourselves having them upon our walls" (*TR*, p. 473). To this point, Esme's letter supports the idea of the work of art as the supreme act of the human spirit, the modernist aesthetic ideal. But Esme questions that aesthetic, emphasizing that any work of art remains a function of the limitations of its human creator, that it cannot fully communicate a vision of God: "they are unreasonably enough, insufficient, because they are not made of ideas, they are made of paint, all else is really us" (*TR*, p. 473). Pessimistically, she concludes, "Paintings are metaphors for reality, but instead of being an aid to realization obscure the reality which is far more profound. The only way to circumvent painting is by *absolute* death" (*TR*, p. 473). Wyatt, too, passes through this confrontation with a strangely religious nihilism before returning to an engagement with life, and perhaps a reacceptance of art.

Before questioning the sufficiency of art, Wyatt, like Joyce's Stephen Dedalus, must learn to escape the confines of his individuality and find his true subject. Wyatt's early attempts at original compositions remain unfinished (*TR*, p. 55), and he quickly accepts Herr Koppel's statement on "that romantic disease, originality, all around we see originality of competent idiots, they could draw nothing, paint nothing, just so the mess they make is original" (*TR*, p. 89). Finding that his real genius lies in "forgeries," Wyatt nonetheless fiercely defends the integrity of his work: "when I'm working, I . . . Do you think I do these the way all other forging has been done? Pulling the fragments of ten paintings together and making one . . . No, it's . . . the recognitions go much deeper, much further back" (*TR*, p. 250). Wyatt assumes the necessity of "the Guild oath, to use pure materials, to work in the sight of God" (*TR*, p. 250). As Salemi observes, however, Wyatt's integrity remains assailable as long as he works with the ulterior motive of financial reward, embodied in his complex relationship with Valentine and Brown. If Wyatt aspires to communicate the highest spiritual recognitions, he cannot base his work on the lie that it is not his work. Therefore, Wyatt's attempt to claim credit for his paintings at Brown's Christmas Eve gathering (*TR*, p. 676) reflects not a return to egotism but an insistence on comprehensive honesty. Prior to his disastrous confrontation with Valentine and Brown, Wyatt explains the impulse behind his work to Esther: "it isn't just expiation, but . . . that's why it is crucial, because this is the only way we can know ourselves to be real, is this moral action, you understand don't you, the only way to know others are real" (*TR*, p. 591). This insight parallels Stanley's less tortured acceptance of the idea that "nothing is self-sufficient, even art, and when art isn't an expression of something higher, when it isn't invested you might even say, it breaks up into fragments that don't have any meaning" (*TR*, p. 617). Both Wyatt and Stanley resist this lack of meaning.

This drive to extend the significance of the work of art beyond itself reflects Gaddis's dissatisfaction with the modernist ideal. Ironically, *The Recognitions* approximates this ideal through Gaddis's godlike manipulation of his characters, a manipulation which evinces little recognition of his own idiosyncratic perspectives. By remaining in the position of an ostensibly impartial arbiter, Gaddis fails to "claim" his own work. Whatever its structural implications, however, *The Recognitions* contains several explicit rejections of "the Modernism heresy" (*TR*, p. 178). Stanley presents the case most clearly when he argues, "When art tries to be a religion in itself . . . a religion of perfect form and beauty, but then there it is all alone, not uniting people, not . . . like the Church does but, look at the gulf between people and modern art" (*TR*, p. 632). The artist, Stanley believes, must serve art only insofar as art unites people; the only true union comes through God. Once removed from the highest purpose, the modernist artist as Stanley sees him confuses medium with message: "It isn't for love of the thing itself that an artist works, but so that through it he's expressing love for something higher, because that's the only place art is really free, serving something higher than itself" (*TR*, p. 632).

Realizing this resolution poses major problems. Even Stanley's faith wavers during his affair with Esme, but his real problem lies in his simple commitment to the Roman Catholic concept of spiritual reality. The collapse of the Fenestrula cathedral which results from Stanley's playing the organ reflects two problems with his position. Gaddis implies first that the attempt to realize the ideal work of art in reality entails the destruction of the artist;

look upon God and die. Second, he implies that institutional religious structures can no longer withstand the expression of their own essential truth. In a world of televised "Lives of the Saints" and movie spectaculars on the life of the "BVM," the Catholic Church appears a willing participant in spiritual decay. Stanley's commitment to an archaic ideal of the Church, dissociated from reality, literally kills him. Similarly, Esme, the other "simple" religious believer in the late stages of the novel, dies from an infection contracted kissing the feet of a holy statue. Once again, overlooking the reality of the church, in an attempt to attain a spiritual comfort it no longer offers, proves fatal.

Perceiving this insufficiency of institutional religion because of his family heritage, abortive theological studies, and contact with the Jesuit Valentine, Wyatt flirts with nihilism after his failure to claim credit for his forgeries. Throughout *The Recognitions*, intimations that human life rests on a void haunt Wyatt. His father perceives a "perfectly ordered chaos" (*TR*, p. 18) and the oxymoron persists. Wyatt fears that his most perfect copies lack contact with any original recognition of reality. When Valentine presses Wyatt to continue forging even after his decision to claim his work, Wyatt responds: "Why are you doing this to me? . . . When you know it doesn't exist? to ask me to copy it? Like he . . . restoring an empty canvas" (*TR*, p. 381). Valentine precipitates his own "murder" by taunting Wyatt with visions of a void beyond God:

> Yes, I remember your little talk, your insane upside-down apology for these pictures, every figure and every object with its own presence, its own consciousness because it was being looked at by God! Do you know what it was? What it really was? that everything was so afraid, so uncertain God saw it, that it insisted its vanity on His eyes? Fear, fear, pessimism and fear and depression everywhere, the way it is today, that's why your pictures are so cluttered with detail, this terror of emptiness, this absolute terror of space. [*TR*, p. 690]

Wyatt's attempt to kill Valentine plunges him directly into the void. After wandering with Sinisterra in Spain, he reaches the monastery where he expresses his nihilistic urges by destroying the art treasures owned by the monks (*TR*, p. 866). Tony Tanner believes that Wyatt "is pushing on to a more comprehensive idea of restoration—namely, the restoring of reality to itself, sym-

bolized by his easing of the interpositions of art, and all the flitter-
ings and fixities which a work of art involves."[8] Tanner's observation underemphasizes the destructive element of Wyatt's action.
In his drive to learn, like El Greco (*TR*, p. 372), not to fear empty
spaces, he loses contact with both art and reality. Wyatt's nihilistic reaction brings him very close to the dissociated position of
the American romantic hero, a position which violates Gaddis's
desire for the active redemption of the debased reality.

Ultimately, Wyatt cannot maintain his nihilism. Attempting to
reject his art, he hesitates and then reaffirms exactly the kind of
artistic reality his nihilistic "restorations" destroy: "I? in a world
of shapes and smells. The things that were real to other people
weren't real to me, but the things that were real to me, they . . .
yes they still are" (*TR*, p. 893). The reacceptance of art leads directly to a second regenerative step, Wyatt's reacceptance of human reality:

> Look back, if once you're started in living, you're born into sin,
> then? And how do you atone? By locking yourself up in remorse
> for what you might have done? Or by living it through. By lock-
> ing yourself up in remorse with what you know you have done?
> Or by going back and living it through. By locking yourself up
> with your work, until it becomes a gessoed surface, all prepared,
> clean and smooth as ivory? Or by living it through. By drawing
> lines in your mind? Or by living it through. If it was sin from
> the start, and possible all the time, to know it's possible and
> avoid it? Or by living it through. [*TR*, p. 896]

Finally he resolves simply "to live deliberately" (*TR*, p. 900) and
departs. The hero sets off for a place where he can attempt to
manifest his mystic awareness in the real world.

Typically, Gaddis provides no concrete image of Wyatt's deliberate life. As with his satire on Pivner, Gaddis focuses on the
symbolic content and deemphasizes the realistic complexities.
While his theory insists on the interpenetration of all aspects
of reality, his practice fails to realize the theoretical demand.
Throughout *The Recognitions* Gaddis expresses his doubt of art's
ability to comprehend the full significance which, he does not
doubt, exists in God's world. Admirably demonstrating the ability
of his own artwork to express his sense of this symbolic spiritual
reality, he falters in his treatment of "simple" physical and social

realities. Halfway from Joyce to Pynchon, Gaddis questions the modernist ideal but retreats to an aesthetically coherent expression of an abstraction. Pynchon completes the rejection of the modernist detached position, embracing Joyce the sympathetic comedian where Gaddis follows Joyce the sober priest.

Thomas Pynchon

Nothing since *Finnegans Wake* cries for commitment like the first sentences of *Gravity's Rainbow*: "A screaming comes across the sky. It has happened before, but there is nothing to compare it to now."[9] Is the screaming human or the inanimate descent of the rocket? Is the coming messianic? Sexual? Is there actually "nothing" to compare it to; are we orphans in a void? Or has nothing else ever been as important as our agony? When we read Pynchon we decide, or They have already decided for us, how we live. Pynchon, shunning the robes of the aesthetic priest, preaches for the preterite, never dogmatic, but doomed (like one of his characters) to know "how phony it looks. Who will believe that in his heart he wants to belong to them out there, the vast Humility sleepless, dying, in pain tonight across the Zone? the preterite he loves, knowing he's always to be a stranger" (*GR*, p. 731). However it looks, *Gravity's Rainbow* belongs to and with the wretched of the earth.

The screaming's human.

If we don't believe it's important now, we never will.

And our decisions are more important than any questions of literary influence or tradition. Our decisions can take us out of our conceptual systems into a life where the issues are worth talking about, where they have something to do with our humanity. Pynchon forces the resolution of modes off the page and into our lives, where it belongs. If we let him.

Joyce did influence *Gravity's Rainbow*, but he did not dominate it or direct it. Several critics have noted parallels between *Gravity's Rainbow* and *Ulysses*: both resolve questions of literary mode by rendering them irrelevant; both extend symbolic and realistic modes until they seem meaningless impositions of abstract systems on a concrete reading experience.[10] Joyce reinforces his stylistic resolution by portraying his characters successfully resolving their experiences. Pynchon, less sure both of his own aesthetic resolution and of the ability of any individual to effect a resolution, demands that any resolution take place in the minds and lives of his real readers—you and me—rather than in an abstract "life" on the printed page. While literature is a part of "real life," it works on us individually; Pynchon challenges us to reach beyond our solipsism and to contact our preterite brothers and sisters.

Inferring Pynchon's "position" on any issue is dangerous. We simply don't know much about him. Still, *Gravity's Rainbow* provides sufficient evidence to suggest that Pynchon reacts to Joyce ambivalently. It alludes to numerous modern novelists, including Kerouac and Henry Miller, Beckett and Proust (*GR*, pp. 675ff.), Ellison (see the cluster of invisibility images, *GR*, pp. 379–82), Gaddis (see the use of the forgery metaphor, *GR*, pp. 464, 610). While Pynchon frequently catalogs the names of important scientists, he *names* few novelists, most notably Ishmael Reed (*GR*, p. 588) and Joyce. The direct reference to Joyce suggests Pynchon's belief that at times Joyce, too, felt drawn to the preterite: "Lenin, Trotsky, James Joyce, Dr. Einstein all sat out at these tables. Whatever it was *they* all had in common: whatever they'd come to this vantage to score . . . perhaps it had to do with the people somehow, with pedestrian mortality, restless crisscrossing of needs or desperations in one fateful piece of street . . . dialectics, matrices, archetypes all need to connect, once in a while, back to some of that proletarian blood, to body odors and senseless screaming across a table, to cheating and last hopes, or else all is dusty Dracularity, the West's ancient curse" (*GR*, pp. 262–63). The small "t" in "they" which Pynchon emphasizes with italics hints that he sees Joyce in essential conflict with the capital T They who have no sense of the screaming of the preterite.[11]

Several other allusions to Joyce in *Gravity's Rainbow*, however, emphasize Joyce's participation in the destructive elitism of western culture. Identifying 1904, the year of *Ulysses'* action, as one of the "critical points" (*GR*, p. 451) of history when some major change might have been possible, Pynchon quickly asserts that, in fact, nothing changed: "1904, Achtfaden. Ha, ha! *That's* a better joke on you than any singed asshole, all right. Lotta good it does *you*. You can't swim upstream, not under the present dispensation anyhow, all you can do is attach the number to it and suffer" (*GR*, p. 452). At times Pynchon openly rejects the entire Joycean dedication to craft, the dedication which drew Joyce to the mythic figure of Daedalus: "Weissmann's cruelty was no less resourceful than Pökler's own engineering skill, the gift of Daedalus that allowed him to put as much labyrinth as required between himself and the inconvenience of caring" (*GR*, p. 428). If Pynchon feels an affinity with Joyce, he qualifies it so as to preclude any temptation to compress *Gravity's Rainbow* into a narrowly Joycean mold. One of the ironies of the reception of *Gravity's Rainbow* has been the development of an image of the book as a new *Finnegans Wake*, inaccessible to all but a highly educated elite. The *Wake* indeed presents the reader with numerous puzzles, some demanding special knowledge for solution. Doomed by his vision of complexity, Pynchon uses a vocabulary no more complex than his content absolutely demands and employs numerous popular cultural references in a way which emphasizes his desire to communicate with the very people who are least likely to read his book. Joyce wanted to be studied as well as read; Pynchon would clearly accept the reading.

Pynchon's "attacks" on Joyce reflect his distrust of attempts to include reality within systems: scientific, literary, religious, whatever.[12] To Pynchon, attempts to impose systematic constraints on experience are murderous: Pointsman (following Pavlov) struggles to explain all life in behaviorist terms because he feels threatened by the idea that another shares his own complexity. Pointsman's meditation on Pavlov reveals that he values his system more highly than human life:

> Pavlov thought that all the diseases of the mind could be explained, eventually, by the ultraparadoxical phase, the pathologically inert points on the cortex, the confusion of the ideas of the opposite. He died at the very threshold of putting these things on an experimental basis. But I live. I have the funding, and the time, and the will. Slothrop is a strong imperturbable. It won't be easy to send him into any of the three phases. We may finally have to starve, terrorize. [*GR*, p. 90]

Weissmann's analogous vision of humanity as simple raw material for propagating his own obsessions inspires some of Pynchon's most bitter prose.

183

What more do they want? She asks this seriously, as if there's a real conversion factor between information and lives. Well, strange to say, there is. Written down in the Manual, on file at the War Department. Don't forget the real business of the War is buying and selling. The murdering and the violence are self-policing, and can be entrusted to non-professionals. The mass nature of wartime death is useful in many ways. It serves as a spectacle, as diversion from the real movements of the War. It provides raw material to be recorded into History, so that children may be taught History as sequences of violence, battle after battle, and be more prepared for the adult world. Best of all, mass death's a stimulus to just ordinary folks, little fellows, to try 'n' grab a piece of that Pie while they're still here to gobble it up. The true war is a celebration of markets.[*GR*, p. 105]

The Daedalus figure (the film director Gerhardt von Göll—der Springer) provides the artistic analog to the scientific and economic systemizer. Von Göll believes that the people he meets are literally his creations: "His film has somehow brought them into being. 'It is my mission,' he announces to Squalidozzi, with the profound humility that only a German movie director can summon, 'to sow in the Zone seeds of reality'" (*GR*, p. 388). Von Göll sees them simply as pieces in a chess game he controls (*GR*, p. 494). Each of these systems is futile; each lacks the control of reality it claims, and each deceives its creator.

Pynchon may believe, as several critics suggest, in an entropic vision of a world doomed to an eventual lack of order and energy.[13] But he recognizes the presence of very important ordering systems at work in the world as we have it, systems which, even if ultimately doomed, pose a much more serious threat than those of individuals such as the Pointsman, von Göll, or even Weissmann. Unlike these systems, the "controlling" system rests not on individual delusion, but on massive social forces which no single person directs. The system which Pynchon images as "They" involves a large number of individuals, most of whom do not consciously endorse the destruction they contribute to. Pirate Prentice, a well-meaning paratrooper capable of acting kindly, listens to Father Rapier's sermon on the nature of "They" (*GR*, pp. 539–40) and realizes that "with everything else, these are, after all, people who kill each other: and Pirate has always been one of them" (*GR*, p. 542). The system, whether or not it reflects individual volition and/or an inherent order of reality, destroys human lives and reduces the survivors to unresisting accomplices.

Pynchon suggests one relatively simple technique for resisting Their pressure: reject Their categories, live on the interface between the terms of Their dichotomies. Roger Mexico, who contrasts directly with Pointsman, commits himself to life and love even when the commitment contradicts the statistical system with which he works: "If ever the Antipointsman existed, Roger Mexico is the man. Not so much, the doctor admits, for the psychical research. The young statistician is devoted to number and method, not table-rapping or wishful thinking. But in the domain of zero to one, not-something to something. Pointsman can only possess the zero and the one. He cannot, like Mexico, survive anyplace in between . . . to Mexico belongs the domain *between* zero and one—the middle Pointsman has excluded from his persuasion—the probabilities" (*GR*, p. 55). The domain between one and zero, the interface between dream and reality, between self and society, the internal and the external, recurs frequently in *Gravity's Rainbow*. Denying the absolute validity of dichotomies—including that of realism and romance—results in a sense of common humanity as a weapon against the solipsism which insists on perceiving situations simply in either/or terms: "Kevin Spectro did not differentiate as much as he between Outside and Inside. He saw the cortex as an interface organ, mediating between the two, but *part of them both.* 'When you've looked at how it really is,' he asked once, 'how can any of us be separate?'" (*GR*, pp. 141–42).

Weakening the sense of separateness, existing on the interface, challenges our basic modes of perception. Pointsman observes that while we accept positions of certainty, yeses and nos, the process of transition frequently frightens us, as it does him, back into solipsistic isolation: "In each case, the change from point to no-point carries a luminosity and enigma at which something in us must leap and sing, or withdraw in fright" (*GR*, p. 396). Nonetheless, as Mondaugen believes, the deepest life transpires precisely in that flow, that process of change:

Think of the ego, the self that suffers a personal history bound to time, as the grid. The deeper and true Self is the flow between cathode and plate. The constant, pure flow. Signals—

sense-data, feelings, memories relocating—are put onto the grid, and modulate the flow. We live lives that are waveforms constantly changing with time, now positive, now negative. Only at moments of great serenity is it possible to find the pure, the informationless state of signal zero. [*GR*, p. 404]

To overcome our fear of the interface, we must break out of our solipsism. This struggle demands both Slothrop's recognition "that the Zone can sustain many other plots besides those polarized upon himself" (*GR*, p. 603) and his later perception that the multiplicity of individual struggles is not taking place in a vacuum: "For the first time now it becomes apparent that the 4 and the Father-conspiracy do not entirely fill their world. Their struggle is not the only, or even the ultimate one. Indeed, not only are there many *other* struggles, but there are also *spectators*, watching, as spectators will do, hundreds of thousands of them" (*GR*, p. 679). In essence, Slothrop learns to read the text of his *Gravity's Rainbow* in human rather than nihilistic terms. Most important, however, is the possibility of human contact which develops when two people find their way beyond the dichotomies and onto the interface at the same time and place: "Well. What happens when paranoid meets paranoid? A crossing of solipsisms. Clearly. The two patterns create a third: a moire, a new world of flowing shadows, interferences" (*GR*, p. 395). Slothrop possesses something of this sense of possibility all along. Following his comic nightmare descent through the toilet (*GR*, pp. 63–66), Slothrop finds himself on what he believes is the deepest level of his psyche. Expecting isolation, he discovers what appear to be archetypes: "only one fight, one victory, one loss. And only one president, and one assassin, and one election. True. One of each of everything. You had thought of solipsism, and imagined the structure to be populated—on your level—by only, terribly, one. No count on any other levels. But it proves to be not quite that lonely. Sparse, yes, but a good deal better than solitary. One of each of everything's not so bad" (*GR*, pp. 67–68). Soon Pynchon reveals even this degree of solipsistic isolation as an illusion:

the plaza is seething with life, and Slothrop is puzzled. Isn't there supposed to be only one of each?
A. Yes.

Q. Then one Indian girl . . .
A. One *pure* Indian. One *mestiza*. One *criolla*. Then: one Ya-
qui. One Navaho. One Apache—. [*GR*, p. 70]

Obviously, if we pursue this path far enough, each of us is unique,
each of us exists even on Slothrop's deepest solipsistic level of
awareness. The secret lies in perceiving and accepting the similarity of our own isolation and that of others.

Gravity's Rainbow devotes a great deal of attention to those
who fail to overcome their fear and perceive this bond, those who
fall off the interface and commit themselves to solipsism. Such a
commitment, Pynchon implies, inevitably contributes to Their
system and results in physical and psychic death. While the end
result may be the same, there are several different ways of retreating into solipsism. General Pudding, whose sexual life centers on
eating and drinking Katje's excrement (*GR*, pp. 231–36), provides
the most striking example of the horrors of solipsism. His behavior, as Paul Fussell demonstrates, stems from his inability to confront the horror of World War I.[14] He allows himself to degenerate
into a perfect symbol of Their success in destroying human brotherhood in the twentieth century.

While Pudding provides the most extreme example, Major
Duane Marvey, Franz Pökler, and Tchitcherine pursue lives leading to a similar dehumanization. Pökler believes he can remain
personally removed from the immorality of the rocket-cartel system. However, "Pökler found that by refusing to take sides, he'd
become Weissmann's best ally" (*GR*, p. 401). Weissmann successfully manipulates Pökler, even while condemning Pökler's daughter to life in a concentration camp adjacent to the laboratory
where her father works. Pökler's "neutrality," based on a naive belief that integrity can survive without reference to external context, results in the very destruction he fears most.

Marvey and Tchitcherine share a fear of blackness which leads
them to personal hells similar to Pökler's. The simpleminded
Marvey sees blacks as bestial threats to American purity, while
the more complex Tchitcherine reacts to his black half-brother
Enzian as a threat to his personal sense of purity. Neither can accept any suggestion of a human bond with blackness, internal or
external. Pynchon connects the inability of most whites in *Grav-*

ity's Rainbow, and in Euro-American culture as a whole, to accept blackness with their (Their?) insistence on ignoring death:

> Shit, now, is the color white folks are afraid of. Shit is the presence of death, not some abstract-arty character with a scythe but the stiff and rotting corpse itself inside the whiteman's warm and private own *asshole,* which is getting pretty intimate. That's what that white toilet's for. You see many brown toilets? Nope, toilet's the color of gravestones, classical columns of mausoleums, that white porcelain's the very emblem of Odorless and Official Death. Shinola shoeshine polish happens to be the color of Shit. Shoeshine boy Malcolm's in the toilet slappin' on the *Shinola,* working off whiteman's penance on his sin of being born the color of Shit 'n' Shinola. [*GR,* p. 688]

Malcolm X's pursuit of Slothrop down the toilet (*GR,* pp. 61–66), which ends with Slothrop in the solipsistic cesspool of his psychic sewer system, emphasizes the white tendency to dehumanize the self rather than accept the ambiguities of any relationship with blackness. While Slothrop recovers a sense of contact, at least in part, most whites in *Gravity's Rainbow* fail. Whether their solipsistic retreat stems from realistic social pressures (Marvey and Pudding) or individual symbolic reactions (Pökler and Tchitcherine), it aggravates both realistic and symbolic problems. By demonstrating the identical outcomes of apparently diverse situations, Pynchon effectively rejects the dichotomy between characters confronting experience on a realistic level and those confronting it on a symbolic level. The mode matters little. The human outcome demands attention.

In addition to the characters who surrender, Pynchon portrays several who struggle to escape their isolation and establish human contact. Significantly, the extent of their success has little to do with their theoretical beliefs. Roger Mexico, the statistician involved in a love affair with Jessica Swanlake, is unable to fit the experience into any of his "normal" categories of perception: "The time Roger and Jessica have spent together, totaled up, still only comes to hours. All their spoken words to less than one average SHAEF memorandum. And there is no way, first time in his career, that the statistician can make these figures mean anything. Together they are a long skin surface, flowing sweat, close as muscles and bones can press, hardly a word beyond her name, or his" (*GR*, p. 121). But he accepts the interface, the unquantifiable love he feels. Conversely, von Göll articulates the theory of human contact well: "Be compassionate. But don't make up fantasies about them. Despise me, exalt them, but remember, we define each other. Elite and preterite, we move through a cosmic design of darkness and light, and in all humility, I am one of the very few who can comprehend it *in toto*" (*GR*, p. 495). But his Daedalian arrogance leads him to force his aesthetic system onto life, leaving him with a perception of himself as one of the elite and negating any realistic application of his compassion.

Small acts of kindness glimmer through *Gravity's Rainbow*. In addition to Mexico's love for Jessica, Tantivy's loyalty to Slothrop (*GR*, pp. 21, 210), Bodine's gift of Dillinger's preterite blood (*GR*, pp. 740–41) and Katje's willingness to submit herself to the desperate needs of several lovers hint that some escape from solipsism into compassion is possible. The small gestures, however, dissolve frequently in frustration and at times generate new retreats into solipsism. Unable to separate herself from her fiance, Jeremy, Jessica abandons Roger after the immediate threat of the external war passes. Neither Tantivy nor Bodine saves Slothrop; Katje's shit kills Pudding.

The fate of the Hereros emphasizes the difficulties of realizing love and points out its tendency to collapse eventually into solipsism. The plot involving the Southwest African blacks who set up an independent rocket-oriented society within the Zone originates in the visit of Enzian's and Tchitcherine's Russian father to Africa in 1904. Old Tchitcherine, AWOL from a Russian ship, attains fleeting contact with a Herero girl: "It was nearly Christmas, and he gave her a medal he had won in some gunnery exercise long ago on the Baltic. By the time he left, they had learned each other's names and a few words in the respective languages—afraid, happy, sleep, love, . . . the beginnings of a new tongue, a pidgin which they were perhaps the only two speakers of in the world" (*GR*, p. 351). Communication demands just this shared experience, a reaching beyond the self and a recognition that another shares both fears and joys. But their communication dissolves when Tchitcherine returns to Russia, leaving his lover and their child, Enzian, to the genocidal German policy. Enzian survives, eventually leading the *Schwarzkommando*, who seemingly promise a creative force counterbalancing the death-oriented Euro-American culture. But Enzian's visions of a redeemed rocket, a rocket of escape rather than of destruction, gradually generate a counterforce among the Hereros: the Empty Ones, devoted to tribal suicide. Preaching "a day when the last Zone-Herero will die, a final zero to a collective history fully lived" (*GR*, p. 318), the Empty Ones are in fact defined by the very intensity of their opposition to European pressure. While symbolically their plan "has appeal" (*GR*, p. 318), realistically it accomplishes exactly what Europeans from the Germans on most desire: the final repression of the black other. The original contact between old Tchitcherine and Enzian's mother simply extends the influence of the death-obsession to those blacks caught up in the political and psychological dichotomy of black and white.

Similarly, Slothrop's attempts to escape his solipsism ultimately fail. Despite his recognition of the bonds of humanity, despite his willingness to accept as full a range of reality as confronts him on whatever terms that confrontation generates, Slothrop simply dissolves (*GR*, p. 742).[15] Neither his symbolic awareness nor acceptance of reality saves him. He falls victim to a sense of emptiness similar to that which affected Wyatt in *The Recognitions*: "If there is something comforting—religious, if you want—about paranoia, there is still also anti-paranoia, where nothing is connected to anything, a condition not many of us can bear for long. Well right now Slothrop feels himself sliding onto the anti-paranoid part of his cycle, feels the whole city around him going back roofless, vulnerable, uncentered as he is, and only pasteboard images now of the Listening Enemy left between him and the wet sky" (*GR*, p. 434). Unlike Wyatt, however, Slothrop does not recover:

> Slothrop, as noted, at least as early as the *Anubis* era, has begun to thin, to scatter. "Personal density," Kurt Mondaugen in his Peenemünde office not too many steps away from here, enunciating the Law which will one day bear his name, "is directly proportional to temporal bandwidth." "Temporal bandwidth" is the width of your present, your *now*. It is the familiar "Δt" considered as a dependent variable. The more you dwell in the past and in the future, the thicker your bandwidth, the more solid your persona. But the narrower your sense of Now, the more tenuous you are. It may get to where you're having trouble re-

membering what you were doing five minutes ago, or even—as Slothrop now—what you're doing *here*. [*GR*, p. 509]

Soon he will be unnameable. Slothrop's disintegration reflects Pynchon's insistence that his characters cannot resolve the experiences of *Gravity's Rainbow*. Pynchon states the limitations of the characters directly:

> Who would have thought so many would be here? They keep appearing, all through this disquieting structure, gathered in groups, pacing alone in meditation, or studying the paintings, the books, the exhibits. It seems to be some very extensive museum, a place of many levels, and new wings that generate like living tissue—though if it all does grow toward some end shape, those who are here inside can't see it. Some of the halls are to be entered at one's peril, and monitors are standing at all the approaches to make this clear. [*GR*, p. 537]

Rather than following the modernist approach by resolving *Gravity's Rainbow* through his own aesthetic structures (imposing his own perceptual system), Pynchon insists that, once we enter the halls, we find the exit for ourselves. He can offer us points of advice, guideposts, but they won't matter if we can't step outside our solipsism, first to confront the reality of *Gravity's Rainbow* and then to take it into our own lives.

When it matters most, Pynchon speaks to us directly. Using the second-person pronoun, Pynchon draws us into *Gravity's Rainbow*; our response depends on both our own experiences and our ability to empathize with others. Frequently, Pynchon attempts to make us participate in his vision through the use of traditional devices such as minutely detailed realistic settings or slapstick parody sequences written in third person. Having drawn us into his fictional world, Pynchon abruptly shifts to a direct form of address, reminding us that his world is also ours, demanding that we surrender our own solipsism and interact with the book. What Pynchon wants us to share, what he employs the second person to communicate, is his vision of a world of the preterite, a world in agony, a world in desperate need of love. The "you" passages occur throughout the book—there are some twenty in all—and when juxtaposed they challenge us to recognize the similarity of our own isolation and that of others, our share of responsibility for Their dominance, the serious consequences of giving in to isolation, and the necessity of extending ourselves to our brothers and sisters among the preterite in order to forge a new sense of moral community.

Slothrop's ancestor William wrote of the preterite as the source of moral value every bit as important as the elect: "'That's what Jesus meant,' whispers the ghost of Slothrop's first American ancestor William, 'venturing out on the Sea of Galilee. He saw it from the lemming point of view. Without the millions who had plunged and drowned, there could have been no miracle. The successful loner was only the other part of it: the last piece to the jigsaw puzzle, whose shape had already been created by the Preterite, like the last blank space on the table'" (*GR*, p. 554). Tyrone clings to the vision, extending it to our own world:

> Could he have been the fork in the road America never took, the singular point she jumped the wrong way from? Suppose the Slothropite heresy had had the time to consolidate and prosper? Might there have been fewer crimes in the name of Jesus, and more mercy in the name of Judas Iscariot? It seems to Tyrone Slothrop that there might be a route back—maybe that anarchist he met in Zurich was right, maybe for a little while all the fences were down, one road as good as another, the whole space of the Zone cleared, depolarized, and somewhere inside the waste of it a single set of coordinates from which to proceed, without elect, without preterite, without even nationality to fuck it up. [*GR*, p. 556]

Straining to break even the dichotomy of elect and preterite, Tyrone refuses simply to invert the terms and condemn the elect; preterition becomes a metaphor for the condition of all of us caught in systems based on arbitrary dichotomies.

Pynchon hymns the preterite, reminding us of our own preterition, of

> men you have seen on foot and smileless in the cities but forget, men who don't remember you either, knowing they ought to be grabbing a little sleep, not out here performing for strangers, give you this evensong, climaxing now with its rising fragment of some ancient scale, voices overlapping three—and fourfold, up, echoing, filling the entire hollow of the church—no counterfeit baby, no announcement of the Kingdom, not even a try at warming or lighting this terrible night, only, damn us, our scruffy obligatory little cry, our maximum reach outward—

praise be to God!—for you to take back to your war-address, your war-identity, across the snow's footprints and tire tracks finally to the path you must create by yourself, alone in the dark. Whether you want it or not, whatever seas you have crossed, the way home. [*GR*, p. 136]

He writes of "Your own form immobile, mouth-breaking, alone face-up on the narrow cot next to the wall so pictureless, chartless, mapless: so *habitually blank*" (*GR*, p. 136). He places us on the target as the rocket descends, staring up with Pökler to confront the physical symbol of the destructive effect of our own attempts to remain uninvolved:

Now what sea is this you have crossed, exactly, and what sea is it you have plunged more than once to the bottom of, alerted, full of adrenalin, but caught really, buffaloed under the epistemologies of these threats that paranoid you so down and out, caught in this steel pot, softening to devitaminized mush inside the soup-stock of your own words, your waste submarine breath? It took the Dreyfus Affair to get the Zionists out and doing, finally: what will drive you out of your soup-kettle? Has it already happened? Was it tonight's attack and deliverance? Will you go to the Heath, and begin your settlement, and wait there for your Director to come? [*GR*, pp. 389–90]

He forces us either to retreat to solipsism or to share the agony, and the responsibility for the agony. If we refuse to see ourselves in the "you" Pynchon addresses, we aren't going to get much out of *Gravity's Rainbow*.

All we have, finally, is love. It may be too much to expect, but nothing's more important than trying to find, to love:

You have waited in these places into the early mornings, synced in to the on-whitening of the interior, you know the Arrivals schedule by heart, by hollow heart. And where these children have run away from, and that, in this city, there is no one to meet them. You impress them with your gentleness. You've never quite decided if they can see through to your vacuum. They won't yet look in your eyes. . . . Tonight's child has had a long trip here, hasn't slept. Her eyes are red, her frock wrinkled. Her coat has been a pillow. You feel her exhaustion, feel the impossible vastness of all the sleeping countryside at her back, and for the moment you really are selfless, sexless . . . considering only how to shelter her, you are the Traveler's Aid. [*GR*, pp. 50–51]

If nothing else, we can shelter strangers. Occasionally we can love like Mexico loves Jessica. Pynchon pulls us deeper than direct address at the end of section one of *Gravity's Rainbow*. He has spoken to us. Here we speak to Jessica. There are no quotation marks, no Joycean distancing techniques. Living under attack, we merge with Mexico: "You go from dream to dream inside me. You have passage to my last shabby corner, and there, among the debris, you've found life. I'm no longer sure which of all the words, images, dreams or ghosts are 'yours' and which are 'mine.' It's past sorting out. We're both being someone new now, someone incredible" (*GR*, p. 177). Pynchon offers us a "we" which can include Roger, Jessica, Pynchon, you and me. Recognizing the fragility, we share our cry with Mexico: "You're catching the War. It's infecting you and I don't know how to keep it away. Oh, Jess. Jessica. Don't leave me . . ." (*GR*, p. 177).

She leaves.

Just as Pynchon refuses to offer us a traditional resolution through Slothrop, he refuses to offer us a vicarious resolution through Mexico. If we love, we love in reality, not on a printed page. We love with our dreams and our bodies, but we love together, not alone with our books. The last words are Pynchon's: "All together now, all you masochists out there, specially those of you don't have a partner tonight, alone with those fantasies that don't look like they'll ever come true—want you just to join in here with your brothers and sisters, let each other know you're alive and sincere, try to break through the silences, try to reach through and connect" (*GR*, p. 415).

Now Everybody.

The Shadow on the Water:
In Praise of Multiplicity

JOYCE'S SHADOW STIPPLES the surface of the big two-hearted river, the mainstream of American fiction. The romantic and realistic currents flow on, whirling, eddying, never quite merging, pulsing in a single rhythm. Without the flow, the river dries up; without the ebb, it floods. Only the balance nurtures. Since Joyce, American writers, aware of the shadow while they work in the sunlight, have recognized that life requires all of the currents, auricles and ventricles, arteries and veins.

From my vantage point on shore, several of the writers I have watched appear to share a heart with the classic American romantics. John Barth loves symbols, metaphysical resonances; William Gaddis confronts theological mystery directly. Others seem to advance in the realistic current. John Updike reworks his memories of a Pennsylvania childhood; James Baldwin re-creates the details of life in Harlem. Still others seem clearly in one stream when seen from one angle, only to switch as clearly to the other when I shift my gaze. Jack Kerouac builds an intensely romantic vision on a seemingly complete immersion in concrete experiences; Saul Bellow's victims struggle against Dreiserian environments on their way to Emersonian retreats.

The resolution of the waterscape depends on the vision of the beholder, whether novelist or critic. If Bellow (or Sylvia Plath or Donald Barthelme) perceives only the stream and not the river, he won't be likely to navigate efficiently. He'll avoid going aground in his own familiar cause, but he won't be able to guide anyone negotiating the other heart. He'll convince the romantics and lose the realists, or vice versa. To the extent that any writer sees the underlying connections between the two hearts, he can move back and forth beween their surfaces, exploiting their motive power. He can hail travelers in either stream, and perhaps convince them that their safety and survival depend on recognizing alternate routes. Joyce's shadow, cast across the water ahead from his standpoint behind, falls across the entire river, drawing the contemporary writer's gaze to the interface between the two hearts. To see Joyce's form, the contemporary writer must shift his own perspective, moving beyond the limitations of narrowly romantic or realistic modes. No single angle of vision explains the shape of the shadow.

Most of the writers I have considered accept the necessity of triangulation in looking at, and reacting to, Joyce. Striving to see reality in its widest sense, they frequently use Joyce as an intermediate focus. Recognizing his importance, they expand their sensibility as a result of studying his achievement and adapt his ideas and techniques to realize their own expanded vision. In some cases this leads to thematic resolutions of the kind that Richard Chase found lacking in the earlier American novel. Ernest Gaines combines political and metaphysical action; Ralph Ellison repudiates the implications of the classic American retreat from society. In other cases Joyce's influence suggests solutions for the stylistic impasse which Richard Poirier sees as the weakness of the American novel. Toni Morrison's magic realism shatters the barriers between dreams and realities; Ronald Sukenick recognizes fiction as the intermediary between solipsistic fantasy and irreducible fact.

A new, or at least newly re-perceived, sense of the breadth of reality connects the thematic and stylistic resolutions. Very few of the novelists I have considered claim *superiority* for either social, individual, or fictional reality. Like Joyce, they seek the most powerful expression of their vision, an expression which they hope will touch each level. Although most emphasize one level more strongly than others, most agree with Russell Banks's conception of fiction as a part of reality, not as some anomalous entity bound by preordained rules concerning the proper interaction of art and life. William Melvin Kelley's insistence on the reality of both dream- and city-scapes mirrors this insistence, as does Raymond Federman's belief in the equivalence of levels of discourse.

Paralleling this conviction of the reality of fiction is a growing demand that fiction participate directly in life. For Norman Mailer, this demand leads to a heightened perception of the importance of his actions as both realistic and symbolic parts of a community life. For William Burroughs, it entails a deep distrust of artistic manipulation, an awareness of fiction as a threat to the community. For Thomas Pynchon, it generates an insistence that the reader *live*, recognizing the limits while realizing the potential of the printed page. Joyce inspired the expanded perceptions of reality, particularly in *Ulysses* and *Finnegans Wake*, but the contemporary American writers perceive implications of the expansion which Joyce never anticipated. Their—our—art returns to life with an immediate passion foreign to its proximate Irish father.

And the river flows on. Since completing the main body of this work, I have read several books which could easily have been included. Guy Davenport's short story cycle *Da Vinci's Bicycle*[1] meditates on the significance of patterns and the artistic imagination and uses Joyce as a character. *The Third Mind*[2] by Burroughs and Brian Gysin may refer to the mind of the "collaborators" whose words form parts of the cut-up artifact; but it may equally well refer to the mind of the reader, cast into a new mode of confrontation with reality through his interaction with the words before him. Like Pynchon, Burroughs and Gysin refuse to allow the reader to distance himself from life through art.

Gilbert Sorrentino's *Mulligan Stew*[3] is at once a part of the mainstream of post-Joycean writing and an important new current. Obviously "Joycean" in approach, the novel alludes frequently to *Ulysses* and *Finnegans Wake*. Sorrentino recalls the publishing difficulties which plagued Joyce in an introductory section consisting of critical and editorial rejections of *Mulligan Stew*. Joyce appears as a character in a "Circe"-style drama where he is introduced as "a grocer's assistant" (*MS*, p. 178). One of the central characters of *Mulligan Stew* is Martin Halpin, "stolen" from a footnote in *Finnegans Wake* by Anthony Lamont, an experimental novelist writing a detective novel while his life falls apart. Halpin complains that he has been spirited away from the rational orderly world of "that gentlemanly Irishman, Mr. Joyce" (*MS*, p. 25), where he lived a simple life as a gardener. Halpin (who, like a Flann O'Brien character, lives an independent life when not under the direct control of his "author") speculates on his fate:

> I can't understand how Mr. Joyce allowed him to take me away! Surely, it can't have been for money! Or does Mr. Joyce even *know* that I have gone? Maybe he's dead. I have no idea of what arrangements have been made, I certainly ought to be given a decent salary, telling, as I am, the whole story. But what possesses this man to make me out such a fool? I would have been delighted to play a small role, even an anonymous role, somewhere in this vulgar work. Some superintendent who lives in a basement apartment, or even the caretaker of this lodge. The smiling roomer down the hall. He could have put me in a rowboat far out on the lake, a man seen from the window. I could troll. If I must be the star why can't I speak intelligent lines? I'm not a robot, I'm not immune to ill treatment. Mr. Joyce, knowing that I could do nothing at all, merely stated, *stated*, mind you, that I performed "odd jobs." That is what one may term nicety of expression. Nowhere was I made to perform, actually *perform* these "odd jobs" for Brophy—who, of course, this shameless man has also taken over and made into some sort of radical author. Perhaps Lamont somehow purchased the entire footnote, or even whole sections of that quiet world in which nothing ever happened—at least in my small area of it. I don't know, I just don't know. [*MS*, p. 26]

Halpin concludes, "If there is one thing I learned while working for Mr. Joyce, it is that one cannot escape for long from a writer" (*MS*, p. 27).

Sorrentino affirms this conclusion in *Mulligan Stew*, although in a circuitous manner. He demonstrates that the "character" Halpin is as much a function of the disintegrating world of the "experimental" writer Lamont as he was of the "quiet world" of the "gentlemanly" Joyce. Sorrentino makes the point that one's view of the universe depends in large part on one's position in that universe; few of the characters in *Finnegans Wake* lead such a sedate life as Halpin. But Sorrentino extends his discussion to indicate that Lamont (and by extension Sorrentino, also an "experimental" novelist) is himself a function of the culture in which he lives.

Mulligan Stew is an extremely funny novel, like *Ulysses* and the *Wake*. It combines exaggeration and deflation, parody and travesty. Frequently humor is allusive, as in the catalog of books in Halpin's house, among which are *"How to Understand the Deaf* by James Joyce," *"Having That Affair* by B. Boylan," *"Say Yes to Love* by Molly Bloom," *"The Layman's Missal* by Buck Mulligan," and *"James: Preserves and Jellies* by Stuart Gorman" (*MS*, pp. 31–34). But, more important, Sorrentino's humor critiques the mythologies, popular and elitist, of its culture. The play in which Joyce participates—"Flawless Play Restored"—is subtitled "The Masque of Fungo," in honor of "a star shortstop who's lost a step" (*MS*, p. 178). Later, William Blake is described as "the Dick Stuart of poetry" (*MS*, p. 433), a reference to the former Pittsburgh Pirate and Boston Red Sox first baseman famed for his tremendous power and total lack of finesse. The last reference occurs in a chapter of Lamont's novel entitled "Making It Up As We Goes Along," yet another allusion to a footnote in the same section of the *Wake* which introduces Martin Halpin to the literary world.

Sorrentino's point seems to be that we do indeed make it up as we goes along, and that one of the results is that our art inevitably reflects our culture and our life. Just as Joyce filled the *Wake* with references to cricket stars, Sorrentino fills *Mulligan Stew* with allusions to baseball players. Similarly, the literary myth of Fitzgerald's Daisy Buchanan is as important to Sorrentino's characters as is the literary myth of Leopold Bloom. Sorrentino, like Joyce, accepts and employs everything which falls within his experience without aesthetic preconceptions either realistic or romantic. He uses the *Wake* as a point of departure for a statement which combines the aesthetic emphasis of Federman and Barthelme with the cultural emphasis of Kelley and Burroughs.

In the end *Mulligan Stew*, like *Finnegans Wake*, insists only that we work with the full range of the experience at our disposal. Echoing the final question of the catechism chapter of the *Wake*, Sorrentino writes:

Q: When is a man not a man?
A: When he is a sham. [*MS*, p. 42]

Halpin, Lamont, Sorrentino, and Joyce may all be shams of a sort, but they are shams who lead us into closer contact with the nature of our culture and our selves. Like the Joyce whom Sorrentino salutes in the closing "credits" to *Mulligan Stew* as "Joky Joyce who lost her undies" (*MS*, p. 440), as "Joyce the Jewel of the merchant fleet" (*MS*, p. 444), and as "Jimmy the Joy of Dublin" (*MS*, p. 445), we all wind up as the many shams and the single man.

Down here next to the river, the shadow sometimes obscures the source. Defracted into as many patterns as there are perceivers, Joyce's influence yields no easy conclusions concerning the nature of his own work. Joyce simply encompasses. Through multiplicity, he unifies. Perhaps the best measure of his greatness is the very welter of life drawing on him for vitality. Joyce waters; our riverruns. He has helped us to understand our tradition, our direction, our rhythm, and our flow.

Notes

CHAPTER ONE

1. In addition to *The American Novel and Its Tradition* (Garden City, N.Y.: Doubleday/Anchor, 1957), the standard work on the American "romance" tradition is Daniel Hoffman's *Form and Fable in American Literature* (New York: Oxford University Press, 1961). Each of these studies acknowledges its debt to F. O. Matthiessen's *American Renaissance* (London: Oxford University Press, 1941), which directly or indirectly exerts a large influence over nearly every subsequent study of American literature, the current one not excepted. Malcolm Cowley's essay on "Naturalism in American Literature," from Stow Persons's anthology *Evolutionary Thought in America* (New Haven: Yale University Press, 1950), provides a good basic statement of the realist position. Donald Pizer's *Realism and Naturalism in Nineteenth-Century American Literature* (Carbondale: Southern Illinois University Press, 1966) and Charles Child Walcutt's *American Literary Naturalism: A Divided Stream* (Minneapolis: University of Minnesota Press, 1956) have developed and expanded on the ideas of Cowley's sketch.

2. Chase, *American Novel*, pp. 12–13. It is important to note that Chase uses "novel" as a synonym for "realism," rather than as a more general term.

3. Richard Poirier, *A World Elsewhere* (New York: Oxford University Press, 1973), p. 16.

4. For extended discussions of the symbolic significance and thematic importance of the "street furniture" of *Ulysses*, see Richard Kain's *Fabulous Voyager* (Chicago: University of Chicago Press, 1947) and Robert Martin Adams's *Surface and Symbol* (New York: Oxford University Press, 1962). For the basic argument in support of a realistic substructure in *Finnegans Wake*, see Bernard Benstock's *Joyce-Again's Wake* (Seattle: University of Washington Press, 1966). Perhaps the book which does the best justice to both approaches is

C. H. Peake's *James Joyce, the Citizen and the Artist* (Stanford: Stanford University Press, 1977).

5. Harry Levin, *James Joyce* (Norfolk, Conn.: New Directions, 1960), p. 221.

6. T. S. Eliot, *Selected Essays: New Edition* (New York: Harcourt, Brace and World, 1950), pp. 124–25.

7. George Kent, *Blackness and the Adventure of Western Culture* (Chicago: Third World Press, 1972), p. 112. This volume provides a penetrating set of insights into Afro-American literary culture and has exerted a large influence over my thought in this study. Although it had not yet been published when I finished the first version of this manuscript, Robert B. Stepto's *From Behind the Veil* (Urbana: University of Illinois Press, 1979) helped me clarify several passages and provides valuable perspectives both on Afro-American literature in general and on questions of literary influence.

8. Eliot's insistence on preexisting universal truths led directly to his famous misreading of *Ulysses* as a savage parody of the insubstantial efforts of degraded modern man. Eliot's essay "*Ulysses*: Myth and Order" (in *Selected Essays*) describes "The Waste Land" admirably, but fails to recognize the human sympathy which forms such a large part of Joyce's treatment of Leopold Bloom.

9. James Joyce, *Ulysses* (New York: Random House, 1961), p. 734. Subsequent quotations refer to this edition and will be noted parenthetically in the text.

10. David Hayman, "Some Writers in the Wake of the *Wake*," in *In the Wake of the Wake*, ed. David Hayman and Elliott Anderson (Madison: University of Wisconsin Press, 1978), p. 36.

11. Despite my belief that Harold Bloom's position on the decline of contemporary poetry does not shed light on the situation of the contemporary novel, *The Anxiety of Influence* (New York: Oxford University Press, 1973) has provided a valuable statement on the mechanics of influence in a self-conscious era. Robert Martin Adams's *AfterJoyce: Studies in Fiction since Ulysses* (New York: Oxford University Press, 1977) is the first full-length study of Joyce's influence involving American writers. Adams, however, devotes himself primarily to stressing the broad range of Joyce's influence on world literature and does not explore particular areas in depth. Vivien Mercier's consideration of Joyce's influence on the new French novelists in *A Reader's Guide to the New Novel* (New York: Farrar, Straus and Giroux, 1971) provides numerous suggestions regarding Joyce's technical contributions to the art of fiction which have influenced my argument in the current study in ways which cannot always be acknowledged through specific references.

CHAPTER TWO

1. William Faulkner, *Mosquitoes* (New York: Liveright, 1927), p. 145.
2. Joseph Blotner, *Faulkner: A Biography* (New York: Random House, 1974), pp. 352, 417–18, 452, 716, 746, 759.
3. Richard Ellmann, *James Joyce* (New York: Oxford University Press, 1959), pp. 308, 782.
4. Faulkner, *Mosquitoes*, p. 128. Subsequent quotations refer to the 1927 Liveright edition and will be noted parenthetically in the text.
5. For an extended comparison of these passages, see Cleanth Brooks, *William Faulkner: Toward Yoknapatawpha* (New Haven: Yale University Press, 1978), pp. 370–72.
6. Joyce Warren, "Faulkner's 'Portrait of the Artist,'" *Mississippi Quarterly* 19 (1966): 121–31.
7. Ibid., p. 121.
8. Ibid., pp. 122–24.
9. See Hugh Kenner, *Dublin's Joyce* (Bloomington: Indiana University Press, 1956), pp. 109–33.
10. Hyatt Waggoner, *William Faulkner: From Jefferson to the World* (Lexington: University of Kentucky Press, 1959), p. 13.
11. Michael Millgate, *The Achievement of William Faulkner* (New York: Random House, 1971), p. 69.
12. Richard P. Adams, *Faulkner: Myth and Motion* (Princeton: Princeton University Press, 1968), p. 43.
13. See Olga W. Vickery, *The Novels of William Faulkner* (Baton Rouge: Louisiana State University Press, 1964), p. 11.
14. Chase, *American Novel*, p. 221.
15. Ibid., pp. 221–24; Adams, *Faulkner*, pp. 83–89; and Michael Groden, "Criticism in New Composition: *Ulysses* and *The Sound and the Fury*," *Twentieth Century Literature* 21 (1975): 265–77.
16. Peter Swiggart, *The Art of Faulkner's Novels* (Austin: University of Texas Press, 1962), pp. 62–63.
17. William Faulkner, *As I Lay Dying* (New York: Vintage Books, 1968), pp. 5, 15, 29, 41. Subsequent quotations refer to this edition and will be noted parenthetically in the text.
18. Adams, *Faulkner*, p. 58.
19. Eliot, *Selected Essays*, p. 177.
20. Carvel Collins, "The Pairing of *The Sound and the Fury* and *As I Lay Dying*," *Princeton University Library Chronicle* 18 (1957): 114–23; Barbara M. Cross, "Apocalypse and Comedy in *As I Lay Dying*," *Texas Studies in Language and Literature* 3 (1961): 251–58; and Millgate, *Achievement of Faulkner*, p. 109.
21. *Writers at Work*, ed. Malcolm Cowley (New York: Viking Press, 1959), p. 129.
22. Vickery, *Novels of Faulkner*, p. 205.
23. Chase, *American Novel*, p. 205.

24. Cleanth Brooks, *William Faulkner: The Yoknapatawpha Country* (New Haven: Yale University Press, 1966), p. 152.
25. Ibid., p. 143.
26. Adams, *AfterJoyce*, p. 88.
27. Vickery, *Novels of Faulkner*, p. 124.
28. William Faulkner, *Go Down, Moses* (New York: Random House, 1942), p. 118. Subsequent quotations refer to this edition and will be noted parenthetically in the text.
29. Irving Howe, *William Faulkner: A Critical Study* (New York: Random House, 1962), p. 258.
30. Critical consensus has gradually moved toward an acceptance of *Go Down, Moses* as a novel rather than a collection of short stories. Faulkner himself was dismayed by the printing of the book under the title *Go Down, Moses and Other Stories*, and the fourth part of "The Bear" relies heavily on information available only in other sections of the book.
31. R. W. B. Lewis, "William Faulkner: The Hero in the New World," in *Faulkner: A Collection of Critical Essays*, ed. Robert Penn Warren (Englewood Cliffs, N.J.: Prentice-Hall, 1966), pp. 204–18.
32. Millgate, *Achievement of Faulkner*, p. 210.
33. *Faulkner in the University*, ed. Frederick L. Gwynn and Joseph L. Blotner (Charlottesville: University of Virginia Press, 1959), pp. 245–46.
34. Howe, *Faulkner*, p. 92.
35. For discussion of the tension between positive and stereotyped elements in Lucius' character, see Charles H. Nilon, *Faulkner and the Negro* (New York: Citadel Press, 1965), and Myra Jehlen, *Class and Character in Faulkner's South* (Secaucus, N.J.: Citadel Press, 1978), pp. 103–10.
36. Jesse Bier, "The Romantic Coordinates of American Literature," *Bucknell Review* 18 (1970): 16–33, discusses the relationship of the resolution of *Go Down, Moses* to the romantic tradition.
37. Richard Wright, *Black Boy* (New York: Perennial Classic, 1967), p. 274.
38. Michel Fabre, in "Richard Wright: Beyond Naturalism?" in *American Literary Naturalism: A Reassessment*, ed. Yoshinabu Hakutani and Lewis Fried (Heidelberg: Carl Winters, 1975), pp. 147–48, comments that "literature [for Wright] is thus less the depiction of the actual world than the representation of emotional experience through words."
39. Michel Fabre, *The Unfinished Quest of Richard Wright* (New York: William Morrow, 1973), pp. 146, 166.
40. Ibid., p. 111.
41. See Edward Margolies, *The Art of Richard Wright* (Carbondale: Southern Illinois University Press, 1969), p. 102, and Katherine

Fishburn, *Richard Wright's Hero: The Faces of a Rebel-Victim* (Metuchen, N.J.: Scarecrow Press, 1977), p. 54.

42. Richard Wright, *Lawd Today* (New York: Walker, 1963), p. 25. Subsequent quotations refer to this edition and will be cited parenthetically in the text.

43. Richard Wright, *Uncle Tom's Children* (New York: Harper and Brothers, 1938), p. 317. Subsequent quotations refer to this edition and will be cited parenthetically in the text.

44. Keneth Kinnamon, *The Emergence of Richard Wright* (Urbana: University of Illinois Press, 1972), p. 116.

45. Richard Wright, *Native Son* (New York: Harper and Row, 1940), p. viii. Subsequent quotations refer to this edition and will be cited parenthetically in the text.

46. Kinnamon, *Emergence*, pp. 136–37. Also see Robert Bone's chapter on Wright in *The Negro Novel in America* (New Haven: Yale University Press, 1965), pp. 140–52.

47. Donald B. Gibson, "Wright's Invisible Native Son," *American Quarterly* 21 (1969): 728–38.

48. This idea was first suggested to me by my colleague Jim Machor at the University of Illinois.

CHAPTER THREE

1. James Joyce, *Stephen Hero* (New York: New Directions, 1963), p. 187.

2. Ibid., p. 211.

3. Forrest L. Ingram, *Representative Short Story Cycles of the Twentieth Century* (The Hague: Mouton, 1971), pp. 13–25.

4. For a discussion of Joyce's use of an expanding narrative perspective in *Dubliners*, see Homer Obed Brown's *James Joyce's Early Fiction: The Biography of a Form* (Cleveland: Western Reserve Press, 1967).

5. Jerry H. Bryant, "From Death to Life: The Fiction of Ernest J. Gaines," *Iowa Review* 3 (1972): 106–8, comments on the Faulknerian influence which Gaines acknowledges in an interview in *Interviews with Black Writers*, ed. John O'Brien (New York: Liveright, 1973), p. 82.

6. *Interviews*, ed. O'Brien, p. 82.

7. Gaines acknowledges the Joycean influence in an interview included in *Fiction! Interviews with Northern California Novelists*, ed. Dan Tooker and Roger Hofheins (New York: Harcourt Brace Jovanovich, 1976), p. 98.

8. See Michel Fabre's comparison of Faulkner and Gaines, "Bayonne d'earnest aule Gaines's Yoknapatapha," *Recherches Anglaises et Americaines* 4 (1976): 208–22.

9. Among critics who have commented on structural patterns unify-

ing *Bloodline* have been Walter R. McDonald, who emphasizes the change in time of day in "'You Not a Bum, You a Man': Ernest J. Gaines's *Bloodline*," *Black American Literature Forum* 11 (1977): 47–49; Jack Hicks, who emphasizes the movement from childhood to old age in "To Make These Bones Live: History and Community in Ernest Gaines's Fiction," *Black American Literature Forum* 11 (1977): 9–18; and William Burke, who cites the role of black history in "*Bloodline*: A Black Man's South," *CLA Journal* 19 (1976): 545–58.

10. Ernest J. Gaines, *Bloodline* (New York: W. W. Norton, 1976), p. 243. Subsequent quotations refer to this edition and will be noted parenthetically in the text.

11. Actually, "Just Like a Tree" was written and published before any of the other stories included in *Bloodline*, so the revaluation process inverts those of Joyce and Wright, who used the concluding stories of *Dubliners* and *Uncle Tom's Children* to alter the out-of-context meanings of earlier works.

12. Burke, "*Bloodline*," p. 558.

13. Flannery O'Connor, *The Complete Stories* (New York: Farrar, Straus and Giroux, 1971), p. 375. Subsequent quotations refer to this edition and will be noted parenthetically in the text.

14. David Aiken, "Flannery O'Connor's Portrait of the Artist as a Young Failure," *Arizona Quarterly* 32 (1976): 248.

15. For a discussion of Joyce's position on the relationship of artist and priest, see Brown, *Joyce's Early Fiction*, pp. 50–54.

16. Thomas F. Gossett, "Flannery O'Connor's Opinions of Other Writers: Some Unpublished Comments," *Southern Literary Journal* 6 (1974): 71.

17. Melvin J. Friedman, "Introduction" to *The Added Dimension: The Art and Mind of Flannery O'Connor*, ed. Melvin J. Friedman and Lewis A. Lawson (New York: Fordham University Press, 1966), p. 9.

18. Forrest L. Ingram, "O'Connor's Seven-Story Cycle," *Flannery O'Connor Bulletin* 2 (1973): 19.

19. Flannery O'Connor, *Mysteries and Manners* (New York: Farrar, Straus and Giroux, 1973), pp. 74–75.

20. Preston Browning, Jr., "Parker's Back: Flannery O'Connor's Iconography of Salvation by Profanity," *Studies in Short Fiction* 6 (1969): 526.

21. Jerome Klinkowitz, *The Life of Fiction* (Urbana: University of Illinois Press, 1977), p. 155.

22. Russell Banks, "Symposium: The Writer's Situation," *New American Review* 9 (1970): 78.

23. Ibid., p. 81.

24. See the interview with Banks in *Fiction International* 2/3 (1977).

25. Russell Banks, *Searching for Survivors* (New York: Fiction Collec-

tive, 1975), p. 1. Subsequent quotations refer to this edition and will be noted parenthetically in the text.

26. Banks, "Symposium," p. 80.
27. Ibid., p. 81.
28. Ibid.
29. Cited in Klinkowitz, *Life of Fiction*, p. 146.
30. Banks, "Symposium," p. 79.
31. Breon Mitchell discusses this issue in *Approaches to "A Portrait of the Artist as a Young Man*," ed. Bernard Benstock and Thomas Staley (Pittsburgh: University of Pittsburgh Press, 1977).
32. See Gordon Lameyer's comments on Joycean details in *The Bell Jar* in "The Double in Sylvia Plath's *The Bell Jar*," in *Sylvia Plath: The Woman and the Work* (New York: Dodd, Mead, 1977), pp. 156, 160, 162.
33. Sylvia Plath, *The Bell Jar* (New York: Harper and Row, 1971), p. 37. Subsequent quotations refer to this edition and will be noted parenthetically in the text.
34. Stan Smith, "Attitudes Counterfeiting Life: The Irony of Artifice in Sylvia Plath's *The Bell Jar*," *Critical Quarterly* 17 (1975): 254.
35. Lameyer, "The Double," p. 159; Marjorie G. Perloff, "A Ritual for Being Born Twice: Sylvia Plath's *The Bell Jar*," *Contemporary Literature* 13 (1972): 521–22.
36. Lameyer, "The Double," pp. 144, 159.
37. Smith, "Attitudes," p. 250.
38. Ann Charters, *Kerouac: A Biography* (New York: Warner, 1974), pp. 21, 155, 265.
39. Jack Kerouac, "Essentials of Spontaneous Prose," in *The Moderns*, ed. LeRoi Jones (New York: Corinth Books, 1963), p. 343.
40. Ibid.
41. See LeRoi Jones, "Introduction" to *The Moderns*, pp. xv–xvi.
42. Jack Kerouac, "Old Angel Midnight Part Two," *Evergreen Review* (September 1964): 68.
43. Ibid. For reactions to the work, see John Tytell, *Naked Angels: The Lives and Literature of the Beat Generation* (New York: McGraw-Hill, 1976), p. 148; Robert A. Hipkiss, *Jack Kerouac: Prophet of the New Romanticism* (Lawrence: Regents Press of Kansas, 1976), p. 84.
44. For further discussion of spontaneous prose, a much-discussed theory which actually resulted in very little important work, see Hipkiss, *Kerouac*, p. 94; Tytell, *Naked Angels*, p. 143; and Charters, *Kerouac*, p. 140.
45. Charters, *Kerouac*, p. 97.
46. Tytell, *Naked Angels*, pp. 67–69.
47. Jack Kerouac, *On the Road* (New York: Viking, 1959), pp. 5, 9, 11. Subsequent quotations refer to this edition and will be noted parenthetically in the text.

48. James Baldwin, *Notes of a Native Son* (New York: Bantam, 1968), p. 138.
49. Ibid., p. 6.
50. Ibid., p. 25.
51. Ibid., p. 5.
52. Kent, *Blackness*, p. 140.
53. James Baldwin, *Go Tell It on the Mountain* (New York: Alfred A. Knopf, 1953), p. 59. Subsequent quotations refer to this edition and will be noted parenthetically in the text.
54. Shirley S. Allen, "The Ironic Voice in Baldwin's *Go Tell It on the Mountain*," in *James Baldwin: A Critical Evaluation*, ed. Therman B. O'Daniel (Washington: Howard University Press, 1977), p. 34; Roger Rosenblatt, *Black Fiction* (Cambridge: Harvard University Press, 1974), pp. 36–54; Donald B. Gibson, "Baldwin: The Political Anatomy of Space," in *James Baldwin*, ed. O'Daniel, pp. 4–7.
55. Gibson, "Baldwin: Political Anatomy," p. 4.
56. See Kent's summary of an uncollected Baldwin short story, "The Death of the Prophet," which concerns John's fall from faith (Kent, *Blackness*, p. 144).
57. See Harold Courlander, *A Treasury of Afro-American Folklore* (New York: Crown, 1976), pp. 306–8; Lawrence Levine, *Black Culture and Black Consciousness* (New York: Oxford University Press, 1978); and Dena J. Epstein, *Sinful Tunes and Spirituals* (Urbana: University of Illinois Press, 1977).
58. Michel Fabre, "Fathers and Sons in James Baldwin's *Go Tell It on the Mountain*," in *James Baldwin: A Collection of Critical Essays*, ed. Keneth Kinnamon (Englewood Cliffs, N.J.: Prentice-Hall, 1974), p. 129.
59. Frank Budgen, *James Joyce and the Making of "Ulysses"* (Bloomington: Indiana University Press, 1973), pp. 151–52.
60. Robert Scholes, *The Fabulators* (New York: Oxford University Press, 1967), p. 171. Scholes writes, "Since so much is known *about* myths and archetypes, they can no longer be used innocently. Even their connection to the unconscious finally becomes attenuated as the mythic materials are used more consciously. All symbols become allegorical to the extent that we understand them. . . . A writer, aware of the nature of categories, is not likely to believe that his own mythical lenses really capture the truth."
61. Adams, *AfterJoyce*, p. 42.
62. *Writers at Work: Fourth Series*, ed. George Plimpton (New York: Viking, 1977), p. 443.
63. John Updike, *The Centaur* (New York: Alfred A. Knopf, 1963), epigraph. Subsequent quotations refer to this edition and will be noted parenthetically in the text.
64. Adams, *AfterJoyce*, p. 42.

65. Edward P. Vargo, "The Necessity of Myth in Updike's *The Centaur*," *PMLA* 88 (1973): 452–60.

66. John Updike, *Picked-Up Pieces* (Greenwich, Conn.: Fawcett, 1975), p. 481.

67. *The New Fiction: Interviews with Innovative American Writers*, ed. Joe David Bellamy (Urbana: University of Illinois Press, 1975), p. 71.

68. Ronald Sukenick, "On the New Cultural Conservatism," *Partisan Review* 39 (1972): 449.

69. Ibid.

70. Ronald Sukenick, "Fiction in the Seventies: Ten Digressions on Ten Digressions," *Studies in America Literature* 5 (1977): 99.

71. Ronald Sukenick, *98.6* (New York: Fiction Collective, 1975), p. 131. Subsequent quotations refer to this edition and will be noted parenthetically in the text.

72. *The New Fiction*, ed. Bellamy, p. 57.

73. Jerome Klinkowitz, *Literary Disruptions* (Urbana: University of Illinois Press, 1975), p. 146.

74. Ronald Sukenick, "Not My Bag," *New York Review of Books*, March 13, 1969, p. 40.

75. Ibid., p. 41.

76. Robert Coover, *The Public Burning* (New York: Viking, 1977), p. 337. Subsequent quotations refer to this edition and will be noted parenthetically in the text.

77. This is only one of several instances where particular Coover styles resemble Joycean styles—in this case, the catalogs of "Cyclops." Coover alludes stylistically to "Circe" on pp. 283–88, to the "Oxen of the Sun" on p. 18, to "Eumaeus" on p. 188, to "Aeolus" frequently in his treatment of events in terms of newspaper headlines, and perhaps to the number play of "Ithaca" on p. 196.

78. See pp. 114–15, 122, 136, 234, 362–63, 470–85.

79. See Rita Guibert, *Seven Voices: Seven Latin American Writers Talk to Rita Guibert* (New York: Vintage, 1973), pp. 136, 154.

80. Toni Morrison, *Song of Solomon* (New York: Alfred A. Knopf, 1977), epigraph. Subsequent quotations refer to this edition and will be noted parenthetically in the text. For a brief indication of Morrison's attitude toward Joyce, see "Intimate Things in Place: A Conversation with Toni Morrison," in *Chant of Saints*, ed. Michael S. Harper and Robert B. Stepto (Urbana: University of Illinois Press, 1979), pp. 213–229.

81. Gilbert Phelps, "The Novel Today," in *The Pelican Guide to English Literature: The Modern Age*, ed. Boris Ford (Aylesbury: Penguin, 1970), p. 477.

82. Philippe Sollers, "Joyce & Co.," in *In the Wake of the Wake*, ed. Hayman and Anderson, pp. 107–21. The argument over the politics of the *Wake* reflects the debate concerning the "correct" relation-

ship between avant-garde art and leftist politics which was raging at the time of the book's composition in the 1930s. For an indication of the basic lines of that debate, see Samuel Hynes, *The Auden Generation: Literature and Politics in England in the 1930s* (New York: Viking, 1977).

83. Donald Barthelme, *The Dead Father* (New York: Farrar, Straus and Giroux, 1975), p. 15. Subsequent quotations refer to this edition and will be noted parenthetically in the text.

84. Donald Barthelme, "After Joyce," *Location* 1 (Summer 1964): 13.

85. Ibid., p. 14.

86. Ibid.

87. Raymond Olderman, *Beyond the Wasteland* (New Haven: Yale University Press, 1972), p. 24.

88. Barthelme, "After Joyce," p. 14.

89. See Morris Dickstein, *Gates of Eden* (New York: Basic Books, 1978), p. 238.

90. Klinkowitz, *Disruptions*, p. 78.

91. Samuel Beckett, "Dante . . . Bruno. Vico . . . Joyce," in *James Joyce/ Finnegans Wake: A Symposium* (New York: New Directions, 1972), pp. 1–22. See also Klinkowitz's discussion of Federman's critical work on Beckett in *Literary Disruptions*.

92. Raymond Federman, *Double or Nothing* (Chicago: Swallow Press, 1971), p. pre-147. The page numbering system in *Double or Nothing* necessitates odd references. The easiest way to find a passage is simply to refer to the book's index. Subsequent quotations refer to this edition and will be noted parenthetically in the text.

93. Mercier, *Reader's Guide*, p. 36.

94. *Concrete Poetry: A World View*, ed. Mary Ellen Solt (Bloomington: Indiana University Press, 1970), pp. 71–72.

95. Ibid., p. 7.

96. Ibid., p. 5.

97. Cf. Pignatari's "Semiotic Poem," ibid., p. 110.

98. Ronald Sukenick, "Double or Nothing," *New York Times Book Review*, October 1, 1972, p. 40.

99. William Melvin Kelley, *Dunfords Travels Everywheres* (Garden City, N.Y.: Doubleday, 1970), epigraph. Subsequent quotations refer to this edition and will be noted parenthetically in the text.

100. Grace Eckley, "The Awakening of Mr. Affrinnegan: Kelley's *Dunfords Travels Everywheres* and Joyce's *Finnegans Wake*," *Obsidian* 1 (1975): 27–41.

101. Kelley, "Oswhole'stalking," *L'Arc* 36 (1969): 94.

102. Addison Gayle, *The Way of the New World* (Garden City, N.Y.: Doubleday/Anchor, 1976), p. 374.

103. Ralph Ellison, *Invisible Man* (New York: Vintage, 1972), p. 16.

104. Jones, *The Moderns*, p. xv.

105. Marshall McLuhan, "Notes on Burroughs," *The Nation* 199 (1964): 519.
106. William Burroughs, *The Ticket That Exploded* (New York: Grove Press, 1968), p. 65. Subsequent quotations refer to this edition and will be noted parenthetically in the text.
107. *Writers at Work: Third Series*, ed. George Plimpton (New York: Viking, 1968), p. 157.
108. Ibid., p. 146.
109. McLuhan, "Notes," p. 519.
110. *Writers: Third Series*, p. 146.
111. Ihab Hassan, *Paracriticisms* (Urbana: University of Illinois Press, 1975).
112. Hassan, *The Dismemberment of Orpheus* (New York: Oxford University Press, 1971), p. 250.

CHAPTER FOUR

1. Sukenick, "Fiction in the Seventies," p. 99.
2. Walt Whitman, *Complete Poetry and Selected Prose*, ed. James E. Miller, Jr. (Boston: Houghton Mifflin, 1959), p. 486.
3. Ibid., p. 497.
4. Tony Tanner, *City of Words* (New York: Harper and Row, 1971), p. 299.
5. Saul Bellow, "The Sealed Treasure," *Times Literary Supplement*, July 1, 1960, p. 3.
6. Gordon Lloyd Harper, "Saul Bellow," in *Saul Bellow: A Collection of Critical Essays*, ed. Earl Rovit (Englewood Cliffs, N.J.: Prentice-Hall, 1975), p. 8.
7. Harold Fisch, "The Hero as Jew: Reflections on *Herzog*," *Judaism* 17 (Winter 1968): 47.
8. Harper, "Bellow," p. 18.
9. Ibid., p. 15.
10. Bellow, "Treasure," p. 336.
11. Sanford Pinsker, "Saul Bellow in the Classroom," *College English* 34 (1973): 978.
12. See Fisch, "Hero," pp. 42–54, and Maurice Samuel, "My Friend, the Late Moses Herzog," *Mainstream* 12 (April 1966): 3–25. See also David D. Galloway, "Moses—Bloom—Herzog: Bellow's Everyman," *Southern Review* n.s. 2 (January 1966): 67.
13. Saul Bellow, *Herzog* (New York: Viking, 1964), p. 243. Subsequent quotations refer to this edition and will be noted parenthetically in the text.
14. John Clayton, *Saul Bellow: In Defense of Man* (Bloomington: Indiana University Press, 1971), p. 186.
15. Galloway, "Moses," p. 70; M. Gilbert Porter, *Whence the Power?*

The Artistry and Humanity of Saul Bellow (Columbia: University of Missouri Press, 1974), p. 147; Clayton, *Bellow*, p. 227; Keith Michael Opdahl, *The Novels of Saul Bellow* (University Park: Pennsylvania State University Press, 1967), p. 141.

16. Tanner, *City*, pp. 302–3.
17. Ralph Ellison, "Society, Morality, and the Novel," in *The Living Novel*, ed. Granville Hicks (New York: Macmillan, 1957), pp. 77–79.
18. Ellison, *Invisible Man*, p. 268.
19. Ellison comments on his reaction to Joyce in *Interviews with Black Writers*, ed. O'Brien, p. 73. Floyd R. Horowitz notes several parallels between the battle royal scene in *Invisible Man* and the beach scene in *Portrait* in "Ralph Ellison's Modern Version of Brer Bear and Brer Rabbit in *Invisible Man*," in *Twentieth Century Interpretations of Invisible Man*, ed. John M. Reilly (Englewood Cliffs, N.J.: Prentice-Hall, 1970), p. 81. George Kent notes several parallels between Joyce and Ellison; *Blackness*, p. 158.
20. *Writers at Work: Second Series*, ed. George Plimpton (New York: Viking, 1963), p. 330.
21. Tanner, *City*, p. 62.
22. John Hersey, "Introduction," in *Ralph Ellison: A Collection of Critical Essays*, ed. John Hersey (Englewood Cliffs, N.J.: Prentice-Hall, 1974), p. 14.
23. *Writers: Second Series*, ed. Plimpton, p. 336.
24. See Horowitz, "Ellison's Modern Version"; Archie D. Sanders, "Odysseus in Black: An Analysis of the Structure of *Invisible Man*," *CLA Journal* 13 (March 1970): 217–28; and Charles W. Scruggs, "Ralph Ellison's Use of the *Aeneid*," *CLA Journal* 17 (March 1974): 268–78, for discussions of the mythic dimensions of *Invisible Man*. For discussions of the use of historical dimensions, relating primarily to the experience of blacks in the United States, see Russell C. Fischer, "*Invisible Man* as History," *CLA Journal* 17 (March 1974): 338–67, and Gayle, *Way of the New World*, pp. 247–58.
25. Kent, *Blackness*, p. 161.
26. Gene Bluestein, "The Blues as Literary Form," in *Black and White in American Culture*, ed. Jules Chametsky and Sidney Kaplan (Amherst: University of Massachusetts Press, 1969), p. 254.
27. Ralph Ellison, *Shadow and Act* (New York: Signet, 1966), p. 90.
28. Larry Neal, "Ellison's Zoot Suit," in *Ellison*, ed. Hersey, p. 71.
29. Ellison, *Shadow*, p. 221.
30. Ibid., p. 248.
31. Neal, "Ellison's Zoot Suit," presents the strongest defense of Ellison's political stance.
32. For the main arguments concerning Ellison's attitude toward Emerson, see Leonard J. Deutsch, "Ralph Ellison and Ralph Waldo Emerson," *CLA Journal* 16 (December 1972): 159–78; and William W.

Nichols, "Ralph Ellison's Black American Scholar," *Phylon* 31 (Spring 1970): 70–75.

33. Tanner, *City*, p. 58.
34. Ellison, *Shadow*, p. 55.
35. Richard Poirier, *The Performing Self* (New York: Oxford University Press, 1971), pp. 48, 45.
36. Ibid., p. 87.
37. John Barth, *Letters* (New York: G. P. Putnam's Sons, 1980), p. 650. Subsequent quotations refer to this edition and will be noted parenthetically in the text.
38. *The New Fiction*, ed. Bellamy, pp. 8–9.
39. Scholes, *Fabulators*, p. 137.
40. Olderman, *Beyond the Wasteland*, pp. 88–89.
41. *The Contemporary Writer*, ed. L. S. Dembo and Cyrena N. Pondrom (Madison: University of Wisconsin Press, 1972), pp. 21, 23.
42. John Barth, *Giles Goat-Boy* (Garden City, N.Y.: Doubleday, 1966), p. 63. Subsequent quotations refer to this edition and will be noted parenthetically in the text.
43. Scholes, *Fabulators*, p. 161.
44. Norman Mailer, *The Deer Park* (New York: Berkley, 1969), p. 194.
45. Norman Mailer, *Advertisements for Myself* (New York: Signet, 1960), p. 285.
46. Ibid., p. 140.
47. *Writers: Third Series*, ed. Plimpton, p. 265.
48. See John W. Aldridge, "The Energy of New Success," in *Norman Mailer: A Collection of Critical Essays*, ed. Leo Braudy (Englewood Cliffs, N.J.: Prentice-Hall, 1972), pp. 109–19; Richard Gilman, "What Mailer Has Done," ibid., pp. 158–66; Michael Cowan, "The Americanness of Norman Mailer," ibid., pp. 143–57; and Laura Adams, *Existential Battles: The Growth of Norman Mailer* (Athens: Ohio University Press, 1976).
49. Norman Mailer, *Cannibals and Christians* (New York: Dell, 1966), p. 95.
50. Ibid., p. 99.
51. Adams, *Existential Battles*, p. 121.
52. Norman Mailer, *The Armies of the Night* (New York: Signet, 1968), p. 107. Subsequent quotations refer to this edition and will be noted parenthetically in the text.
53. Adams, *Existential Battles*, p. 121.
54. Tanner, *City*, p. 365.
55. Ibid., p. 358.
56. Ibid., p. 366.
57. Adams, *Existential Battles*, p. 124.
58. To the extent that Mailer fails to establish his image as a representative figure, he undercuts his own performance, which risks seeming

simply egotistical. Both Gilman and Robert Meredith in "The 45-Second Piss: A Left Critique of Norman Mailer and *The Armies of the Night*," *Modern Fiction Studies* 17 (1971): 433–49, reject the figure of Mailer in the novel and find his message unconvincing.

59. See Adams, *Existential Battles*, p. 133, and Robert Solotaroff, *Down Mailer's Way* (Urbana: University of Illinois Press, 1974), p. 225.

CHAPTER FIVE

1. William Gaddis, *The Recognitions* (New York: Harcourt, Brace and World, 1955), p. 114. Subsequent quotations refer to this edition and will be noted parenthetically in the text.

2. Peter William Koenig, "Recognizing Gaddis's Recognitions," *Contemporary Literature* 16 (1975): 64.

3. Bernard Benstock, "On William Gaddis: In Recognition of James Joyce," *Wisconsin Studies in Contemporary Literature* 6 (1965): 177–89.

4. David Madden, "On William Gaddis's *The Recognitions*," in *Rediscoveries*, ed. David Madden (New York: Crown, 1971), p. 304.

5. Fuller and Reverend Dick are among the other characters treated as emblems rather than as "real" characters.

6. Joseph S. Salemi, "To Soar in Atonement: Art as Expiation in Gaddis's *The Recognitions*," *Novel: A Forum on Fiction* 10 (1977): 130.

7. Ibid., p. 127.

8. Tanner, *City*, p. 398.

9. Thomas Pynchon, *Gravity's Rainbow* (New York: Viking, 1973), p. 3. Subsequent quotations refer to this edition and will be noted parenthetically in the text.

10. See Edward Mendelson's excellent "Introduction," in *Pynchon: A Collection of Critical Essays*, ed. Edward Mendelson (Englewood Cliffs, N.J.: Prentice-Hall, 1978), pp. 1–16; and Richard Poirier, "The Importance of Thomas Pynchon," in *Mindful Pleasures*, ed. George Levine and David Leverenz (Boston: Little, Brown, 1976), pp. 15–30. Mendelson's ideas on Pynchon and the genre of "encyclopedic fiction" are seminal to further discussion of *Gravity's Rainbow*.

11. The most important allusion to Joyce in *The Crying of Lot 49* reinforces the conclusion that Pynchon sees Joyce, at least potentially, as a writer of the preterite. The character who sets the protagonist Oedipa Maas on her quest is named Pierce Inverarity. The name alludes to the following passage in *Portrait*: "The pages of his time-worn Horace never felt cold to the touch even when his own fingers were cold: they were human pages and fifty years before they had been turned by the human fingers of John Duncan Inverarity and by his brother William Malcolm Inverarity. Yes, those were noble names

on the dusky flyleaf and, even for so poor a Latinist as he, the dusky verses were as fragrant as through they had lain all those years in myrtle and lavender and vervain: but yet it wounded him to think that he would never be but a shy guest of the world's culture and that the monkish learning, in terms of which he was striving to forge out an aesthetic philosophy, was held no higher by the age he lived in than the subtle and curious jargons of heraldry and falconry" (*P*, pp. 179–80). Stephen, like Oedipa, devotes his efforts to decoding "subtle and curious jargons." But both Pynchon and Joyce recognize that the key for unlocking the deepest meanings of their characters' experiences is a recognition of the "humanity" of the pages. The major problem stems from the multiplicity of potential readings of the clues. Stephen chooses to focus on the "nobility" of the name Inverarity, rather than on the shared humanity emanating from Horace. Similarly, when Oedipa attains a brief moment of human contact holding the old sailor, her attention wavers and returns to her obsession with piercing the mystery of the "noble" Inverarity.

12. Nonetheless, several critics have attempted to explain Pynchon as a "closed system" writer, most notably William Plater in *The Grim Phoenix: Reconstructing Thomas Pynchon* (Bloomington: Indiana University Press, 1978). Lawrence C. Wolfey claims a "controlling" influence of Norman O. Brown on *Gravity's Rainbow* in "Repression's Rainbow: The Presence of Norman O. Brown in Pynchon's Big Novel," *PMLA* 92 (1977): 873–89. Robert Martin Adams argues that "Pynchon appears to have less than no interest in morals, in politics, in religion, in what used to be called 'human nature'" (*AfterJoyce*, p. 179). Adams, however, represents an extreme minority position. Critics who see a good deal more openness in Pynchon include Thomas H. Schaub in *Pynchon: The Voice of Ambiguity* (Urbana: University of Illinois Press, 1981), and Mark Richard Siegal in *Pynchon: Creative Paranoia in "Gravity's Rainbow"* (Port Washington, N.Y.: Kennikat Press, 1978).

13. See Speer Morgan, "*Gravity's Rainbow:* What's the Big Idea?" *Modern Fiction Studies* 23 (1977): 199–216, and David Leverenz, "On Trying to Read *Gravity's Rainbow,*" in *Mindful Pleasures,* ed. Levine and Leverenz.

14. Paul Fussell, *The Great War and Modern Memory* (New York: Oxford University Press, 1977), pp. 328–34.

15. For a provocative discussion of Slothrop's dissolution as Pynchon's rejection of modernism, see Mendelson, *Pynchon,* p. 2.

EPILOG

1. Guy Davenport, *Da Vinci's Bicycle* (Baltimore: Johns Hopkins University Press, 1979).

2. Gilbert Sorrentino, *Mulligan Stew* (New York: Grove Press, 1979). Subsequent quotations refer to this edition and will be noted parenthetically in the text.
3. William Burroughs and Brian Gysin, *The Third Mind* (New York: Viking, 1979).

Bibliography

Adams, Laura. *Existential Battles: The Growth of Norman Mailer.* Athens: Ohio University Press, 1976.

Adams, Richard P. *Faulkner: Myth and Motion.* Princeton: Princeton University Press, 1968.

Adams, Robert Martin. *AfterJoyce.* New York: Oxford University Press, 1977.

——. *Surface and Symbol.* New York: Oxford University Press, 1962.

Aiken, David. "Flannery O'Connor's Portrait of the Artist as a Young Failure." *Arizona Quarterly* 32 (1976).

Aldridge, John W. "The Energy of New Success." In *Norman Mailer: A Collection of Critical Essays.* Ed. Leo Braudy. Englewood Cliffs, N.J.: Prentice-Hall, 1972.

Allen, Shirley S. "The Ironic Voice in Baldwin's *Go Tell It on the Mountain.*" In *James Baldwin: A Critical Evaluation.* Ed. Therman B. O'Daniel. Washington: Howard University Press, 1977.

Approaches to "A Portrait of the Artist as a Young Man." Ed. Bernard Benstock and Thomas Staley. Pittsburgh: University of Pittsburgh Press, 1977.

Baldwin, James. *Go Tell It on the Mountain.* New York: Alfred A. Knopf, 1953.

——. *Notes of a Native Son.* New York: Bantam, 1968.

Banks, Russell. *Searching for Survivors.* New York: Fiction Collective, 1975.

——. "Symposium: The Writer's Situation." *New American Review* 9 (1970).

Barth, John. *Giles Goat-Boy.* Garden City, N.Y.: Doubleday, 1966.

——. *Letters.* New York: G. P. Putnam's Sons, 1980.

Barthelme, Donald. "After Joyce." *Location* 1 (Summer 1964).

——. *The Dead Father.* New York: Farrar, Straus and Giroux, 1975.

Beckett, Samuel. "Dante . . . Bruno. Vico . . . Joyce." In *James Joyce/Finnegans Wake: A Symposium.* New York: New Directions, 1972.

Bellow, Saul. *Herzog.* New York: Viking, 1964.

——. "The Sealed Treasure." *Times Literary Supplement,* July 1, 1960.

Benstock, Bernard. *Joyce-Again's Wake*. Seattle: University of Washington Press, 1966.

———. "On William Gaddis: In Recognition of James Joyce." *Wisconsin Studies in Contemporary Literature* 6 (1965).

Bier, Jesse. "The Romantic Coordinates of American Literature." *Bucknell Review* 18 (1970).

Bloom, Harold. *The Anxiety of Influence*. New York: Oxford University Press, 1973.

Blotner, Joseph. *Faulkner: A Biography*. New York: Random House, 1974.

Bluestein, Gene. "The Blues as Literary Form." In *Black and White in American Culture*. Ed. Jules Chametsky and Sidney Kaplan. Amherst: University of Massachusetts Press, 1969.

Bone, Robert. *The Negro Novel in America*. New Haven: Yale University Press, 1965.

Brooks, Cleanth. *William Faulkner: The Yoknapatawpha Country*. New Haven: Yale University Press, 1966.

———. *William Faulkner: Toward Yoknapatawpha*. New Haven: Yale University Press, 1978.

Brown, Homer Obed. *James Joyce's Early Fiction: The Biography of a Form*. Cleveland: Western Reserve Press, 1978.

Browning, Preston. "Parker's Back: Flannery O'Connor's Iconography of Salvation by Profanity." *Studies in Short Fiction* 6 (1969).

Bryant, Jerry H. "From Death to Life: The Fiction of Ernest J. Gaines." *Iowa Review* 3 (1972).

Budgen, Frank. *James Joyce and the Making of "Ulysses."* Bloomington: Indiana University Press, 1973.

Burroughs, William. *The Ticket That Exploded*. New York: Grove Press, 1968.

——— and Gysin, Brian. *The Third Mind*. New York: Viking, 1979.

Chants of Saints. Ed. Michael S. Harper and Robert B. Stepto. Urbana: University of Illinois Press, 1979.

Charters, Ann. *Kerouac: A Biography*. New York: Warner, 1974.

Chase, Richard. *The American Novel and Its Tradition*. Garden City, N.Y.: Doubleday/Anchor, 1957.

Clayton, John. *Saul Bellow: In Defense of Man*. Bloomington: Indiana University Press, 1971.

Collins, Carvel. "The Pairing of *The Sound and the Fury* and *As I Lay Dying*." *Princeton University Library Chronicle* 18 (1957).

Concrete Poetry: A World View. Ed. Mary Ellen Solt. Bloomington: Indiana University Press, 1970.

The Contemporary Writer. Ed. L. S. Dembo and Cyrena N. Pondrom. Madison: University of Wisconsin Press, 1972.

Coover, Robert. *The Public Burning*. New York: Viking, 1977.

Courlander, Harold. *A Treasury of Afro-American Folklore*. New York: Crown, 1976.

Cowan, Michael. "The Americanness of Norman Mailer." In *Norman*

Mailer: A Collection of Critical Essays. Ed. Leo Braudy. Englewood Cliffs, N.J.: Prentice-Hall, 1972.

Cross, Barbara M. "Apocalypse and Comedy in *As I Lay Dying.*" *Texas Studies in Language and Literature* 3 (1961).

Davenport, Guy. *Da Vinci's Bicycle.* Baltimore: Johns Hopkins University Press, 1979.

Deutsch, Leonard J. "Ralph Ellison and Ralph Waldo Emerson." *CLA Journal* 16 (December 1972).

Dickstein, Morris. *Gates of Eden.* New York: Basic Books, 1978.

Eckley, Grace. "The Awakening of Mr. Affrinnegan: Kelley's *Dunfords Travels Everywheres* and Joyce's *Finnegans Wake.*" *Obsidian* 1 (Summer 1975).

Eliot, T. S. *Selected Essays: New Edition.* New York: Harcourt, Brace and World, 1950.

Ellison, Ralph. *Invisible Man.* New York: Random House, 1952.

———. *Shadow and Act.* New York: Signet, 1966.

———. "Society, Morality, and the Novel." In *The Living Novel.* Ed. Granville Hicks. New York: Macmillan, 1957.

Ellmann, Richard. *James Joyce.* New York: Oxford University Press, 1959.

Epstein, Dena J. *Sinful Tunes and Spirituals.* Urbana: University of Illinois Press, 1977.

Fabre, Michel. "Bayonne d'earnest aule Gaines's Yoknapatapha." *Recherches Anglaises et Americaines* 4 (1976).

———. "Fathers and Sons in James Baldwin's *Go Tell It on the Mountain.*" In *James Baldwin: A Collection of Critical Essays.* Ed. Keneth Kinnamon. Englewood Cliffs, N.J.: Prentice-Hall, 1974.

———. "Richard Wright: Beyond Naturalism?" In *American Literary Naturalism: A Reassessment.* Ed. Yoshinabu Hakutani and Lewis Fried. Heidelberg: Carl Winters, 1975.

———. *The Unfinished Quest of Richard Wright.* New York: William Morrow, 1973.

Faulkner, William. *As I Lay Dying.* New York: Vintage, 1968.

———. *Go Down, Moses.* New York: Random House, 1942.

———. *Mosquitoes.* New York: Liveright, 1927.

Faulkner in the University. Ed. Frederick L. Gwynn and Joseph L. Blotner. Charlottesville: University of Virginia Press, 1959.

Federman, Raymond. *Double or Nothing.* Chicago: Swallow Press, 1971.

Fiction! Interviews with Northern California Novelists. Ed. Dan Tooker and Roger Hofheins. New York: Harcourt Brace Jovanovich, 1976.

Fisch, Harold. "The Hero as Jew: Reflections on *Herzog.*" *Judaism* 17 (Winter 1968).

Fischer, Russell G. "*Invisible Man* as History." *CLA Journal* 17 (March 1974).

Fishburn, Katherine. *Richard Wright's Hero: The Faces of a Rebel-Victim.* Metuchen, N.J.: Scarecrow Press, 1977.

Friedman, Melvin J. "Introduction." In *The Added Dimension: The Art and Mind of Flannery O'Connor.* Ed. Melvin J. Friedman and Lewis A. Lawson. New York: Fordham University Press, 1966.

Fussell, Paul. *The Great War and Modern Memory.* New York: Oxford University Press, 1977.

Gaddis, William. *The Recognitions.* New York: Harcourt, Brace and World, 1955.

Gaines, Ernest. *Bloodline.* New York: W. W. Norton, 1976.

Galloway, David D. "Moses—Bloom—Herzog: Bellow's Everyman." *Southern Review* n.s. 2 (January 1966).

Gayle, Addison. *The Way of the New World.* Garden City, N.Y.: Doubleday/Anchor, 1976.

Gibson, Donald B. "James Baldwin: The Political Anatomy of Space." In *James Baldwin: A Critical Evaluation.* Ed. Therman B. O'Daniel. Washington: Howard University Press, 1977.

———. "Wright's Invisible Native Son." *American Quarterly* 21 (1969).

Gilman, Richard. "What Mailer Has Done." In *Norman Mailer: A Collection of Critical Essays.* Ed. Leo Braudy. Englewood Cliffs, N.J.: Prentice-Hall, 1972.

Gossett, Thomas F. "Flannery O'Connor's Opinions of Other Writers: Some Unpublished Comments." *Southern Literary Journal* 6 (1974).

Groden, Michael. "Criticism in New Composition: *Ulysses* and *The Sound and the Fury.*" *Twentieth Century Literature* 21 (1975).

Guibert, Rita. *Seven Voices: Seven Latin American Writers Talk to Rita Guibert.* New York: Vintage, 1973.

Harper, Gordon Lloyd. "Saul Bellow." In *Saul Bellow: A Collection of Critical Essays.* Ed. Earl Rovit. Englewood Cliffs, N.J.: Prentice-Hall, 1975.

Hassan, Ihab. *The Dismemberment of Orpheus.* New York: Oxford University Press, 1971.

———. *Paracriticisms.* Urbana: University of Illinois Press, 1975.

Hayman, David. "Some Writers in the Wake of the *Wake.*" In *In the Wake of the Wake.* Ed. David Hayman and Elliott Anderson. Madison: University of Wisconsin Press, 1978.

Hersey, John. "Introduction: A Completion of Personality." In *Ralph Ellison: A Collection of Critical Essays.* Ed. John Hersey. Englewood Cliffs, N.J.: Prentice-Hall, 1974.

Hipkiss, Robert A. *Jack Kerouac: Prophet of the New Romanticism.* Lawrence: Regents Press of Kansas, 1976.

Hoffman, Daniel. *Form and Fable in American Fiction.* New York: Oxford University Press, 1961.

Howe, Irving. *William Faulkner: A Critical Study.* New York: Random House, 1962.

Horowitz, Floyd R. "Ralph Ellison's Modern Version of Brer Bear and Brer Rabbit in *Invisible Man.*" In *Twentieth Century Interpretations of*

Invisible Man. Ed. John M. Reilly. Englewood Cliffs, N.J.: Prentice-Hall, 1970.

Hynes, Samuel. *The Auden Generation: Literature and Politics in England in the 1930s*. New York: Viking, 1977.

Ingram, Forrest L. "O'Connor's Seven-Story Cycle." *Flannery O'Connor Bulletin* 2 (1973).

———. *Representative Short Story Cycles of the Twentieth Century*. The Hague: Mouton, 1971.

Interviews with Black Writers. Ed. John O'Brien. New York: Liveright, 1973.

In the Wake of the Wake. Ed. David Hayman and Elliott Anderson. Madison: University of Wisconsin Press, 1978.

Johlen, Myra. *Class and Character in Faulkner's South*. Secaucus, N.J.: Citadel Press, 1978.

Jones, LeRoi. "Introduction." In *The Moderns*. Ed. LeRoi Jones. New York: Corinth Books, 1963.

Joyce, James. *Dubliners*. New York: Viking, 1973.

———. *Finnegans Wake*. New York: Viking, 1968.

———. *A Portrait of the Artist as a Young Man*. New York: Viking, 1969.

———. *Stephen Hero*. New York: New Directions, 1963.

———. *Ulysses*. New York: Viking, 1961.

Kain, Richard. *Fabulous Voyager*. Chicago: University of Chicago Press, 1947.

Kelley, William Melvin. *Dunfords Travels Everywheres*. Garden City, N.Y.: Doubleday, 1970.

———. "Oswhole'stalking." *L'Arc* 36 (1969).

Kenner, Hugh. *Dublin's Joyce*. Bloomington: Indiana University Press, 1956.

Kent, George. *Blackness and the Adventure of Western Culture*. Chicago: Third World Press, 1972.

Kerouac, Jack. "Essentials of Spontaneous Prose." In *The Moderns*. Ed. LeRoi Jones. New York: Corinth Books, 1963.

———. "Old Angel Midnight Part Two." *Evergreen Review* (September 1964).

———. *On the Road*. New York: Viking, 1957.

Kinnamon, Keneth. *The Emergence of Richard Wright*. Urbana: University of Illinois Press, 1972.

Klinkowitz, Jerome. *The Life of Fiction*. Urbana: University of Illinois Press, 1977.

———. *Literary Disruptions*. Urbana: University of Illinois Press, 1975.

Koenig, Peter William. "Recognizing Gaddis's Recognitions." *Contemporary Literature* 16 (1975).

Kostelanetz, Richard. "The Politics of Ellison's Booker: Invisible Man as Symbolic History." In *A Casebook on Ralph Ellison's Invisible Man*. Ed. Joseph F. Trimmer. New York: Crowell, 1972.

Lameyer, Gordon. "The Double in Sylvia Plath's *The Bell Jar*." In *Sylvia Plath: The Woman and the Work*. New York: Dodd, Mead, 1977.

Leverenz, David. "On Trying to Read *Gravity's Rainbow*." In *Mindful Pleasures*. Ed. George Levine and David Leverenz. Boston: Little, Brown, 1976.

Levin, Harry. *James Joyce*. Norfolk, Conn.: New Directions, 1960.

Levine, Lawrence. *Black Culture and Black Consciousness*. New York: Oxford University Press, 1978.

Lewis, R. W. B. "William Faulkner: The Hero in the New World." In *Faulkner: A Collection of Critical Essays*. Ed. Robert Penn Warren. Englewood Cliffs, N.J.: Prentice-Hall, 1966.

Madden, David. "On William Gaddis's *The Recognitions*." In *Rediscoveries*. Ed. David Madden. New York: Crown, 1971.

Mailer, Norman. *Advertisements for Myself*. New York: Signet, 1960.

———. *The Armies of the Night*. New York: Signet, 1968.

———. *Cannibals and Christians*. New York: Dell, 1966.

———. *The Deer Park*. New York: Berkley, 1969.

Margolies, Edward. *The Art of Richard Wright*. Carbondale: Southern Illinois University Press, 1969.

Matthiessen, F. O. *American Renaissance*. London: Oxford University Press, 1941.

McLuhan, Marshall. "Notes on Burroughs." *The Nation* 199 (1964).

McDonald, Walter R. "'You Not a Bum, You a Man': Ernest J. Gaines's *Bloodline*." *Black American Literature Forum* 11 (1977).

Mendelson, Edward. "Introduction." In *Pynchon: A Collection of Critical Essays*. Ed. Edward Mendelson. Englewood Cliffs, N.J.: Prentice-Hall, 1978.

Mercier, Vivien. *A Reader's Guide to the New Novel*. New York: Farrar, Straus and Giroux, 1971.

Meredith, Robert. "The 45-Second Piss: A Left Critique of Norman Mailer and *The Armies of the Night*." *Modern Fiction Studies* 17 (1971).

Millgate, Michael. *The Achievement of William Faulkner*. New York: Random House, 1971.

Morgan, Speer. "*Gravity's Rainbow*: What's the Big Idea?" *Modern Fiction Studies* 23 (1977).

Morrison, Toni. *Song of Solomon*. New York: Alfred A. Knopf, 1977.

Neal, Larry. "Ellison's Zoot Suit." In *Ralph Ellison: A Collection of Critical Essays*. Ed. John Hersey. Englewood Cliffs, N.J.: Prentice-Hall, 1974.

The New Fiction: Interviews with Innovative American Writers. Ed. Joe David Bellamy. Urbana: University of Illinois Press, 1975.

Nichols, William W. "Ralph Ellison's Black American Scholar." *Phylon* 31 (Spring 1970).

Nilon, Charles H. *Faulkner and the Negro*. New York: Citadel Press, 1965.

O'Connor, Flannery. *The Complete Stories.* New York: Farrar, Straus and Giroux, 1971.
———. *Mysteries and Manners.* Ed. Sally and Robert Fitzgerald. New York: Farrar, Straus and Giroux, 1973.
Olderman, Raymond. *Beyond the Wasteland.* New Haven: Yale University Press, 1972.
Opdahl, Keith Michael. *The Novels of Saul Bellow.* University Park: Pennsylvania State University Press, 1967.
Peake, C. H. *James Joyce, the Citizen and the Artist.* Stanford: Stanford University Press, 1977.
Persons, Stow. *Evolutionary Thought in America.* New Haven: Yale University Press, 1950.
Perloff, Marjorie G. "A Ritual for Being Born Twice: Sylvia Plath's *The Bell Jar.*" *Contemporary Literature* 13 (1972).
Phelps, Gilbert. "The Novel Today." In *The Pelican Guide to English Literature: The Modern Age.* Ed. Boris Ford. Aylesbury: Penguin Books, 1970.
Pinsker, Sanford. "Saul Bellow in the Classroom." *College English* 34 (1973).
Pizer, Donald. *Realism and Naturalism in Nineteenth-Century American Literature.* Carbondale: Southern Illinois University Press, 1966.
Plath, Sylvia. *The Bell Jar.* New York: Harper and Row, 1971.
Plater, William. *The Grim Phoenix: Reconstructing Thomas Pynchon.* Bloomington: Indiana University Press, 1978.
Poirier, Richard. "The Importance of Thomas Pynchon." In *Mindful Pleasures.* Ed. George Levine and David Leverenz. Boston: Little, Brown, 1976.
———. *The Performing Self.* New York: Oxford University Press, 1971.
———. *A World Elsewhere.* New York: Oxford University Press, 1973.
Porter, M. Gilbert. *Whence the Power? The Artistry and Humanity of Saul Bellow.* Columbia: University of Missouri Press, 1974.
Pynchon, Thomas. *Gravity's Rainbow.* New York: Viking, 1973.
Rosenblatt, Roger. *Black Fiction.* Cambridge: Harvard University Press, 1974.
Salemi, Joseph S. "To Soar in Atonement: Art as Expiation in Gaddis's *The Recognitions.*" *Novel: A Forum on Fiction* 10 (1977).
Samuel, Maurice. "My Friend, the Late Moses Herzog." *Mainstream* 12 (April 1966).
Sanders, Archie D. "Odysseus in Black: An Analysis of the Structure of *Invisible Man.*" *CLA Journal* 13 (March 1970).
Schaub, Thomas H. *Pynchon: The Voice of Ambiguity.* Urbana: University of Illinois Press, 1981.
Scholes, Robert. *The Fabulators.* New York: Oxford University Press, 1967.
Scruggs, Charles W. "Ralph Ellison's Use of the *Aeneid.*" *CLA Journal* 17 (March 1974).

Siegel, Mark Richard. *Pynchon: Creative Paranoia in "Gravity's Rainbow."* Port Washington, N.Y.: Kennikat Press, 1978.

Smith, Stan. "Attitudes Counterfeiting Life: The Irony of Artifice in Sylvia Plath's *The Bell Jar.*" *Critical Quarterly* 17 (1975).

Solotaroff, Robert. *Down Mailer's Way.* Urbana: University of Illinois Press, 1974.

Sorrentino, Gilbert. *Mulligan Stew.* New York: Grove Press, 1979.

Stepto, Robert. *From Behind the Veil: A Study of Afro-American Narrative.* Urbana: University of Illinois Press, 1979.

Sukenick, Ronald. "Double or Nothing." *New York Times Book Review,* October 1, 1972.

———. "Fiction in the Seventies: Ten Digressions on Ten Digressions." *Studies in American Literature* 5 (1977).

———. *98.6.* New York: Fiction Collective, 1975.

———. "Not My Bag." *New York Review of Books,* March 13, 1969.

———. "On the New Cultural Conservatism." *Partisan Review* 39 (1972).

Swiggart, Peter. *The Art of Faulkner's Novels.* Austin: University of Texas Press, 1962.

Tanner, Tony. *City of Words.* New York: Harper and Row, 1971.

Tytell, John. *Naked Angels: The Lives and Literature of the Beat Generation.* New York: McGraw-Hill, 1976.

Updike, John. *The Centaur.* New York: Alfred A. Knopf, 1963.

———. *Picked-Up Pieces.* Greenwich, Conn.: Fawcett, 1975.

Vargo, Edward P. "The Necessity of Myth in Updike's *The Centaur.*" *PMLA* 88 (1973).

Vickery, Olga W. *The Novels of William Faulkner.* Baton Rouge: Louisiana State University Press, 1964.

Waggoner, Hyatt. *William Faulkner: From Jefferson to the World.* Lexington: University of Kentucky Press, 1959.

Walcutt, Charles Child. *American Literary Naturalism: A Divided Stream.* Minneapolis: University of Minnesota Press, 1956.

Warren, Joyce. "Faulkner's 'Portrait of the Artist.'" *Mississippi Quarterly* 19 (1966).

Whitman, Walt. *Complete Poetry and Selected Prose.* Ed. James E. Miller, Jr. Boston: Houghton Mifflin, 1959.

Writers at Work. Ed. Malcolm Cowley. New York: Viking, 1959.

Writers at Work: Second Series. Ed. George Plimpton. New York: Viking, 1963.

Writers at Work: Third Series. Ed. George Plimpton. New York: Viking, 1967.

Writers at Work: Fourth Series. Ed. George Plimpton. New York: Viking, 1977.

Wolfey, Lawrence C. "Repression's Rainbow: The Presence of Norman O. Brown in Pynchon's Big Novel." *PMLA* 92 (1977).

Wright, Richard. *Black Boy*. New York: Perennial Classic, 1967.
———. *Lawd Today*. Chicago: Avon, 1963.
———. *Native Son*. New York: Perennial Classic, 1966.
———. *Uncle Tom's Children*. New York: Perennial Classic, 1970.

Index

Abernathy, Milton, 11
Adams, Laura, 156, 157, 162
Adams, Richard P., 15
Adams, Robert Martin, 6, 14, 18, 70, 72
Advertisements for Myself, 154, 155
"Aeolus," 24, 68, 209n77
Aesop, 122
Aesthetic theory: Faulkner's, 12–13; Joyce's, 166
Africa: Morrison and, 92–93; Kelley and, 109, 114; Ellison and, 138
Afro-American folk culture: in *Lawd Today*, 24; in *Song of Solomon*, 89–94 *passim*; in *Dunfords Travels Everywheres*, 111–14; in *Invisible Man*, 134, 135–38, 140. *See also* Blues; Jazz; Spirituals
Afro-American literature. *See names of individual writers and works*
"After Joyce," 98, 99
Aiken, David, 40
Allegory: and romance, 2; in Banks, 47–48, 50; and myth, 69; in Barthelme, 99, 100, 101, 102; in *Giles Goat-Boy*, 146, 147, 149. *See also* Myth; Romance; Symbolism
Allen, Shirley S., 63
ALP. *See* Plurabelle, Anna Livia
American Dream, An, 157, 158–59
American humor: in *The Public Burning*, 85–88
American Novel and Its Tradition, The, 1–2. *See also* Chase, Richard
Anderson, Sherwood, 9, 11, 13, 35
Animal fable, Afro-American, 111, 114
Appointment in Samara, 70
Aquinas, Thomas, 168
"Araby," 42
Armies of the Night, The: "aesthetic" of, 156, 163–64; resolution of, 156–

57, 162–64; images of irresolution in, 157; Mailer's self-indulgence in, 159; media in, 159–60; Mailer's arrest in, 161–62; middle class in, 162–63
Armstrong, Louis, 137–38, 140, 141–42
As I Lay Dying: stream of consciousness in, 14–15; myth in, 14, 15–16; realistic detail in, 15; symbols as unifying devices, 15; Faulkner's plan for, 16; central themes of, 16–17; conclusion of, 17–18; and *Bloodline*, 36
As You Like It, 46
Asurias, Miguel Angel, 89
At Swim-Two-Birds, 106
Austen, Jane, 51

Baldwin, James: critique of Joyce, 51–52, 60–68 *passim*; on history, 60–61; on social forces, 61; on categories, 61; political awareness, 64–65; resolution of modes, 66–68; on racism, 67; mentioned, 7, 195. *See also Go Tell It on the Mountain*
Banks, Russell: and *Dubliners*, 35, 45–46; stylistic movement, 46–50; relation to Joyce, 46; concern with survival, 46; as romantic, 47; reconciliation of dream and reality, 50; mentioned, 7, 196. *See also Searching for Survivors*
Barbary Shore, 155
Barth, John: and encyclopedic impulse, 120, 121, 122, 144–54 *passim*; as formalist, 144–45; and Joyce, 145–46, 147, 150–51, 152, 153; as performer, 144, 145, 150–54 *passim*; on own sensibility, 146, 150; mentioned, 7,

Index

James, Henry: Isabel Archer, 2; Lambert Strether, 5; mentioned, 6, 28–29, 41, 51
Jazz: Gaines on, 35; and Kerouac's style, 57; Ellison's use of, 136, 137–39, 140, 141
Johnson, Lyndon Baines, 49
Jones, LeRoi, 114
Joyce, James: as mediator, 3; emphasis on particular, 4; and contemporaries, 9; stylistic development of, 33–34; mystique, 50–52; criticism of Stephen Dedalus, 51–52; deflation of epiphanies, 54–55; crafting and aesthetic distance, 123–24; as performer, 143; aesthetics, 166; classical sensibility, 167; post-Joycean tradition, 195–97, 200
—Relation to artistic movements, modes: redefines symbolism and realism, 3; and Superfiction, 46; and *Bildungsroman*, 50–52; and magic realism, 89; and encyclopedic fiction, 120–22; and epistolary tradition, 152; and modernism, 165–66; symbolism in, 168, 169; realism in, 168, 169
—Relation to individual writers: to Faulkner, 9–10, 10–22 *passim*; to Wright, 9–10, 22–32 *passim*; to Gaines, 35–36, 40; to O'Connor, 40–41, 45; to Banks, 46; to Plath, 52–56 *passim*; to Kerouac, 56–57, 58, 60; to Baldwin, 60–61, 68; to Updike, 70–71, 74–75; to Sukenick, 75–76, 82; to Coover, 83, 209n77; to Morrison, 89–90, 94–95; to Barthelme, 98–102 *passim*; to Kelley, 108–9; to Burroughs, 115–16, 117, 119; to Ellison, 133–35; to Barth, 145–46, 147, 150–51, 152–53; to Mailer, 154–55; to Gaddis, 169, 170–73, 174, 177, 181; to Pynchon, 181–83, 194, 214–15n11; to Sorrentino, 197–200
—mentioned, 7, 92, 97, 108, 132, 138, 142, 143. *See also individual works, chapters of Ulysses, and characters' names*
Joyce, John, 68
Jung, Carl Gustav, 138

Kafka, Franz, 99–100, 121
Kelley, William Melvin: and *Finnegans Wake*, 97, 98, 108–14 *passim*; and Joyce, 108–9; compared to

Ellison, 112; mentioned, 7, 115, 197, 199. *See also Dunfords Travels Everywheres*
Kennedy, John Fitzgerald, 49
Kennedy, Robert, 99–100
Kent, George, 4, 62, 135
Kerouac, Jack: Banks on, 48; critique of Joycean mystique, 51–52, 56–60 *passim*; "Old Angel Midnight," 57; spontaneous prose, 57; critique of spontaneity, 58–60; mentioned, 7, 182, 195. *See also On the Road*
Kinnamon, Keneth, 27
Klinkowitz, Jerome, 46, 80, 100
Künstlerroman, 50, 58
Kupferberg, Tuli, 161, 163

Lameyer, Gordon, 53, 55
Last Days of Louisiana Red, The, 90
Lawd Today: as Wright's *Ulysses*, 23–24; variety of styles, 24–25; symbolism in, 24–25, 26; realism in, 24–25, 26; stream of consciousness in, 25–26; compared to *Uncle Tom's Children*, 28
Lawrence, David Herbert, 121
Lenin, Nikolai, 182
Letters: Joyce in, 150–53 *passim*; generational patterns in, 150–51; writing of history in, 151–52; letters in, 151–52; characters challenging author in, 152; initials in, 153; resolution of, 153–54; mentioned, 121, 144, 145
Levin, Harry, 3
Lewis, R. W. B., 20
Light in August, 18
Longfellow, Henry Wadsworth, 87
Lost in the Funhouse, 145, 150
Love and Death in the American Novel, 85

McLuhan, Marshall, 115, 116
McTeague, 25
Madden, David, 174
Magic Mountain, The, 171
Magic realism, 89, 90, 94–95, 196
Mailer, Norman: and encyclopedic impulse, 120, 121, 122; and performance, 144, 154–55, 156, 157, 160–64; and Joyce, 154–55; on American literature, 156; writing style, 157–58; relation to middle class, 162–63; mentioned, 7, 197. *See also The Armies of the Night*
Malamud, Bernard, 145

Index

patterns in, 58–60; resolution of, 60; mentioned, 51

Pangram, 80, 82

Parody, 24, 46, 98, 100–102

Pater, Walter, 143, 144

Pavlov, 183

Performance: "allegorical," 69; Sukenick and, 69, 76, 77, 80, 81–82; and encyclopedic art, 122; Poirier's definition, 143–44; Barth and, 144, 145, 150–54 *passim*; Mailer and, 154–55, 156, 157, 160–64

Perloff, Marjorie, 53

Physiology: and style of *Ulysses*, 24, 82; and style of *98.6*, 82; Burroughs and, 118–19

"Pilot Plan for Concrete Poetry," 103–4

Plath, Sylvia: critique of Joycean mystique, 51–52; recreation of experience in art, 52, 53; and Dostoevsky, 53–54; use of epiphany, 54–56; relation to Esther Greenwood, 56; mentioned, 60, 195. *See also The Bell Jar*

Plurabelle, Anna Livia, 3, 101, 152

Poe, Edgar Allan, 29, 86, 128

Poirier, Richard, 2, 143–44, 155, 196

Porter, M. Gilbert, 127

Portrait of the Artist as a Young Man, A: and *Mosquitoes*, 12–14; and Joyce's stylistic development, 33–34; as Joyce's *Bildungsroman*, 50–51; romantic view of, 51; technical sources, 51; and Plath, 52; Joyce and Stephen in, 56; related to spontaneous prose, 57; individual and community in, 60–61; fatherhood in, 65–66; and *Invisible Man*, 134; echoed in *Letters*, 150, 151; and *The Crying of Lot 49*, 214–15n11; mentioned, 3, 9, 23, 58, 63, 135

Pound, Ezra, 9

"Preface to Lyrical Ballads," 46

Prometheus, 70–74 *passim*, 77

"Proteus," 12

Proust, Marcel, 121, 182

Public Burning, The: Nixon in, 82–88 *passim*; incarnation in, 82–83, 88; Uncle Sam in, 83–88 *passim*; doubles in, 84–85; immaturity in, 85; American humor in, 85–88; mentioned, 69, 94

Pynchon, Thomas: and Beckett, 7; and modernism, 165–67; and the Vic-

torian novel, 167; denial of aesthetic unity, 167–68; realism in, 168, 169; symbolic systems in, 168–69; 181–94 *passim*; and Joyce, 181–83, 194, 214–15n11; mentioned, 173, 175, 197. *See also Gravity's Rainbow*

Racism: in *Uncle Tom's Children*, 27; Baldwin on, 67; Kelley on, 112–13; Pynchon on, 187–88, 189–90

Realism: in Joyce's style, 1–6 *passim*, 33–34, 168–69; and novel form, 1; and symbolism, 2, 5; and Superfiction, 46; "magic" realism, 89, 90, 94–95, 196; and concrete art, 97, 103; and encyclopedic fiction, 123–24; and modernism, 165–66; and post-Joycean tradition, 195–97 —Relation to specific writers: Faulkner, 13–14, 16–18, 19–20, 21–22; Wright, 22–23, 24, 25, 27, 29–32; Gaines, 38–39; Banks, 46, 47, 48, 50; Kerouac, 60; Baldwin, 66, 67; Updike, 70–74 *passim*; Sukenick, 75, 79, 81–82; Coover, 82, 88; Morrison, 89, 94, 95–96; Barthelme, 99, 100, 102; Federman, 104, 106–7; Kelley, 112, 114; Burroughs, 116, 119; Bellow, 126–33 *passim*; Ellison, 133–34, 138–39, 141–43; Barth, 146, 149, 150, 153–54; Mailer, 156–57, 158, 160–64; Gaddis, 168, 170–75 *passim*, 178–80; Pynchon, 168, 181–82, 185, 188, 190, 194 —mentioned, 8, 10, 22, 69, 82. *See also* Naturalism; Resolution of modes

Recognitions, The: stylistic sources, 167, 169–81 *passim*; myth in, 170–71, 174; art as religion in, 170, 176–80; heroism in, 172; realistic detail in, 173–74; satire on Pivner, 174–75; view of science, 175; art and reality in, 175–80 *passim*; forgery and plagiarism in, 176–79; aesthetic of, 176–81; critique of religious institutions, 178–79; destruction of artist in, 178–79; resolution of, 180; mentioned, 166, 190

Reed, Ishmael, 90, 182

Resolution of modes: Joycean, 1–8 *passim*, 168–69, 195–97; in Faulkner, 20–22; Wright's, 32; in Gaines, 36–37, 39–40; in O'Con-

234

A Note on the Author

CRAIG HANSEN WERNER teaches in the English Department, the Black Studies program, and the Center for the Study of Southern Culture at the University of Mississippi. He has published articles on subjects ranging from Dickens to David Rabe and Amiri Baraka. A native of Colorado, he currently resides in rural Lafayette County, Mississippi.